COMMUNICATING IN THE SMALL GROUP

Theory and Practice

BEATRICE G. SCHULTZ

University of Rhode Island

HARPER & ROW, PUBLISHERS, New York
Cambridge, Philadelphia, San Francisco,
London, Mexico City, São Paulo, Singapore, Sydney

1817

Sponsoring Editor: Barbara Cinquegrani
Project Editor: Joan Gregory
Text Design Adaptation: Lucy Krikorian
Cover Design: Katherine von Urban
Text Art: Fineline Illustrations, Inc.
Photo Research: Mira Schachne
Production Manager: Jeanie Berke
Production Assistant: Paula Roppolo
Compositor: ComCom Division of Haddon Craftsmen, Inc.
Printer and Binder: R. R. Donnelley & Sons Company
Cover Printer: The Lehigh Press, Inc.

Communicating in the Small Group: Theory and Practice

Library of Congress Cataloging in Publication Data

Schultz, Beatrice G.
  Communicating in the small group.

  Includes bibliographies and index.
  1. Communication in small groups.   2. Small groups.
I. Title.
HM133.S348 1989   302.3′4   88-16246
ISBN 0–06–045815–1

88 89 90 91 9 8 7 6 5 4 3 2 1

To my husband, Mike,
and to our children—
Claudia,
Richard,
Jeffrey,
and
Amy—
a very special group.

Contents

Preface

Communicating in the Small Group: Theory and Practice combines theories of small group behavior and experiential exercises in one text. The premise of the book is that people can learn the basic principles and dynamics of group participation by exploring the processes that improve a group's functioning.

Using the task group as a framework, the book emphasizes experiential learning. Realistic, practical exercises illuminate both the theoretical and experimental knowledge for understanding group behavior. Thus the book provides important dimensions of group participation and effectiveness: interpersonal relationships within and among groups, social roles, problem solving, decision making, leadership skills, conflict management, and intervention and change strategies.

Each chapter asks a key question: What does a person need to know to be an effective participant in a group? In response, you will find in each chapter dialogues of group interaction, elaborated examples, and experiential exercises that reveal valuable concepts, principles, and procedures—the essential features for understanding how groups work. The exercises are especially designed to reinforce critical aspects of the participation process. In this way you can learn new skills, develop new attitudes, and become a more effective participant in a variety of group situations.

Communicating in the Small Group: Theory and Practice offers training in the skills necessary to perform as a contributing member of a group. The textual content and experiential exercises are not limited to use in the college classroom, however. Any member of a group, whether it is a group that shares an apartment or belongs to a social club, a policy-making organization, or a citizen's advocacy task force, will find this book useful in many group settings. By interacting and reflecting upon group experiences, anyone who wishes to learn how to organize a group, influence decisions, and carry out group tasks in organizations, can learn how to participate more effectively and skillfully.

The book begins with a chapter outlining the historical roots and assumptions of small group study. The chapter emphasizes the contributions of significant individuals from a number of disciplines. It offers a definition of the small group and distinguishes the small group from the larger group. It is a short but useful explanation of what has been learned from an interdisciplinary study of small groups.

Chapter 2 discusses individual roles and functions in the group. An exercise is introduced that explores the impact of occupation, religion, gender, family, and socioeconomic groupings on members' behavior in group situations. In this chapter you are encouraged to view your experiences in groups more broadly than either classroom or work groups. You will be asked to think about the effect of communication climate and group norms on your participation within the group: your role, the role of others, and some of the constraints of role behavior on interaction patterns with others.

The goal of Chapter 3 is to lead you to question your own pattern of participation. The chapter focuses on how ideas are processed. Two especially helpful exercises are provided to illustrate how styles of participating—whether you are a high or a low talker; and how you respond to an idea, critically but not evaluatively—affect both the flow of information and the well-being of participants.

Chapter 4 examines some important dimensions of a group's environment—spatial and structural relationships, gestures and paralinguistic cues, and some special problems affecting group ecology: physical facilities, group size, use of time, and group development.

Learning to incorporate desirable leadership behaviors is the central point of Chapter 5. The chapter details major theoretical approaches to the study of leadership, with particular attention to leadership emergence. Exercises are included for examining your own leadership behavior and the impact of leadership style on group effectiveness.

Chapter 6 outlines methods of probing and analyzing a problem. It includes an extended discussion of problem analysis, exploring the demands as well as the difficulties of effective problem solving. A training exercise and a step-by-step commentary emphasize how group members can use systematic inquiry to help them reach workable solutions.

Chapter 7 looks at how decisions are made and in what ways they can be structured more effectively. The chapter explores decision-making methods and emphasizes the characteristics of good decision making. It also includes a discussion of "groupthink" and the principles for counteracting faulty decision processes.

Chapter 8 discusses the nature, forms, and levels of conflict. It explores the myths and realities of conflict and the ways in which conflict can be used to promote good decision making in the group. Of special interest is an exercise showing how conflict is created between groups.

The basic concepts of managing conflict is the concern of Chapter 9. The chapter discusses styles of conflict and how both individuals and the group can serve as managers of conflict. A model that has great utility for providing negotiation positions illustrates how to prepare for the management of conflict.

Chapter 10, the final chapter, presents a comprehensive treatment of diagnostic and change strategies. Basic concepts in the training of groups—how to give and receive help, how to observe and intervene in the group—are illustrated with examples, exercises, and questionnaires for assessing individual and group performance.

An Appendix contains additional materials for observing, analyzing, and evaluating communication in the small group. Included are focused case studies, role-play suggestions, and dialogues of problem-solving groups.

No book is ever written without help. I want to express my deepest gratitude to my daughter, Amy, for being my first and premier editor. Without her encouragement, I might not have been so persistent in completing this book. To my colleagues at the University of Rhode Island, and especially to Judith Anderson, thanks for your patience and your support. I want to thank my assistants, Colleen Hastings and Sherry Giarrusso, for helping me complete so many small group projects, and all my students, who let me know which exercises were worth putting in this book.

During almost 15 years of pursuing my interest in small group processes, I have read voraciously and have been influenced by many sources. A substantial influence has been the heritage provided by Kurt Lewin and the people who gathered and worked at the National Training Laboratory. I am especially grateful for the training I received from William Sattler, at the University of Michigan, and Kenneth Benne and Max Birnbaum, of the Center of Applied Social Science, Boston University. Their influence on my thinking about small groups has made this book possible. I have tried to acknowledge my debt to others. To those who influenced me, but were inadvertently overlooked, I apologize.

Many people at Harper & Row have helped in the development and publication of this book. My appreciation goes to Barbara Cinquegrani, for her overall editorial supervision; to Joan Gregory, for her production supervision; and to Susan Joseph, for her copyediting expertise. For their careful reading at various stages of the manuscript, I wish to acknowledge Rod Carveth, University of Hartford; Anthony J. Clark, University of Florida; Loren Dickinson, Walla

Walla College; Tom Jenness, University of Idaho; and David E. Walker, Jr., Middle Tennessee State University.

Finally, I want to thank my husband, Mike, who not only kept my computer running no matter where I happened to be but whose love and support has sustained me throughout this project.

Beatrice G. Schultz

COMMUNICATING
IN THE SMALL GROUP

chapter 1

An Introduction to the Study of Small Groups

This book is about the small group—more particularly, about communication in the small group. The focus is on task groups—groups that have information to share, goals to set, decisions to make. The theory and concepts, along with the exercises developed in each chapter, are designed to help you acquire the knowledge and skills of group interaction that you can use in the many groups to which you belong.

WHY STUDY SMALL GROUPS?

Why, you may wonder, should you want to study about communication in the small group? For one reason, you are literally surrounded by small groups: family groups, groups of close friends, colleagues at work, social and recreational clubs, athletic teams, and many more. In one way or another you are bound to find yourself in some type of group—a collection of individuals with whom you will be working, interacting, transacting, making decisions, and taking action. Since you spend a significant portion of your life in groups, why not learn how communication in the small group affects your behavior and your sense of well-being?

Second, the world of work—government, politics, health, busi-

Note: Much of the material in the first part of Chapter 1 reflects the thinking of K. D. Benne.

ness—has placed more and more reliance on small groups of experts to gather, interpret, and present data to the decision makers in their organizations. Whether participating in *quality circles*—small decision groups in organizations—citizens' committees, juries, or advocacy and protest groups, individuals are required to understand both the people with whom they are working and the ways in which they can accomplish goals they feel are important. Unless individuals have purposely removed themselves from society, they cannot avoid participating in groups. Indeed, our society could be described as one large group made up of many small, diverse, and overlapping groups. Without such groups, the larger society could not sustain itself. This is an important reason for learning about groups—how they influence the larger society of which they are a part, how they affect you in your own life, and how you can participate effectively.

Throughout our lives we are bound to find ourselves in some type of group.

Third, learning how to act and react in a group can help you overcome some of the anxiety and uncertainty of participating in a group. Sometimes being in a group is a frightening experience. You may feel threatened by a particularly aggressive member, or you may not be able to participate because you fear exposing your lack of information about the subject to others. Or you may find that you have a greater need for achievement than other people in the group. When this happens, you find you are doing more of the work, when what you had expected was that the work would be shared. These feelings and outcomes occur because most people have had little training in how to function in a group and have even less understanding of the fact that what they say or how they say it may determine whether a group accomplishes its goals.

In addition to these reasons for learning about participating in groups, you can acquire an intellectual knowledge of the theories of small group communication that can help you diagnose and improve your own performance. Psychology, sociology, speech communication—among other disciplines—have found new possibilities for understanding human behavior by studying small group behavior. Without the context of the small group, psychologists were dependent on rat laboratories to learn about human motivation, perception, and sensory and cognitive systems. While many theories were formulated from observations of rat behavior, not all of these data were readily transferable to humans. The small group made it possible to examine behavior in a laboratory setting. In that setting, the conditions of environment and behavior could be manipulated, leading to better predictions of how individuals would behave in particular situations.

The conclusions that sociologists reached were constrained by the limitations of studying cultures, religions, and families in very large groups. Extracting data from large groups often meant omitting important facts about individual behavior. With a more focused examination of people in small groups, sociologists have been able to evaluate the effect of environment, sex, age, and social and economic status on individual and group behavior.

Communication scholars have also found small group study valuable for evaluating the effect of communication on behavior. By focusing on the small group they have learned how individuals develop social relationships and how groups solve problems and reach decisions. In their exploration, these researchers consider the entire conversation or discussion of the communicators as a single process. They are prepared to draw inferences about the communication process—to evaluate statements, responses to statements, the frequency and patterns of participation, the communicative functions of the leaders who emerge, and the communicative acts that encourage effective problem solving and decision making.

With access to the small group, and the diverse social and economic status, personalities, and motivations of its members and their varied patterns of communication, researchers and theorists have been able to expand our knowledge of human interaction. The content of this book is based on the data that they have gathered from their observations and studies of the small group. It is a rich and varied data base, from the development of instruments for measuring and evaluating group performance to the effect of cultural differences in conflict management; from the impact of communicator style on leadership selection to the consequences of seating patterns on group interaction; from the influence of problem-solving skills on achieving quality decisions to the effect of environment on group productivity and satisfaction.

Even more important, small group data have been useful for predicting what people are likely to do in a variety of situations—in panic or under stress, or when subjected to influence of the powerful, to majority rule, to authoritarian leadership, and to competitive environments. It is not so surprising, when one considers the research potential of the small group, that there has been such fascination with learning about human performance by studying small group behavior.

This chapter is an introduction to the study of small group processes. First, we will explore what is meant by the small group and outline the components that comprise a group. Second, we will examine the strengths and weaknesses of group participation. Then we will discuss the historical roots and theories of small group behavior that have contributed to our understanding of small group processes.

DEFINING THE SMALL GROUP

What makes a group a small group? The definition that has received the widest use is one offered by Shaw: "Two or more people who are interacting with one another in such a manner that each person influences, and is influenced by, each other person" (Shaw 1981, 8). Other scholars have also provided definitions and, although there are differences, the definitions share essential components (Shaw 1981, 4–7).

A small number of people. For some scholars, the minimum is two; for others, three is the preferred minimum. Those who reject that two people (a dyad) constitute a group recognize that when two people are interacting, they reflect many of the characteristics of a group; nevertheless, these scholars opt for a minimum of three because that number exemplifies more clearly the complexity of a larger social system.

Perhaps the most useful approach for defining size is contained in the following phrase: a group large enough for a variety of views to be shared but small enough for people to be able to talk to each other. Some scholars suggest that for solving problems, an ideal-size group would be 5 to 7. Most agree that the small group should not exceed 20. But no scholar would claim that there is a single right size for a group. Nonetheless, as will be discussed in Chapter 4, the size of a group does affect how members participate in the group (James 1951).

Interaction. Most scholars insist that a group is not a group unless members interact face to face (eyeball to eyeball). Although group members can communicate through written messages and telephone, and even through teleconferencing—a rapidly growing form of communication—the important linkage appears to be the ability to talk to each other, to communicate with each other verbally, in a setting that allows a mutual sharing of ideas and reactions, and in which members can observe facial expressions and bodily gestures to estimate the extent to which ideas are being communicated effectively.

A common purpose. People come together in a group because they are motivated by a collective goal—a problem to solve, a mission to accomplish. They believe that they share a common fate. They participate with a mutual concern for achieving the objectives of the group as well as a concern for the needs of others. Although members may share a common purpose, this does not imply that group members think alike. Indeed, the group does better problem solving if members can contribute their different perspectives. But when groups fail, it is often because members have not identified a common purpose that would motivate them to stay together.

Mutual influence. When members talk and listen to each other, they influence each other's attitudes, thoughts, and actions. How each member behaves—whether cooperatively or hostilely, actively or passively—affects every other member. When members work together, they come to share values, expectations, and resources. Their exchange of verbal and nonverbal messages influences the collective behavior of the group. As they continue to work, relationships develop and members sense that a group exists—they identify the group as their group. Thus they are interdependent. They are related by their common purpose and their intent to accomplish a goal.

These components should help you differentiate between a group of people who experience a sense of "groupness" and other collections of people who, although they may resemble a group, do not meet these specifications. A collection of people waiting for an elevator may have a common purpose, but would you classify them as a group? What is missing is an expression of collectivity, a decision reached by the group that they will work together to achieve a common goal. They are not a group in the way scholars have defined a group. The definition of a small group that we will use is this: A group is a limited number of people who communicate face to face, share a common purpose, influence one another, and express a sense of belonging to the group.

THE DISTINCTIVE FEATURES OF A GROUP

As the definition of a small group suggests, a group is more than a collection of individuals. What individuals do when working alone is distinctively different from what happens when individuals work together in a group. Sometimes you are advantaged by being part of a group. On other occasions, you would be better off working alone.

THE INDIVIDUAL AND THE GROUP

Procedure 1

A. Working alone, think of as many parts of the body as you can that can be spelled with only three letters (slang terms are not acceptable). You have approximately three minutes for this task.
B. Now call out the number of words on your list. Did anyone discover the 10 or 11 items that are possible? If not, try Procedure 2.

Procedure 2

A. Form into groups of five or six people each. As you work together, see if you can increase your individual totals. The first group to finish calls out its list. If no group has a complete list, then the groups share their lists. (The complete list can be found at the end of the chapter.)
B. After returning to your individual places, compare your experiences. Aside from having gained a larger list, what else did you experience when you worked with others? Your discussion should allow you to account for some of the distinctive features of group participation.

The exercise "The Individual and the Group" can help you discover some of these differences. Any number of people can participate, whether in a classroom or other setting.

The Benefits of Group Participation

Participating in small groups provides a number of important advantages.

A group offers greater learning and satisfaction. When you worked alone, you may have felt a certain degree of tension—the kind of anxiety you feel when you take a test. If you were completely alone doing this task, you might sit and work a bit longer, trying to think of additional items. What is more likely is that you would decide not to continue. It is, after all, not the most compelling exercise. But when you joined a group, the atmosphere changed. Clearly you had more resources to count on—and something else.

In the process of exchanging and combining individual answers, you shared ideas with others and probably had more fun. You may have felt less demand on you to succeed, simply because the task was a group project. Possibly you learned something about other people and something about yourself—a social dimension that made your participation more pleasurable. Although working with people can be difficult as well as enjoyable, having others with whom to share can usually lead to a bonding between individual members (Heslin and Dunphy 1964). It can provide a sense of interdependence and stimulate group cohesiveness. By removing the "I'm all alone and helpless" feeling, the group serves to enhance a feeling of well-being.

People join a group when they are motivated by a collective goal.

A group offers more resources for creative problem solving. To be in a group means having the resources of many to work on a problem. When individuals join a group, something new is formed. They create what Buckminster Fuller, the architect of the geodesic dome, called a "synergistic" effect. *Synergy* connotes that the sum is greater than its parts. It is the product of interacting individuals stimulating one another so that what emerges is something that no one member could accomplish working alone. When individuals bring a variety of backgrounds and perspectives to bear on a problem, the group gains. The special commission appointed by President Ronald Reagan to examine the *Challenger* shuttle disaster in 1986, for example, was composed of a group of experts in engineering, physics, technology, and aviation. Only by considering the analyses of a variety of experts could the committee reach a conclusion about the causes of that tragedy.

For complex tasks, a group can make better decisions (Steiner 1972). Although decision making by a group is not always preferable to an individual decision, what is known is that as the task gets more complex, the multiple resources of the group offer an advantage. Several research studies comparing decisions made by individuals working alone with those made by a collaborating group of individuals suggest that groups often make better decisions. Groups will consider more ideas, a process that is likely to improve the quality and originality of the decision. And because of its opportunities for increased communication, a group's decision-making ability is enhanced (Gouran 1982).

There are also psychological advantages—an individual can be affirmed for having made a contribution to the group. When many perspectives are taken into account, especially the views of those who would be affected by the decision, group members are more likely to be satisfied with the decision and more committed to implementing it (Gouran 1969).

The Disadvantages of Group Participation

In our discussion so far we have praised groups for offering such advantages as more satisfying social experiences, more opportunities for creative problem solving, and more effective decision making. There are also pitfalls, however.

A group can pressure members to conform to the majority's view (Asch 1951). One of the important issues in working in a group is the extent to which members are willing to give up their decision-making rights to others. Another question is, How willing are members to surrender their own individual style of working to meet the standards established by the group? The group may rush through a discussion while one member would have liked a more contemplative analysis. Some members may even have ideas that the group will not consider. Irving Janis (1982), a social psychologist, has written insightfully about the power of a group to influence each individual to support the collective "wisdom" of the group, a concept he calls "groupthink." Janis' view is an important one. He reminds us that a group can hold a power over us if we find it attractive enough to want to be a member. He underscores how often the "shared stereotypes" of the group interfere with a careful analysis of an issue.

One of the many examples Janis cites is the Bay of Pigs invasion of Cuba, which took place in 1961. President John F. Kennedy's advisors assured him that when the American-supported force of Cuban exiles landed in Cuba, the Cuban people would rise up in support of them and oust their leader, Fidel Castro. As events subsequently showed, the Bay of Pigs invasion was a fiasco. Kennedy got poor advice because his advisors discounted the evidence indicating that the Cuban people by and large supported the Cuban revolution, which had brought Castro to power in 1959. Janis believes that if an individual had been solely responsible for the Cuban decision, it would have been made differently. In Chapter 7 we will analyze how "groupthink" affects decisions, but as this example indicates, the power of a group is awesome—sometimes facilitating but at other times jeopardizing good decision making (Janis and Mann 1977).

A group takes longer to complete a task than an individual. In terms of efficiency, the group does less well than an individual. A group needs more time to discuss issues and to analyze and resolve problems than an individual working alone. According to David Berg (1967), a group does not have a large attention span. Members are more likely to move from idea to idea, rehashing points brought up earlier. There is also a tendency to get sidetracked, as topics that do not pertain to the discussion at hand may be brought up. Sometimes it seems that a group can spend hours on what turn out to be irrelevant topics. It does take time, of course, for people to hear each other's perspectives. Moreover, it is hard to get agreement on where and when to meet. Groups necessarily must allow time for arranging when the next meeting will take place.

On the other hand, time may be more important than efficiency when important decisions are at stake. A jury taking the time to deliberate may make the difference between a guilty and not-guilty verdict. (Chapter 8 discusses the responsibilities of group decision making.) What is important is which decisions are better handled by an individual and which would be better made by a group. Some decisions, such as routine decisions or those needing immediate responses, should probably be made by an individual. When critical issues must be interpreted and decided, a decision by a group is best.

Interpersonal interactions as well as personal agendas may interfere with getting the job done. Members in a group often are subjected to an individual who wants to take over. Although other members do not feel the need for someone to tell them what to do—at least not until they have had a chance to understand the problem—one or two individuals may decide that they know how to run a meeting and begin to dominate others. A group must learn to deal with a dominant member, because when one person takes over, others will feel less satisfied. They may not think that they have made a contribution to the group.

Groups may also face a situation in which some members do not take on their share of the work. Some individuals do not make good group members. They seem all too willing to let someone else do the work. The situation in which some members don't contribute their share was first documented by a German psychologist named Ringelmann. He had asked groups to pull on a rope attached to a pressure gauge. While he found that groups were clearly "stronger" than individuals, he also found that as groups added individual members, the efforts of some individuals seemed to decline. Thus the term *Ringelmann effect* has been used to signify an inverse relationship between the number of people in a group and the size of an individual's contribution (Shaw 1981).

When members give up their share of the task, there is a loss to the group. The group loses the benefit of having the resources of many individuals working together as well as a division of labor to make the group's work easier. These and other interpersonal problems are recurring features of group interaction.

Small Groups and Individuals—A Comparison

In summary, as we distinguish between what an individual can do and what a group can do, the data appear to fall into a number of "On the one hand/On the other hand" comparisons. Unquestionably, there are both gains and losses when groups decide. When individuals work alone, they have the power to decide for themselves, to take the necessary time to come to decision. Thus individuals can accomplish much, especially as the result of philosophical thinking. But, as lone individuals, they are missing the stimulation, motivation, and other resources that come from human interaction.

Unlike the individual, groups can divide the labor among many members. The greater resources they can call upon may lead to more innovative solutions to problems. But with group decisions, there can also be problems—more conflict, more pressure for uniformity, more difficulty in coming to decision. Because groups are generally more willing to take risks, a decision at its best could be of high quality; at its worst, it could reflect the mentality of the "lynch mob."

In this brief discussion of the features of the small group, you can surmise why scholars have made the small group a focus of their research. A great deal of what we now know about how individuals behave in groups has come from researchers and theorists representing various disciplines—sociology, psychology, education, social work, speech communication, counseling, and political science.

THEORIES OF SMALL GROUP BEHAVIOR

The following section examines in more detail the contributions of several scholars from diverse fields to our understanding of small group behavior. Five theoretical perspectives are presented, beginning with the foundations laid down by Kurt Lewin and concluding with a much used model in current studies of small groups. Although no single approach is sufficient to explain the complexity of group interaction and group processes, these perspectives, collectively, offer insight into what has been learned from small group studies.

Theories Focusing on the Individual in the Group

Principles of Field Theory Kurt Lewin, aptly called the "father of group dynamics," was a significant contributor to our understanding of interpersonal interaction in groups (Lewin 1951). One distinguishing feature of Lewin's work was the assumption that the study of group behavior requires an examination of how individuals see their reality, rather than how observers report that reality. Lewin emphasized that individuals should examine their own experiences and then discuss their mutual experiences with other members to learn about group behavior. By making commitments in this way, members could learn to behave in more skillful and effective ways.

Lewin adapted a number of concepts from the physical sciences; his field theory, in particular, was influenced by principles from physics. He developed field theory to emphasize that behavior must be looked on as a function of an individual's personal characteristics and the characteristics of the environment, such as the features of the group, the interactions of group members, and the situation. He illustrated this idea with the formula $B = f(P, E)$—behavior is a function of personality and environment (Shepherd 1964). All of these factors, examined as a totality, formed what Lewin called one's *lifespace.*

Lewin believed that individuals share space with other individuals within a field. In this lifespace, they live in a subjective world in which they are motivated by their needs and goals. But as individuals "locomote"—that is, move toward their goals—they encounter barriers, forces that keep them from achieving their goals. Any change in a person's lifespace (for example, taking a new job, moving to a different town, graduating from college, losing a loved one) will have some effect on reaching goals. Thus, to succeed, individuals must learn how to surmount obstacles, by changing either goals or lifespace, or both.

In adapting field theory to groups, field theorists substituted the term "group" for "individual" (Shepherd 1964). A key concept of field theory is that members of a group are interdependent; they share some of their lifespace with each other. Field theorists also added new terms to help them deal with the reality of groups. Many of these terms are the stuff of small group research: *norms*—the rules of behavior that members establish; *roles*—the position a member has in a group and its relative status within the group; *power* and *influence*—the type and extent of control that members have; and *cohesion*—the sense of attachment that members feel for the group.

As a refugee from Nazi Germany, Lewin was greatly influenced by democratic principles, which in turn led to his developing theories about individual performance in a group. Lewin believed that individuals within a group should be allowed to determine their own goals and to work out their differences. This would help create the sense of belonging, or cohesiveness, that Lewin believed was essential if group members were to stay together in a common lifespace. The concept of cohesion became one of the more important areas of study for field theorists. Lewin's students and colleagues focused on the forces that created greater or lesser cohesion in the group. Their inquiry led to an exploration of the relationship of cohesion to goals, norms, leadership, satisfaction, and productivity (Shepherd 1964).

Implications of Field Theory   Lewin's work helped to define the essential attributes of group work. To work in a group is to understand roles, norms, interaction patterns, and the bonding that leads to satisfaction and productivity. What group members learn from field theory is the concept of multiple forces that must be reckoned with in the group. The group is affected by the individual needs of members and, at the same time, the individual is influenced by the standards of the group. Additionally, Lewin's initial work in the 1930s and the work of his followers in subsequent years signified that small group research was a legitimate focus for the study of human behavior.

Principles of Sociometric Theory   A fundamental premise of sociometry is that a group composed of people responsive to one another will produce a more effective outcome than either uninvolved or hostile people. Jacob L. Moreno (1953) was one of the first theorists to explain interpersonal behavior by using visual diagrams to illustrate the relationships that members have with each other. He developed a theory of attraction–repulsion to explain how interpersonal conflicts that exist in a group affect interpersonal relationships.

A visual diagram, called a *sociogram,* can enable us to collect data about a group's climate. Moreno theorized that visual diagrams would map who each member likes or dislikes in the group. People who are liked are called "stars," and those who are disliked are called "isolates." We can learn about the internal dynamics of a group by drawing a sociogram based on questionnaires that explore patterns of acceptance and rejection within the group, or we can examine and record the communication flow within a group to determine its dynamics. For example, a sociologist seeking information about relationships within the group might ask questions such as these (Phillips 1973):

1. Which three people in your group would you prefer to work with most?
2. Which people would you prefer not to work with?
3. Who would you like to be your leader?
4. With whom would you like to socialize outside of this meeting?

From these data, a researcher can draw a diagram illustrating which people are accepted or rejected, who has power in the group, and where the cliques, the coalitions, the stars, and the isolates are.

Communication scholars, in adapting this concept, diagram the flow of communication—who is speaking to whom, and with what frequency. Such a diagram can also reflect patterns of acceptance and rejection, leaders and isolates, as the following example illustrates.

Suppose you were able to observe a family group interacting during dinner for a one-hour period. This is a six-person group—a mother; a father; a daughter, Carol, age 16; a son, Robert, age 15; another son, John, 13; and another daughter, Anne, 11. On the basis of your observation of who talks to whom, and with what frequency—that is, your recording of the flow of communication—you could produce a diagram similar to the one in Figure 1.1.

What inferences can you draw from this diagram? For one

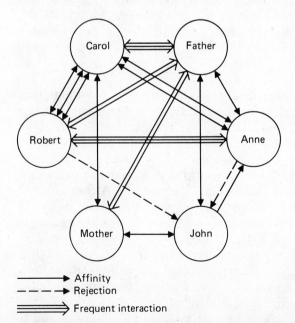

Figure 1.1 A sociogram showing how the members of a family—the parents and their four children—interacted during one dinner. The arrows between circles representing the individuals indicate the frequency of communication and the emotional quality of the communication (friendly or hostile).

thing, everyone likes Anne; she gets the majority of messages. Father and mother seem to give messages equally to all the children, but the children have developed special patterns of their own. Carol does not speak to John, and it appears that Robert and Anne are also ignoring John. Carol, Robert, and Anne, on the other hand, show an affinity for one another.

Implications of Sociometric Theory   What we gain from a sociometric approach is information about patterns of affinity and rejection (liking and disliking), who is allied with whom, which members are stars (in the example we used, Anne), and which members are isolates (John). While the interpersonal dynamics of a group are far more complex than merely who affiliates with whom and who rejects whom, this method can assist us in interpreting interpersonal conflicts in the group.

The method also permits an evaluation of the effect of acceptance and rejection on the group's structure. We may not know the reasons for an individual's particular feelings or behavior toward another member of the group (people are often unaware that they are bringing a "hidden agenda"—their personal goals and feelings—to the group), or we may not be able to establish whether the interactions that have been diagrammed would be different in another episode. Nevertheless, the sociogram is a useful method for illustrating interpersonal interactions in the group. By pointing to some ongoing problems within a group, a sociometric analysis, despite its limitations, allows us to understand the impact of rejection and isolation, as well as affection, on the communicative patterns of group members.

Principles of Psychoanalytic Theory   Intuitively, you can recognize that different personalities influence the behavior of people in a group. The work of Wilfred R. Bion (1961), whose research was carried out with therapy groups, provides some fresh insights about how and why people do what they do when they are working with others.

Bion's psychoanalytic theory assumes that everyone has personal needs that only other individuals can satisfy. Although Bion believed that work and emotionality are two functions of group behavior, his primary concern was with the second of these, emotional needs (Thibaut and Kelley 1959). Bion used four terms to describe what happens emotionally in a group: "fight," "flight," "pairing," and "dependency." Bion presumed that as a group worked, one of these emotional states would keep a group from doing productive work. The terms "fight" and "flight" were used to describe the way people approach a task. When members "fight," they tend to respond negatively, or even with hostility, to whatever idea or action is proposed. When members are in "flight," they appear uninterested in completing a task. They may fool around or discuss nonrelevant issues—anything to keep the group from getting the task accomplished. In either condition, the group is hampered.

When "pairing" occurs, one or more pairs, or twosomes, work on their own agenda. The pairs focus on their conversation and seem oblivious to the needs of the group. "Dependency" represents the effort of a group to rely on the leader or to find someone else or some other way to get the work done—any way that will relieve them of the burden of doing it themselves. Both "pairing" and "dependency" can defeat the ability of groups to get something done.

Other theories of emotionality focus on two emotions, intimacy and control. For example, Bennis and Shepard (1956), in their theory of group development, suggest that group members are preoccupied with two interrelated issues: How close are they to get to each other? Who is to control the group? Bion's classification certainly includes the concept of intimacy and control.

Implications of Psychoanalytic Theory   Although it is difficult to measure a group's emotional state, it is important to be aware of how emotions do affect a group. Bion's psychoanalytic approach shows us that a group's internal state and the stresses it faces should also be considered in diagnosing how a group is doing. As you work with others in a group, you need to be aware of the different standards, the different ways of interacting, and the different ways that people have of responding to the needs of other members. Bion's insights provide a way of understanding important issues affecting many types of groups:

1. How do members respond to a task?
2. How dependent or independent are members as they work on a task?
3. How indifferent are members to the needs of the group?
4. How do relationships of members hinder a group's ability to get a task accomplished?

Theories Focusing on the Group

Principles of Interactionist Theory   Lewin, Moreno, and Bion stressed the individual and his or her relationship to other members of a group. Interactionist theory, largely based on the work of Robert Bales (1950), focuses more on the group. Bales' analysis of the task and social activities of groups, the phases in group development, and the types of roles that members play in a group provides substantial data about the internal functions of a group.

Bales' impact on our knowledge of group interaction comes primarily from his development of an observational scheme labeled

Interaction Process Analysis (IPA). The IPA evolved from observations and analyses that Bales undertook with hundreds of groups. Because it provided an economical system for measuring verbal and nonverbal communication within a group, it became one of the most widely used research methods for analyzing small group behavior.

The emphasis of IPA is on the types of statements participants make in a discussion. Bales developed a classification scheme in which statements are divided into two major categories. Either participants are engaged in task activities, such as giving or asking for information, suggestions, and opinions; or they are contributing positively or negatively to the social-emotional climate of the group by showing solidarity toward, or withdrawing from, the group. Table 1.1 presents the main characteristics of each of the areas of the IPA system.

Implications of Interactionist Theory   One of the major points we can learn from the interactionist approach is how communicative acts function to produce effective or ineffective groups. From Bales' data we learn that groups on average spend 56 percent of their communication time providing answers, 25 percent offering positive reactions, 7 percent asking questions, and the remaining 12 percent en-

Table 1.1   INTERACTION PROCESS ANALYSIS

Social-emotional area: **Positive reactions**	1.	Shows solidarity, raises status of others, gives help, rewards
	2.	Shows tension release, jokes, laughs, shows relief
	3.	Shows agreement, understands, concurs, complies
Task area: **Attempted answers**	4.	Gives suggestions and direction, implying autonomy for others
	5.	Gives opinions, evaluation, analysis; expresses feeling or wish
	6.	Gives information, orientation, repetition, confirmation
Task area: **Questions**	7.	Asks for information, orientation, repetition, confirmation
	8.	Asks for opinions, evaluation, analysis; expresses of feelings or wishes
	9.	Asks for suggestions, direction, and possible ways of action
Social-emotional area: **Negative reactions**	10.	Disagrees, passively rejects, withholds help
	11.	Shows tension, withdraws, daydreams
	12.	Deflates others' status, shows antagonism, defends or asserts self

Based on Robert F. Bales, *Interaction Process Analysis: A Method for the Study of Small Groups* (Reading, Mass.: Addison-Wesley, 1950), p. 59. The terminology has been modified slightly.

gaging in negative reactions. How useful is such information? Although there is very little differences in most groups' profiles, impressive differences occurred in positive and negative reactions. Bales found that though satisfied groups tend to have twice the number of suggestions as dissatisfied groups, what is striking is that dissatisfied groups will have three times the number of disagreements as satisfied groups (Shepherd 1964).

By examining the ratio of attempted answers and positive reactions to questions and negative reactions, you can determine to what extent your group matches Bales' satisfied groups. If, for example, the percentage of answers in your group far exceeds the number in Bales' groups and, at the same time, the number of questions raised is exceedingly low, this could mean that your group has fallen into the "groupthink" trap. On the other hand, if you find that the percentage of answers and positive reactions is too low, you might want to find out why there was so little communicative interaction.

Using the IPA system encourages you to ask: What is the proper balance among types of communication acts? (Chapter 10 provides instruction in how to use this system.) You can learn who the high participators are and who receives most of the messages. You can discover differences in individual contributions—people who help move the group toward completion of a task, people who help soothe tensions in the group. It can help you evaluate what is going on in your group, just as Judith found when she coded the communication exchanges in her group:

> My IPA results came out significantly different from Bales' outcome. Thirty-eight percent of the acts were answers, and 36 percent were positive expressions. The significant decrease in answers and the increase in positive reactions shows that our group, although very productive, was more inclined toward the social dimension.

The theories and models proposed by Bales, although valuable for understanding how communicative acts influence group effectiveness, do not account for all that is going on within a group. Many valuable data are necessarily lost when the communicative acts within a group are reduced to twelve statements. It may also be difficult to categorize messages as either task or social-emotional, since they may be combinations of both (Fisher 1975, 116). Nonetheless, the contributions of Bales to small group theory are significant. In addition to the IPA system for studying small groups, his research has provided other models and theories for examining interpersonal behavior and the way groups develop over time (Bales and Strodtbeck 1951). These issues will be discussed in later chapters.

Bales' research also stimulated the research of many scholars who explored the way specific communicative patterns in groups affect group interaction (Janis and Mann 1977), male and female relationships (Wheeler and Nezlek 1977), consensus in group discussion (Gouran 1969), and many more. As an example, the research of Ernest Bormann (1975), a contemporary communication scholar, owes much to the work of Bales. Bormann and his students at the University of Minnesota explored what Bales described as a continuous tension between the task and social dimensions of a group.

Using groups that were initially leaderless and without a prior history of working together as a group, Bormann and his team found that groups experience two forms of tension: primary and secondary. *Primary tension* occurs when a group first meets. Members display a general uneasiness, an inability to get started. They tend to speak softly and are very polite. *Secondary tension,* a more serious problem because of its recurring nature, takes place after the group's discussion is under way and typically reflects conflicts in the group—a struggle over leadership, for instance, or a disagreement over ideas or roles. Primary tension is more easily dissipated—a joke or a suggestion could help—but if neither primary nor secondary tensions are resolved, the group is in potential trouble. (Remedies for dealing with the issues of conflict are discussed in Chapter 9.) Bormann's research is significant in its own right, but his research also illustrates how Bales' theories stimulated other fruitful investigations of group processes.

Principles of Systems Theory   One other approach remains to be discussed, that of systems theory. Although the concept of general systems theory has been employed in many fields—from biology to computer science—as adapted by communication theorists, systems theory represents a synthesis of field theory and interaction theory (Fisher 1975, 1980). It has been an especially productive way of examining small group variables. The advantage of a systems approach is that we can see the interactive effects of both the internal and external demands placed on group members.

The several concepts used in systems theory—interdependence, open, input, process, output, feedback—have yielded important data when applied to the small group. This approach assists us in examining how groups express goals, work toward these goals through cooperative action, and formulate decisions regarding group action, and enables us to determine how effectively they use feedback to assess their accomplishments.

Interdependence   Underlying the concept of interdependence is the concept of *wholeness* (Fisher 1980, 109). Wholeness suggests that every component of a system affects, and is affected by, every other component. Since all participants (or all objects) in a system are interrelated, a change in any one part of the system will have an effect on other parts. Interdependence leads to a ripple effect—one event brings about another, in ways often not anticipated.

As an example, consider the condition of farmers in recent years. The decreasing value of farmland in the 1980s led to a dramatic change in the welfare of independent farmers. This situation brought about increasing debts, the loss of many farms, the subsequent closing of many local banks that provided loans, and the failure of many businesses that depended on farmers for their income.

The small group may be looked on as a system, an entity that behaves collectively because of the interdependence of its members (Fisher 1980, 109). Group members are continually affected by the way other members interact. If a task group fails to set an agenda, this may interfere with its ability to accomplish a group goal. Members who are overly social can have a negative impact on a group's productivity. If a message is not directly relevant to the issues under consideration, it may add to the group's frustration. A dominant leader, listless members, a drafty room—all of these can affect a group's work.

Open In addition to the interdependence of variables, systems theorists look at the boundaries of a system—whether it is an open system or a closed system—to determine how it is functioning. Our bodies, in one sense, can be classified as open systems. Although as humans we are ingeniously designed to grow and develop, we cannot do so without taking in food, air, and water. In this way we are an open system. But in another sense, if we were to close ourselves off from outside stimulation, become so engaged in routinized behavior that no new element could influence us, we would be operating more like a closed system, shutting ourselves off to anything remotely different from what is familiar. An unwillingness to be open to change can seriously affect the development of an individual or a group.

Input, process, and output variables What constitutes *input* variables in the small group are such components as group members and their resources (their expertise, their desire to work, their ability to articulate goals), the task they are working on, their purpose or goal, the relationships they have established within their own group as well as with other groups or organizations, and their interaction with the external environment. These elements represent the interdependencies that members have as participants in group work.

When groups choose the procedures they will follow, they are engaged in *process* behavior. How groups choose is determined by the standards that members practice—the norms or expectations that members have for each other and the group. Members may consider such factors as how much time they will devote to a task or to socializing, the roles that each member will undertake, the responsibilities of leaders, and how to negotiate among conflicting views.

Output variables refer to group outcomes, the product of a group's work. Did the group work on and solve a problem, determine policies, make recommendations? The output is the result of a group's use of its resources to accomplish its agenda. Other outcomes may be the perception of progress toward group goals, the opportunity for participation in the group's decision, and members' satisfaction with their personal relationships and the group's achievement (Heslin and Dunphy 1964).

Feedback   Feedback refers to the process of giving both positive and negative responses. The concept of feedback comes from the field of cybernetics—the study of how machines (and humans) develop normal functioning by responding to and controlling deviations from what is considered "normal" (Fisher 1980, 110). When we learn that our actions are not appropriate to a situation, then we are in a position to alter our behavior. Negative feedback can be useful if there is a need to extinguish undesirable behavior, while positive feedback offers encouragement to continue an activity.

Feedback loops enable a system to respond to change. A fundamental assumption of general systems theory is that all systems must change if the system is to survive. If a system fails, it does so because it has become insensitive to the forces of change or has no adequate internal processes for dealing with change. For a group to complete its task, to build consensus—to grow and develop—it is essential that feedback processes occur.

Implications of Systems Theory   The tenets of a systems approach offers by far the most comprehensive look at the complexity of the small group. It provides promising leads for studying small group communication. By examining a group as a system, we can focus on communicative exchanges—what is said, to whom it is said, how it is said, and, even more important, when it is said—as interdependent components (Fisher 1980, 75). From a systems perspective we can ask the following questions:

How does individual behavior influence group satisfaction?

How does a group's handling of information affect decision making?

How do patterns of participation affect the quality of the decision?

How does the need for achievement affect leadership choice?

Systems theory expands the way you can look at communicative exchanges. It allows you to see that groups are dependent on the acts and messages of their members. But it also enables you to recognize that as old members leave and new members join, or as different projects are undertaken, the group's process is altered. The theory encourages an analysis of statements and their responses, interactions and reactions, perceptions, belief systems, group processes, and group structure. You learn that it is not one isolated act or message that affects the group. The meaning of an act or message is understandable only when examined as a pattern of acts and messages. Whether the group is responding to internal conflict or occurrences outside the group—events over which members have little control—a systems approach allows you to analyze how a group's decisions and goals are altered through a dynamic process that exemplifies a group system.

A FINAL COMMENT

This chapter has taken you through some important theoretical perspectives for understanding small group behavior. As you examined each theorist's explanation of the "reality" of a group, you confronted those elements that each one considered the most important. Because we have focused on one group of contributors—the historical roots of small group studies—we have had to leave out other important theorists—for example, Thibaut and Kelley's social comparison theory (1959), George Homans' system theory (1950), Peter Blau's social exchange theory (1964), and Leon Festinger's conformity theory (1957), among others. Their contributions will be referred to in other chapters.

The primary interest in this chapter has been to acquaint you with the richness of data—the ingredients—that small group research has made available. In one sense, you have been examining and defining how theorists have constructed the "reality" of a group (Berlo 1960). In constructing reality, theorists choose to organize their perceptions in one way or another, but from each of these you can construct the dynamics of group participation.

In another sense, as you examined the various theoretical perspectives, you were doubtless aware that no one perspective answers all the questions about the reality of a group. Although no one theory can explain small group communication, the combination of theories and perspectives has provided significant insights into small group processes.

The information in this book owes a debt to the wisdom and insights provided by both historical studies and contemporary research. You can learn from your examination of these theories which components of group interaction lead to effective group performance. But learning how to be effective in a group requires more than reading about theories. You must have a chance to try out these theories, to apply these principles to your small group experiences.

The chapters in this book offer you information about how groups function as well as experiential exercises that you may practice in your groups. To improve your understanding of, and performance in, small groups, you will need to examine both your expectations of what groups can accomplish and the expectations that groups have of you. The combination of intellectual understanding and experiential exercises should help you deal with the ordinary frustrations of group participation.

After you have studied and practiced, you will have a better understanding of how groups develop, how they are influenced by their environment, how to solve problems and make decisions in groups, how to manage conflicts, how to develop leadership skills, and how to evaluate and improve both your own and your group's performance.

The purpose of this book is to help you become more comfortable and competent as a group member. A great deal is being asked of you. But as you read, learn, and practice, you will become aware of how your behavior will affect everyone else in your group. By interacting and reflecting on your group experiences, by taking the responsibility to do your best, you can learn to participate more skillfully and effectively. If you accept the challenge, and I hope you do, then everyone in the group will prosper.

SUMMARY

This chapter has introduced you to the study of small groups. Since you are surrounded by, and will participate in, many types of groups, learning about how you can be an effective participator in this everyday event should be valuable to you.

Examining the small group is a mechanism for enriched study. You can learn about the multiple functions of group members, the effect of individual behavior on group outcome, and the implications of group problem solving and decision making on the larger society. You can also acquire an intellectual understanding of the theories and practice of effective group performance.

The group is defined as a small number of people who interact face to face, share a common purpose, are mutually influential, and express a sense of belonging. Working in a group has advantages: the stimulation of social relationships, the multiple resources available for more creative problem solving, the potential for more effective decisions. On the other hand, working in a group carries certain disadvantages: the pressures for conformity, the inefficiencies of individual interactions, and the difficulties of dealing with personalities.

Five theoretical perspectives are analyzed as a way to understand the applications of small group study. From Lewin's field theory you learn that the individual is affected by the group, but that the group is also affected by individual behavior. Lewin's work introduces the fundamental components of the small group—norms, roles, power, influence, and cohesion.

The visual diagrams of Moreno allow you to evaluate the climate of a group. By studying the flow of communication, you can observe who relates to whom, who is a likely star or leader, and who is an isolate. Moreno's sociometric theory offers insight into the effect of attraction and rejection on group interaction.

Bion's study of therapy groups provides an understanding of the role of a group's emotional states. You learn that members may engage in fight or flight, pair off with other members, and show dependency on other members or the leader. Each of these states affects the overall performance of a group.

Bales' interactionist approach focuses on communicative acts that can be coded to reflect socioemotional activity—behavior involving interpersonal relationships and task activity, behavior that helps a group solve a problem. Using the Interaction Process Analysis provides information about group interaction, about changes in a group's development, and about satisfied and dissatisfied groups.

From systems theory you gain an understanding that a group must be examined as a whole, for each act influences every other act. Examining the group as a system means looking at the inputs from the environment, the processes a group uses to communicate information, and the outputs of its deliberations.

In sum, the theories and theorists, beginning with the roots of small group study to general systems theory, are applicable to the study of many types of groups. As you move through this book, you will acquire a theoretical knowledge of small group communication. You will gain, as well, a practical understanding of how to participate in a group: how to be an effective participant, how to manage the interpersonal relationships and conflicts within and outside the group, how to solve problems and formulate decisions, how to diagnose problems and offer remedies—the bases of small group participation.

Exercise Answers

Following are the answers for "The Individual and the Group" exercise on page 6: arm, ear, eye, lip, gum, rib, toe, leg, hip, jaw, lid (as in eyelid).

REFERENCES

Asch, S. 1951. "Effects of Group Pressure Upon Modification and Distortion of Judgment." In Harold Guetzkow (ed.), *Groups, Leadership and Men.* Pittsburgh: Carnegie Press, pp. 68–76.

Bales, R. F. 1950. *Interaction Process Analysis: A Method for the Study of Small Groups.* Reading, Mass.: Addison-Wesley.

Bales, R. F., and F. L. Strodtbeck. 1951. "Phases in Group Problem-Solving." *Journal of Abnormal and Social Psychology* 46: 485–495.

Bennis, E. G., and H. A. Shepard. 1956. "A Theory of Group Development." *Human Relations* 9: 415–437.

Berg, D. M. 1967. "A Descriptive Analysis of Distribution and Duration of Themes Discussed by Task-Oriented Groups." *Speech Monographs* 34: 172–175.

Berlo, D. K. 1960. *The Process of Communication.* New York: Holt, Rinehart and Winston.

Bion, W. R. 1961. *Experience in Groups.* New York: Basic Books.

Blau, P. M. 1964. *Exchange and Power in Social Life.* New York: Wiley.

Bormann, E. G. 1975. *Discussion and Group Methods: Theory and Practice.* (2nd ed.) New York: Harper & Row.

Festinger, L. 1957. *A Theory of Cognitive Dissonance.* Evanston, Ill.: Row, Peterson.

Fisher, B. A. 1975. "Communication Study in System Perspective." In B. Rubin and J. Y. Kim (eds.), *General Systems Theory and Human Communication.* Rochelle Park, N.J.: Hayden, pp. 191–206.

Fisher, B. A. 1980. *Small Group Decision Making.* (2nd ed.). New York: McGraw-Hill.

Forsyth, D. R. 1983. *An Introduction to Group Dynamics.* Monterey, Calif.: Brooks/Cole.

Gouran, D. S. 1969. "Variables Related to Consensus in Group Discussions of Questions of Policy." *Speech Monographs* 36: 387–391.

Gouran, D. S. 1982. *Making Decisions in Groups: Choices and Consequences.* Glenview, Ill.: Scott, Foresman.

Heslin, R., and D. Dunphy. 1964. "Three Dimensions of Members' Satisfaction in Small Groups." *Human Relations* 17: 99–112.

Homans, G. C. 1950. *The Human Group.* New York: Harcourt, Brace.

James, J. 1951. "A Preliminary Study of the Size Determinant in Small Group Interaction." *American Sociological Review* 16: 474–477.

Janis, I. L. 1982. *Victims of Groupthink.* New York: Houghton Mifflin.

Janis, I. L., and L. Mann. 1977. *Decision Making: A Psychological Analysis of Conflict, Choice, and Commitment.* New York: Free Press.

Lewin, K. 1951. *Field Theory in Social Science.* New York: Harper & Row.

Moreno, J. L. 1953. *Who Shall Survive?* (rev. ed.). Beacon, N.Y.: Beacon House.

Phillips, G. M. 1973. *Communication and the Small Group.* Indianapolis: Bobbs-Merrill.

Shaw, M. E. 1981. *Group Dynamics: The Psychology of Small Group Behavior.* (3rd ed.). New York: McGraw-Hill.

Shepherd, C. R. 1964. *Small Groups: Some Sociological Perspectives.* San Francisco: Chandler.

Steiner, I. D. 1972. *Group Process and Productivity.* New York: Academic Press.

Thibaut, J. W., and H. H. Kelley. 1959. *The Social Psychology of Groups.* New York: Wiley.

Wheeler, L., and J. Nezlek. 1977. "Sex Differences in Social Participation." *Journal of Personality and Social Psychology* 35: 742–754.

chapter *2*

Membership in the Group

How do you choose the groups you join? How do you explain why you would join one group rather than another? Are there groups you would like to be a member of, but you are not given the chance? Or are you a member of some groups that you wish you could leave but, for a variety of reasons, you cannot?

These are a few of the questions concerning membership in a group. To be a member means deciding not only which groups to join but also how you will interact with other members, what rules you will uphold, and what roles you will play. Membership also includes expectations—those you have for yourself and those you have for others, as well as the expectations other members have for you.

The words *group* and *membership* tend to be used synonymously, with one being defined in terms of the other. What membership indicates, however, is a relationship between an individual and a group. It involves a recognition of the quality of the individual's relationship to the group. If you are a member of a group, whether by choice or by accident of birth, the questions become, How are you supposed to act? What is to be your status? What do others expect of you? Although, from time to time, your individual needs and the group's needs may come into conflict, you and the group are nevertheless interdependent entities. Thus membership becomes a frame of reference. Your interactions with others will influence both how you function and what actions and decisions the group may take.

This chapter explores how individuals affect, and are affected by, membership in a group. We will examine the diverse groups, both voluntary and nonvoluntary, of which you are a member. The focus will be on why individuals join groups and the ways in which groups influence and fulfill individual needs. Then we will analyze the various roles that individuals perform—those that are vital for group survival, those that foster a good climate and good relationships, and those that discourage meaningful group activity. The final section will consider how individuals can help create a functioning group.

WHAT GROUP MEMBERSHIP MEANS

Kurt Back (1951), in his inquiry into whether the reasons for joining a group alter the way individuals behave in a group, made some interesting observations. He found that if a person is primarily seeking friendship, then he or she spends more time talking with others and working harder at trying to establish good relationships. In contrast, if the individual's interest is in getting something accomplished, then there is more effort directed toward finishing the task as quickly as possible. On the other hand, when prestige is the important factor, the person will probably be more cautious about speaking out. The fear of losing credibility or of jeopardizing standing in the group may keep the individual from expressing ideas that may not be acceptable to others (Mortensen 1972).

Think of the many groups of which you are a member. You could begin with those groups close to home—your family, friends, people at work, and in your classes. You could expand this list by putting down all the activities you participate in—sports, politics, government, business, special clubs. Were these all voluntary choices? Or are you a member of a group through little or no choice of your own?

For any group of which you are a member, you should ask what you expect from membership and what others will expect of you (Lindesmith and Strauss 1968). You can be actively involved, very influential, and consequently awarded high status by your group. On the other hand, you can be inactive, and only nominally considered a part of the group. As your involvement varies, so will your impact on the group and the group's impact on you. Sometimes you will encounter problems about the aims and direction of the groups to which you belong. Inevitably, the choices you make about your role in the group—how much you participate and which groups you appreciate—will be determined by two factors: the values the group represents and the reasons you have for joining (Quey 1971).

Some of the groups you are part of you did not choose—race,

sex, and nationality are obvious ones; and, as a member of a family, you become a part of the family's religious, regional, and socioeconomic groups. It is not only that you join with people who accept and support you; it is that the association with a particular group defines you as an individual and gives you an identity.

Your individual identity is closely associated with patterns of acceptance and rejection by the groups in which you are or would like to be a member (Lindesmith and Strauss 1968). This is why you may feel a sense of anxiety when you enter a new group. Will you be accepted and paid attention to, or will you be ignored? Most of the time you can tell whether you have been accepted, whether you are "in" and not "out." But for some people it is such an important issue that they look for tangible evidence to verify that they belong to a desired group. The Green Book, which identifies "Who's Who in Society" in Washington, D.C., is one the more eagerly sought-after publications. Joseph Kennedy, Sr., father of John, Robert, Edward, and other members of the Kennedy clan, moved his family from Boston to New York because he thought they would never be accepted into Boston's "high society." Since they were Catholic and did not represent "old money," he felt they would not be included (McTaggart 1983).

If you would like to learn more specifically about the effect of group labels on the individual, the exercise "The Effect of Gender on Individuals and Groups" will help you discover your reactions.

THE EFFECT OF GENDER ON INDIVIDUALS AND GROUPS

Assemble groups of six to ten members, divided according to gender. Any number of groups can participate. Each group is to have two large sheets of paper and a marking pen. The groups of women and the groups of men are to respond to two questions.

The first question concerns women's and men's perceptions of themselves. As a group of women or a group of men representing the "class" of women or the "class" of men, give your first thoughts to the question, "How do you think women (men) see themselves as women (men)?" The responses of each group are to reflect a world view rather than an individual perspective.

Each group brainstorms—any phrase, adjective, feeling is recorded on paper (or blackboard) and posted. (One of the group members serves as a recorder, writing down all comments.) No response is to be censored—all are worth recording.

Each group should then look over its list and mark with an

asterisk those items members believe would apply to 75 percent of the population of women (or men). The starred items represent a reasonable generalization, labels that would be applicable to roughly three-quarters of the population.

The same process is used for the second question: "How do you think (women/men) view (men/women)?"

A recorder for each group summarizes the group's thinking and shares the results with all participants. A discussion is then held on what the groups have experienced and what has been learned.

Comments on the Exercise

If your group is similar to others that have done this exercise, perhaps you discussed and answered questions similar to the following:

Why are the men's lists shorter than the women's?

Do men tend to see themselves more positively than women see themselves?

Do groups of men and groups of women believe that the others see them in more negative ways?

Do the lists reflect current views about men and women?

The results, although probably not unexpected, can still be puzzling. As you discuss your responses in this exercise, you will discover how a gender label affects the attitudes of participants and consequently group interactions. Although we would like to believe that we are no longer affected by ideas from our past, our behavior may reflect something different from our cognitive beliefs. In a provocative experiment, a teacher demonstrated the arbitrariness, as well as the subjectivity, of labels when she divided her class into brown-eyed and blue-eyed groups. She created antagonism between the two groups merely by giving more favors to the brown-eyed children.

As the gender exercise demonstrates, many of us are still susceptible to stereotypical reactions. A group label not only establishes expectations but creates stereotypical reactions. While some of the responses reflect views that should have been put aside long ago, one important learning from this exercise is that membership in groups carries with it the responsibility for evaluating your responses to, and the interactions with, group members. As you examine your membership in voluntary and nonvoluntary groups, you will find that both groups affect interaction patterns, roles undertaken, and decisions made.

WHY PEOPLE JOIN GROUPS

One of the important questions to consider is, Why do you choose to join a particular group? As discussed in Chapter 1, an advantage of being in a group is that it can enlarge the members' potential for accomplishment. The data indicate another important reason for joining a group: membership may confer prestige—members may gain access to important people and their own status may thereby be enhanced (Napier and Gershenfeld 1985). Of the many motivations for joining a group, three appear to be universal (Quey 1971).

A group can help you do what would ordinarily be difficult to do alone.

1. You join because you are attracted to individuals in the group. The bonds of friendship—the particular people you like to be with—motivate you to join with them.
2. You join because the activities of the group are activities you wish to pursue. A group can help you accomplish what would ordinarily be difficult to do alone. It is doubtless comfortable to be surrounded by other people with similar interests who support you and help you meet your goals.
3. You join because being a member of a group offers other potential benefits outside the group—job opportunities, the chance to meet new people, the opportunity to travel, and so on.

Some theorists have formulated specific reasons why people join groups. We will examine two of these theorists' work.

Fulfilling Individual Needs

Eric Berne (1963), a psychoanalyst, gives a more fundamental reason for joining groups—that of survival. He claims that the need for joining a group is even more basic than the desire for friendship and activities. Moreover, a group may be the only way to fulfill individual needs. Rather than being merely a voluntary choice, the motivation, or drive, for joining is biological. Every individual needs stroking, literally and symbolically, as Berne explains with an example of infants in a foundling hospital:

> In infants, the withholding of caresses and normal human contact . . . [that is] "emotional deprivation," results directly or indirectly in physical as well as mental deterioration. (p. 157)

In addition to a biological need, Berne indicates that psychological needs must also be met. People long for social contact because they do not prosper when they are alone for too long a time. Idleness is too demoralizing for most people; therefore, they look for help. As an example, consider the enormous salaries paid to entertainers who help us spend our time. Moreover to offset the feeling of loneliness, we may be willing to give up many of our individual preferences to experience the satisfaction that association with others can bring. As Berne puts it, it is not only the activities of the group that attract us. It is what group activity can bring—people to interact with, ideas to exchange, the chance to gossip and to play. In sum, according to Berne's view, we become members of groups to fulfill such needs as these:

1. A biological need for stimulation—touching, stroking, hugging.
2. A psychological need for time structuring—talking, working, playing.
3. A social need for intimacy—being close, sharing thoughts and feelings.
4. A physiological need for safety—a longing for the security and safety of childhood.

Fulfilling Interpersonal Needs

William Schutz (1958) affirms that basic needs motivate individuals to become members of groups, but he offers different terms to describe what individuals need. Schutz states that the drive to meet interpersonal needs is the most compelling. He identifies these needs as inclusion, control, and affection.

Inclusion refers to the need to be wanted, to be "in" and not "out"—the need to be recognized as an individual of some worth. People want to be consulted, to be told what is going on, to be asked for their suggestions and opinions. In this way they are confirmed as worthy individuals.

Control represents a desire for personal influence, a chance to have a say in the group's decisions. The control need is most visible when a group is considering proposals. When your ideas are accepted, when you realize that you have been influential, then your being in a group becomes rewarding.

Affection in its most basic sense is the need to be liked, to be able to establish close personal relationships with others. It is in part the desire to be close to others, and in part the desire for others to want to be close to you. People want to be able both to give and to receive emotional warmth and esteem.

When a group first forms, Schutz contends, members most desire to know that they are accepted. The need for inclusion predominates. Control needs are more apparent as the group continues its work. When members begin to develop proposals, to argue over issues, and to reach a decision, they are then focusing on control needs. As members work on their differences, they look for reassurance. Despite any friction that might occur in the group, they would like to know that they are still liked and accepted. This is when affection needs are most important.

The movement from inclusion, to control, and to affection is a progression that is not limited just to a group's early stages; it is a continuous process (Maslow 1954). As individuals communicate with one another, they are able to provide for the continuing needs of all. In this respect the interpersonal needs are both cyclical and interdependent. They will recur throughout the life of the group, as the following excerpts relate:

> In our group there was no risk involved in speaking, whether on the task or off the task, because we were continually reinforced positively by other members. Without this social interaction there would have been no interest or enthusiasm. There would have been more pressure on us to contribute to the group. We might have been bored and uneasy with each other. We spent much of the time socializing, yet we always managed to get back to the topic at hand and complete what we started. Sometimes we socialized more than we worked, but it helped the cohesiveness of the group. On the whole our group came together because there was always someone to redirect us back to the problem.

In these examples you can appreciate that groups prosper when members feel that the group pays attention to their interpersonal needs. Schutz (1958) believes that when members give what is needed as well as ask for what is needed—matching one another in their *expressed* (to others) and *wanted* (from others) interpersonal needs—they will form compatible groups. If you meet the complementary needs of others, Schutz feels, you will be able to work with a minimum of friction. Although individuals vary in the intensity of their interpersonal needs, groups are at risk when they fail to satisfy the needs of members for inclusion, affection, and control.

NONVOLUNTARY GROUPS AND REFERENCE GROUPS

Although we choose groups to satisfy interpersonal needs, we also belong to groups that we have not directly chosen. While such groupings—by race, sex, religion, age, and even family—can be thought of as *nonvoluntary* (and sometimes even the category "compulsory" may apply), it is important to recognize the influence they have on our perceptions of who we are and how we interact with others (Napier and Gershenfeld 1985). Frequently, in the absence of any specific information about us as individuals, people may still formulate expectations about us based on what Joseph Berger labeled "specific-status characteristics" (Forsyth 1983). For example, a grouping by age is an indicator of different expectations. The classification "senior citizens," while it carries some privileges, often signifies a closing down or an ending of vigorous activities. On the other hand, being classified as a "young adult" implies continuing growth.

Similarly, geographic location—city, state, region, nation—affects the way others perceive us. If you have grown up in New York City, the expectations about you will vary considerably from the expectations about a person raised in a small town or rural area. Some state and regional identifications are perceived positively; others get a negative reaction. And as the flags of nations indicate, they suggest a host of divergent perceptions and identifications.

Let's look at the implications of the multiple groups to which you belong. The "Multiple Membership Identification" exercise will allow you to consider the importance of such groups and their impact on you.

MULTIPLE MEMBERSHIP IDENTIFICATION*

Procedure

For each of the dimensions in the left-hand column below, choose only *one* of the terms from the right column and circle it. If you choose "other," then write in the term that you find more appropriate.

After you have made choices for all the dimensions, in-

---

*This exercise was developed in the Human Relations Laboratory, Center for Applied Social Science, Boston University.

cluding the last category, a "forced choice" (you must choose only one of the dimensions), share your choices for all categories with other participants. You can do this either by a facilitator asking for a show of hands, or by assembling with people who have chosen the same label and discussing your reasons for your choice with them.

Family relations:	Parent, child, spouse, lover, single, sibling, other
Age:	Ageless, mature, childlike, young, middle-aged, adult, other
Sex:	Man, woman, male, female, person, human being, other
Origin:	American, Jewish, black, white, wasp, ethnic, other
Religion:	Protestant, Catholic, Jewish, humanist, atheist, searcher, other
Status:	Educated, professional, helper, influential, student, worker, other
Political/economic orientation:	Liberal, radical, conservative, apolitical, independent, leftist, other
Dimensions (forced choice):	Family relations, age, sex, origin, religion, status, political/economic orientation

Reaction

As you discuss why individuals choose one category rather than another, consider the explanations for their choice. As an example, for the dimension "Sex," why did some people choose the label "Male" and others "Man"? Similarly, what were the reasons for choosing "female" rather than "woman"? What meaning did "person" or "human being" have for those who chose that label?

Comments on the Exercise

The exercise depends on your making a "forced choice" among categories. By doing so, you learn about the different perceptions, values, and associations people make when choosing a term. You learn that your beliefs and behavior reflect social forces as well as personal development. Gender, age, ethnicity, status, and cultural background serve as ways to differentiate one individual from another. The implication of learning about the effect of multiple groups is that, more often than not, you will have incorporated both the personal and the social expectations into your interactions with other people (Phillips and Erikson 1970).

Reference Groups   As you discuss the choices you made in the Multiple Membership Identification exercise, you will find that another concept has been identified. It will become evident that the groups you choose, as well as the groups you have not chosen, serve as a "reference group" for you. A *reference group* is any group—current, past, admired—that significantly shapes the way you feel, think, and believe. Reference groups influence both attitudes and relationships with other members within a group as well as with other groups. For example, Hyman (1960), in a study evaluating the impact of reference groups on the way students view their status, found that students relied largely on their family's economic position in determining their status. Thus economic position was the reference group students used as a guide in judging their own status.

Inevitably, members' reference groups affect how members deal with each other. The more important the group, the more likely it will serve as a reference group. Even when individuals are unaware that they are being influenced by a particular reference group, they will react and respond on the basis of their identification with these groups (Festinger 1957). Indeed, as you examine your reference groups, you will learn a great deal about your beliefs.

COMPARATIVE AND NORMATIVE PERSPECTIVES IN GROUP CHOICE

There are other important conclusions to be learned from the exercise. We can learn about the principles, or perspectives, people use in making their choices. As an illustration, let's look at the results of several small groups discussing the labels they chose in the Political/Economic Orientation dimension. There were 15 people who divided themselves according to the following categories:

Liberal (5)

Radical (0)

Conservative (2)

Apolitical (2)

Independent (6)

Leftist (0)

The reasons they gave for their choices were these.

We're *liberal* because we are more open, more willing to look at what's happening. Only then do we decide what should be done. We're not fixed—rigid—like the conservatives. We don't think that everything in the past is the only way things should be. We are much more interested in changing things when they need to be changed. As *conservatives* we are more interested in preserving our way of life. We believe in tradition. Some people think we're old-fashioned, but that doesn't bother us. We don't believe that we have to change things just for the sake of change—something the liberals do all the time. We take our time, we think about things more, we don't get caught up in the latest fad. When we say that we are *apolitical* it doesn't mean that we don't know anything about politics. It's just that we can't believe in the promises of the political parties. We really don't think that either party offers anything different. Sometimes we vote, but we don't think that our vote really changes anything. As *independents* we don't want to be taken for granted. We will not vote for a candidate just because he or she has a label "Republican" or "Democrat." It's a lot harder to be an independent than a Republican or Democrat. We have to look at the issues and then decide. We are not just going to vote without thinking.

These responses illustrates a significant point. When members choose particular dimensions, they rely on two principles. The first is the *comparative* perspective. The standards for judgment each group uses is based on the individuals' estimates of the value of their group compared with other groups. Liberals and conservatives saw themselves pitted one against the other. Independents compared themselves to both groups, and apoliticals suggested that they differed from everyone else; they judged who they were by comparing themselves to their opposite number.

Kelley (1952) and Thibaut and Kelley (1959) introduced the terms *comparison level* and *comparison level for alternatives* to describe how the values and costs of group interaction determine group satisfaction. Overall, one's preferences for a group will conform to a *minimax* principle—people will choose groups that provide them with the maximum number of rewards and the minimum number of costs (Forsyth 1983). *Comparison level* (CL) is the standard by which we evaluate the desirability of group membership. We might simply ask, "Do I want to be a member of this group?" Comparison level for alternatives (Clalt) is the standard by which we compare groups with other available groups. Here we ask, "From what I know about this group, am I better off here or with some other group?"

The comparative perspective applies to all three types of groups—voluntary, involuntary, and reference. For example, if you are given a choice of doing a research project working alone or with a group, you will undoubtedly try to estimate the likely benefits and costs of each. If you decide to choose the group approach, you might weigh such issues as the fact that you could develop friendships, there would be social interaction, more people would help get the job done, and so on. You also would think about negative experiences in groups—a lot of time is wasted, it's hard to get people together, not everyone does his or her share of the work, you might not like your assignment, and so on. By using a comparative perspective, you define the worth of a group. You will remain a part of a group that has a favorable reward-to-cost ratio.

The question for any group member is what you can expect from membership and what others will expect of you.

The second principle is the *normative* one. By choosing to identify with a specific category, you uphold the values associated with that category. "Are you with us or against us?" is a typical rallying cry. People who do not reflect the beliefs implicit in a particular group are judged harshly. The expectation that people will conform to the values of the group makes it difficult for anyone to dissent from a group action. Because the reward of being "in" rather than "out" is so desirable, the group is able to exact a price. Members will expect acceptance of what the group represents. As a member, you can either go along—and pay the price—or give up membership in the group (Festinger 1957).

THE FUNCTION OF ROLES IN A GROUP

That we are different people with our friends than with our parents, and different with an intimate friend than with an acquaintance is readily observed. Social scientists refer to the different behaviors we display in our interactions with others as *roles* (Forsyth 1983). How is a "role" to be defined? The concept of role, borrowed from the theater, refers to the character an actor portrays in a play. Similarly, in a group, it is a position an individual takes, a "part," that is performed during the life of a group, including all interactions and contributions to the task and social needs of the group. In every group various roles evolve that differentiate the functions group members perform or need to perform.

Roles in groups are worked out through communication with other members (Zander 1971). Your individual way of behaving in a group, rather than how the group as a whole behaves, is your undertaking of a role. Erving Goffman (1959), in his discussion of role performance, shows that a large number of communication devices and interaction tactics are used when a person takes on a role. The role or roles you perform are influenced by the expectations that you have set for yourself. As you become part of a group, your individual way of interacting affects how others view you and react to you. The impressions that members have of you and of your abilities help form the expectations of what roles you will fulfill. And, like roles in a play, group roles are independent of the personal characteristics of specific individuals. They can be filled by any person willing to perform them.

Groups vary in what they consider necessary roles in the group and in the way these roles will be distributed. Some groups are highly structured—roles such as leader and recorder are assigned (Lindesmith and Stauss 1968). In less formal groups, members may interchange roles, although after a group continues to meet, role specialization usually occurs. Even in social groups, where roles are to a large extent flexible, members come to expect certain behaviors from individuals. Interactions with other members are predicated on members filling certain roles. If a member fails to meet a role expectation, the group may become disorganized. Consider the following example:

A neighborhood group in a town near a nuclear energy plant took on the task of getting information about the safety of the plant. At the same time the group was exploring whether any nuclear energy plant should be located near major cities. One of the members, Dan, a computer software specialist, who had once been employed by the Environmental Protection Agency, was very knowledge-able about nuclear energy. At their meetings, the members listened to Dan's recitation of facts and his explanations of difficult concepts; they looked to him for leadership.

For one of their meetings, the members invited a few officials from the local plant to attend, so that they could begin discussions about issues that involved them both. They had planned to provide the officials with the information they

had gathered. The group assembled before the meeting was to start, and Dan
was not present. The group panicked. How could they carry on without him, they
wondered?

Dan's role as information provider was crucial to the welfare
of the group. It was not that others in the group did not understand
the problem. Rather, it was that Dan had more specialized knowledge and would be better able to answer any questions directed at
the group. Although many members can fill the roles a group needs,
sometimes a group is unable to function when one individual is
unavailable or fails to meet its requirements.

Role Differentiation

When members of a group begin meeting, they probably see themselves as fairly similar to each other. But in their continuing deliberations, they start to take on different roles. This process researchers
have called *role differentiation* (Forsyth 1983). What we have
learned from research on role differentiation is that some roles are
absolutely essential for a group's good health—indeed, even its survival. Other roles seem to discourage a group from completing its
task.

Task Specialist and Social-Emotional Specialist   Robert Bales (1950), in
his laboratory studies of role differentiation, found that roles could
be classified into three basic types: (1) the role in which individuals
try to achieve their goals; (2) the role of assisting the group to accomplish group goals; and (3) the role in which the individual tries to
build harmonious relations.
    Individuals trying to attain their goals can have either a posi-
tive or a negative impact on the group. If the individual's goals and
the group's goals mesh, then both the individual and the group may
find their task somewhat easier. On the other hand, if the individual's goals deviate from those of the group, say, somebody has a
personal agenda, then the ensuing friction will take the group away
from its task. What is essential is that the group have a person who
performs as a *task specialist.* This person takes the responsibility
for performing the substantive work of the group. A group also
needs someone to play a supportive, nurturant role, what Bales labeled a *social-emotional specialist.* This role helps the group reduce
tension and the strain of interpersonal hostilities.
    As Bales explained, the roles of task specialist and social-emo-
tional specialist are interdependent. Nevertheless, he believed that
one person would find it difficult to perform both roles. His reasoning was that someone who is oriented to getting a task accomplished
necessarily gives more directions, prods the group along, and re-

strains some members from interacting. Although a task specialist may get a negative reaction and increase the tension in the group, without the prodding to get the task done, the group may not succeed. On the other hand, a social-emotional specialist, concerned about the relationships of people, will not likely exert pressure on individuals to move toward their goals. Yet this person serves a vital function in helping the group maintain harmonious relationships. (The concept of dual roles is also considered in the discussion of leadership in Chapter 5.)

Task Roles, Maintenance Roles, and Personal Roles The earliest classification of roles, developed by Benne and Sheats (1948), itemized three broad categories of roles played in groups—task roles, maintenance roles, and personal roles. Essentially, task roles include such communicative behavior as these:

1. Offering new ideas.
2. Asking for clarification of ideas.
3. Contributing relevant information.
4. Keeping the discussion on track.
5. Evaluating the adequacy of the group's information.

Maintenance roles focus on these functions:

1. Providing support or acceptance for ideas of others.
2. Suggesting an idea that everyone will like.
3. Helping provide a good climate for the group.

Personal roles are individual roles that detract from what the group is trying to do, such as attacking other members, not being involved in the group, taking up the group's time with irrelevant comments, and opposing ideas brought up by others. These roles and their influence on communicative interaction are discussed more extensively in Chapter 3 as an illustration of the kinds of interaction that go along with certain types of roles.

The categories identified by Benne and Sheats have been widely used to show how the content and style of communication is strongly influenced by an individual's role. Although people can undertake several roles in a group, frequently they settle for one predominant role. In the following excerpt, members are discussing proposals for altering the image of their university. Several roles stand out.

> LAURA: O.K. Is there a proposal we can make about the minority population?
>
> DARLENE: Rather than saying "minority population," can't we just discuss minority events?

MADELINE: Or events in general . . .

LAURA: Or weekend events in general.

MICHAEL: The thing is, we shouldn't restrict it to just minority students. I think a major point is weekend activities, because that has a lot to do with our image as a suitcase school, and that really hurts the school a lot.

JONATHAN: I think Mike has a great point. The student entertainment committee has come a long way, but it should do more.

LINDA: Well, the dorms are doing a lot. The type of thing that bothers me is when they hold events, really publicize them, get everyone psyched to go, and then hold it in a place too small, so that not everyone can get in.

MICHAEL: But they do that because they figure everyone's going home on the weekend. They also hold concerts on Sunday because they figure everyone would be back then. Maybe they should hold activities like that on Saturdays instead. Maybe the way to get people to stay around campus is to generate more enthusiasm for what goes on here during the weekend.

MADELINE: Well, I always stay for Spring Weekend, and others do too. So I guess people will stay if they think it's worth it.

MICHAEL: As a matter of fact, one point is that here we put on everything for entertainment during the week. If these were put on during weekends, more people would stay and we wouldn't have the reputation of being a party school.

DARLENE: I agree with you, Michael. If we had more events on weekends, we would establish some kind of intellectual tradition.

LINDA: I think we have some important ideas for further consideration. Weekends should be as much a part of the experience of going to college as working and studying are.

LAURA: It sounds to me as if the problem that we should focus on is how to create the events to keep people here on weekends and also to counteract an image that all we do here on weekends is drink.

LINDA: Great point, Laura. Can we brainstorm some ideas?

In this very brief segment of a group at work, how many roles can you identify? If you were to use these roles to evaluate the dialogue of the group above, you would conclude that both task and maintenance roles were present. Darlene, Madeline, and Laura are helping to define the task by clarifying the goal of the group. Michael and Linda provide relevant information. In addition, Laura gives direction to the group and Darlene and Jonathan give support to others.

Necessary Roles   Cragan and Wright (1986), basing their approach on the analysis of Benne and Sheats but offering some distinctive titles for the roles that are important to a group, give us an economical way to recognize roles and the expectations as to how they are to be fulfilled.

1. *The leader role.* This role, perceived as both a task role and a maintenance role, carries with it both status and expectations. A major expectation for the task leader is that he or she will be in the forefront of the group's discussion, helping others to process ideas, giving directions, settling differences as they occur, and generally assisting the progress with the task. A maintenance leader is expected to provide encouragement to group members, helping them to feel included and effective as they work on the group's task.

2. *The tension releaser role.* The person in this role knows when and how to reduce the tension in the group. By telling a good story, cracking a joke, or making a pertinent comment, the individual provides temporary relief to the group. This role is typically valued. But when a group is working hard and looking seriously at a problem, an untimely joke may not be acceptable. While the tension releaser can contribute to the health of a group, inappropriate or badly timed humor can bring hostility to the person who plays the clown.

3. *The information provider role.* The information provider brings in data, in the form of research, readings, interviews, expert opinion, observations, and so forth. While many individuals can and should perform this role, it is a role that calls for critical skills, especially the ability to analyze the reasoning and inferences made by members. Because of the demands of the role, some groups tend to let one skilled individual predominate. A more effective group would share the role. This would allow many people to contribute. And as one member expressed her reaction to being an information provider, the role has several unexpected benefits.

> The interaction with the other students has been great. I can't believe the many different ideas that can come from just a small group of seven. This has been especially good for me because I usually don't say very much. But being in a group like this has made me feel more confident about bringing up my ideas.

4. *The central negative role.* In this role the person challenges either the leader or members when he or she believes they are moving too rapidly over the data or when uninformed opinion seems to be swaying the group. Although a person in this role may criticize a particular action, it need not be a destructive role. On the

contrary, if played well, the central negative assists the group in thinking critically about both the task and the group's process.

Another value is that the role introduces conflict. The group is thereby encouraged to consider other ideas and, perhaps as a result, may come to a higher-quality decision. (The importance of conflict in the nourishing of ideas is discussed in Chapter 8.) If, however, the role is not well performed, it may be seen as obstructing the group's progress, because the person either is blocking the group from taking an agreed-upon action or is trying to impose his or her views on the group.

Four Remaining Roles   The four roles outlined by Cragan and Wright are most important in helping a group reach its goals. Four other roles, although of lesser potency, are still necessary for group interaction.

Questioner. In this role, the concern is more with seeking clarification; in asking for information, a questioner assists the group in clarifying and evaluating ideas.

Silent observer. In every group there is likely to be a person who sits quietly but is also evaluating what is going on. The role is not a passive one, however. Through nonverbal action or by making comments after all voices have been heard, the silent observer becomes a valued resource in the group. An excerpt from a member's diary illustrates how this role may affect a group.

> This meeting was great! We got through so many items. I couldn't believe Kim. She was so quiet in our first meeting, but totally opened up in our third. Kim and I had the most solutions to the parking problem on campus. The more we discussed solutions, the more she came up with. Everyone, it seemed, breathed a sigh of relief and relaxed after we discussed all of our proposals.

Active listener. In many ways this role overlaps with the silent observer role. Yet it is distinctive and a role that everyone can perform. By head-nodding, by statements of agreement, and other forms of reinforcement, members in this role invite others to explain their views. The importance of the role lies in the way it encourages people to participate. With more active listening going on, and more rather than fewer members participating, the group's discussion of ideas is greatly enhanced.

Self-centered follower. Unlike the central negative, a role intended to be a positive force in the group, the self-centered follower is truly a negative influence. It is the "blocking" role identified by Benne and Sheats. The self-centered follower offers a group what it does not need: special pleading, negative responses, lack of concern about what the group is doing, or communication that blocks group action.

The dialogue below is of a group discussing how to choose

topics for a lecture series. You can discern the self-centered follower rather easily, yet even when you can identify the role, it is difficult to know how to handle it. But if the other positive roles are in abundance, then even this type of obstruction can be surmounted.

TRICIA: We have to determine what is of most interest to college students. We need to know what will affect their lives most directly. We can do this by developing a questionnaire. We can give students our list of potential topics, and they can rate them.

BETH: It will never work, Tricia! Questionnaires are never returned. You never reach enough people to satisfy the requirements of a random survey.

TRICIA: I understand what you are saying, Beth, but the idea of a questionnaire is a good, solid place to start.

JOE: It certainly could give us the information we need.

BETH: Oh, this is ridiculous. We obviously need to do something, but a questionnaire hardly seems like the way for us to go ahead.

TRICIA: Can you suggest some other way, then?

BETH: I think this meeting is a farce! If all you can think of is "questionnaires," then we'll never get anywhere.

As you can surmise, a group fortunate enough to have members performing positive roles, with negative roles kept to a minimum, is a group likely to be productive and effective.

ROLES, STATUS, AND IDENTITY

Although members assume a number of roles in groups, they are not always clearly defined. Which role is necessary and how a role is to be performed are often unstated expectations, a situation that leads to *role ambiguity*. There may also be *role conflict*. When a group's expectations about roles differ from that of an individual's, some roles may not be performed. For example, when members do not support each other, important social-emotional roles may be missing. When information is needed and the person to provide it cannot be present, a group may have difficulty coming to a decision. Unless members discuss with each other their needs and expectations, role problems can interfere with the way a group functions.

Roles and Status

The roles you perform have an impact on a group in another way. They influence your status in the group (Wofford, Gerloff, and Cummins 1977). Some people enter a group with characteristics that confer status even before they have spoken. This is an *ascribed* status, based on such factors as an individual's age, gender, position,

or wealth. Others will be awarded status because of their abilities—
for instance, the ability to express ideas and offer suggestions and
advice. This is an *acquired* status. Status has important consequences for group communication, whether it is acquired through
hard work or ascribed because of inherent characteristics.

Status influences how often members will speak, to whom they
will speak, and what they will say. For example, higher-status people are given more leeway to speak more frequently. They receive
more messages and thus are seen as more powerful and influential
(Zander 1971). Patterns of communication are also affected. Higher-
status individuals tend to speak more frequently to other higher-
status persons. Lower-status individuals may withhold their opinions and beliefs; either they are uncertain about the reaction their
responses would receive, or they feel that they have not earned the
right to speak. Since status creates ambiguous cues affecting the
number as well as the quality of ideas exchanged, groups need to
become aware of the effect of status on their interpersonal relationships.

Roles and Identity

The roles you perform in a group are important for still another
reason. They help form your identity (Phillips and Erikson 1970).
Recognizing the connection between role behavior and an individual's quest for identity is an important factor in understanding how
groups work. Bormann (1972), in his investigation of how groups
survive, states that an individual's identity is a large component of
a group's ability to maintain itself. Thus, when someone engages in
behavior that seems to be inconsistent with what the group needs,
that person may be indicating the uncertainty of his or her identity
in the group.

The issue of identity is so strongly embedded in our self-con-
cepts that not only do we go to great lengths to protect the image we
have of ourselves, but we also look for ways to confirm that identity.
(Chapter 3 discusses at greater length the issue of individual identity and group performance.) The need for maintaining an acceptable image of self will influence the role or roles we are willing to
perform, how much we are willing to participate, and the types of
interaction we will initiate.

WHAT INDIVIDUALS CAN CONTRIBUTE TO THE GROUP

As a member of a group, you will ask yourself an important question: "What can I do to help make the group perform well? There are
three areas in which you as an individual can make a difference: in
your ability to recognize—and, if necessary, change—a group's
norms; in your willingness to help the group develop appropriate

goals; and in the qualities of credibility and sensitivity you can bring to the group.

Group Norms

Early in a group's development, members establish a pattern of behavior. These become group *norms*—standards of values or beliefs that in turn influence a person's behavior (Wofford, Gerloff, and Cummins 1977). While members may not be conscious of the norms they are instituting, they are doubtless communicating them. Norms can be identified in almost everything group members do— the kinds of clothes they wear, their patterns of speech and choice of words, the way they use information, and the energy they devote to a task. Every time a group takes a coffee break or begins a meeting late or uses small talk to delay getting down to business, members are illustrating the effect of norms.

Although some members may not conform to the norms of the group—and norms may not even be applied in the same way to everyone in the group—nonetheless, norms affect group behavior. In a positive sense, groups can use norms to improve the way they function. For instance, they can arrange self-critiquing sessions that will allow them to explore ways to run meetings more efficiently. In addition, norms permit groups to develop standards of fairness and cooperation. An appeal to fairness is a good antidote to conflict. For example, rather than fixate on win–lose solutions, groups with a norm of confronting conflict will try to settle their differences openly. (Chapter 9 discusses more fully methods for handling conflict in the group.)

Norms are not always positive for a group, however. When they are so rigidly enforced that a group is unable to respond to new circumstances, they affect the group negatively. In Chapter 7, you will learn how a norm of "no criticism" disadvantages a group by leading it to adopt the assumptions of groupthink—a situation in which overly cooperative and conforming members make poor decisions. Other hindrances to the group occur when members always take on the same roles, follow the same procedures, and continue to make the same errors without questioning whether they should consider changing their way of operating. Norms that interfere with creativity and flexibility, and those that discourage individual contributions, need to be questioned and, it is hoped, changed for the better.

An individual contributes to a group when he or she helps to change unproductive norms into more productive ones. One way to help is to be aware of the effect of norms on the communicative behavior of members. If you notice that some members seem not to talk very often, you can serve as a questioner to help bring out their views. By example, you can help give them the opportunity—the time and the space—to express their views. Or you can move to change a norm that is disadvantageous by altering the environment. Instead of meeting in the same place, suggest another location. Your task group may become more social and less conflicted if you meet for dinner, for example.

You can also alter standards by not always honoring them. For instance, if your group has a standard of not allowing social interaction, you can deviate from this norm by engaging in some informal conversation. You can also seek the aid of another member to help you establish a more beneficial norm. In this way, you may be able to gain sufficient strength to institute a desired change. What is important is that you understand that norms can be used to benefit a group and—although it may be difficult to do and sometimes even problematic—it is worth considering changing norms if a change will help. When members subscribe to norms that enrich the interactions of members, the group gains.

Group Goals

As you think about where you are today—which of your goals you have achieved and which ones you are still working toward—you can realize the place that goals have had in motivating you. Indeed, the desire to achieve, to self-actualize, is considered a primary motivating force for individual growth and development (Maslow 1954). Just as with individuals, groups also are motivated by the need to accomplish some aim, whether it is a long-range goal or several short-term objectives. In ideal circumstances your goals would correspond with the group's goals (Baird and Weinberg 1981). But when you join a group, you are confronted with the schism among diverse interests. You have the choice of going after your own interests, the interests of the group, accommodating both sets of interests, or none of these (Forsyth 1983).

It is not unreasonable to assume that most members will be as interested in helping a group achieve its goals as they are in satisfying their own personal needs, and yet this assumption should be tested. It would be useful for group members to clarify and explain their personal goals as well as their understanding of the group's goals. Patton and Giffin (1978) suggest that the explanations members provide about their perception of what is to be accomplished will help establish the "mutual concerns" of members.

What affects the realization of goals is that most people enter a group with an idealized expectation of what is to be attained. As Lewin and his colleagues (1944), explained after members have participated in a group for a while, they usually revise their expectations. Lewin suggested a theory of *level of aspiration* (LOA) to account for the compromises that have to be made about goals.

    Most groups try to choose goals that are neither too difficult nor too easy to achieve, although members may have to go through trial and error before selecting goals that match their abilities (Zander and Medow 1963). In this sense, goals must be doable—groups have to believe that they are capable of achieving their aims. Otherwise, members will become disillusioned. On the other hand, goals that do not challenge may bring about a lack of interest. Moreover, even when groups are clear about their goals in the beginning of their discussions, members can lose sight of what they are supposed to do (Zander 1971). By continually clarifying, defining, and redefining what the group is trying to get done, members have a better chance of reaching their goals. When members commit themselves to the group and understand and accept the group's objectives, working on a task can be rewarding.

Personal Qualities

What is also important to a group's success are the personal qualities a person brings to a group. Cragan and Wright (1986) suggest that credibility and two other closely related personal qualities, trustworthiness and competence, make a difference to a group. A fourth quality, sensitivity, is also a necessary trait for members to possess if the group is to function well.

Credibility   How knowledgeable you are and how well you articulate your knowledge will determine your reputation and your status in the group. Your ability to share information, to support your ideas with evidence, and to display fairness to others will, more than the characteristics of age, sex, occupation, and ethnicity, establish your credibility. The qualities of trustworthiness and competence will influence perceptions of your credibility.

   Trustworthiness   A judgment of how fair you are in your presentation of data and how you react to the opinions and ideas of others affects whether you will be seen as trustworthy. When you first join a group, little may be known about you. Trust develops as you continue to work in the group, disclosing bits of information about yourself and letting people know who you are by going beyond superficial facts. While trust takes time to build, you will become trustworthy when others learn to have confidence in your judgment and style of interacting with them.

   Competence   To be perceived as competent means that others respect your ability to direct a group and to move the group toward its goals. Competence is closely related to the task activities—initiating, planning, coordinating—that a group must perform. Directing a group is not dominating them. Rather, a competent person is highly interactive and serves as a vital force in attaining group goals. Many researchers, in fact, equate competence with a group's perception of an emergent leader. (Chapter 5 discusses the relationship between competence and leadership perception.)

Sensitivity The personal quality of sensitivity should be emphasized. What makes a difference to a group is having people who are responsive to the values and opinions of others. A sensitive person is one who is able to listen well. Sensitivity requires finely tuned antennae, an alertness to the views, feelings, frustrations, and fears that other persons may have. Sensitivity consists of insight into what creates a group's well-being and the ability to deliver an appropriate response, whether it is a pat on the shoulder, a smile, reinforcement of a view, or praise where needed.

A FINAL COMMENT

You enter a group with some anxiety; you are concerned about losing your identity, about being accepted by the group, and about maintaining some control over your destiny. You discover that, as a member of a group, you bring your personal predispositions to the group. You have the choice of being actively involved or of being cautious and withholding. But you also come as a member of several groups. These groups, made up of multiple social forces, influence your attitudes and beliefs as well as your receptivity to the attitudes and beliefs of other individuals and groups. But despite your anxiety and uncertainty, you will participate in groups, many of them, serving different purposes.

If you expect to gain from your group membership, you must be prepared to make some personal investments in the group (Forsyth 1983). These investments come in the form of helping the group accomplish its task goals and its maintenance goals. As an individual you can undertake several approaches to help with the task: You can keep the goals in the forefront of the group's discussion, and you can remind the group of its stated goals when members tend to move away from the group's primary purpose.

You can improve the climate of the group by your attention to such things as complimenting members on their ideas, stressing how much the group is getting done, encouraging individuals to participate, and inspiring a "we" feeling in the group. The important question to ask about your contribution is: "Am I willing to work substantially for the group's goal achievement?"

When you work with group members, helping them create realizable norms and goals, you forward the group's progress. As you display helpful personal qualities such as credibility and sensitivity, you enhance the group's functions. Each of these contributions brings favorable responses from others because they indicate your willingness to commit yourself to the group's activities. Cragan and Wright (1986) argue that your ethical behavior is at stake when you enter a group. They urge, therefore, that every person express a commitment to do his or her best to promote the good of the group. When you bring to the group your unique self—with your own special knowledge, ability, and skills—along with your resolve to work in the group's best interest, then something magical occurs.

In his novel *Sometimes a Great Notion* (1964), Ken Kesey describes a working group cutting timber. In so doing he captures the spirit of a group in which each person is committed to do the best that he or she knows how to do.

> Until the three of them meshed, dovetailed . . . into one of the rare and beautiful units of effort sometimes seen when a jazz group is making it completely, swinging together completely, or when a hometown basketball squad, already playing over its head, begins to rally to overtake a superior opponent in a game's last minute . . . and the home boys can't miss; because everything—the passing, the dribbling, the plays—every tiny piece is clicking perfectly; when this happens everyone watching knows . . . that, be it five guys playing basketball, or four blowing jazz, or three cutting timber, that this bunch—right now, right this moment—is the best of its kind in the world! But to become this kind of perfect group a team must use all its components, and use them in the slots best suited, and use them with pitiless dedication to victory that drives them up to their absolute peak, and past it.

This peak may be achieved only rarely, but when it does happen, it can be among the most gratifying experiences for anyone who participates and works in groups.

SUMMARY

This chapter has discussed the issue of individual behavior in the group. We examined the various groups to which people belong, in which membership may be voluntary or nonvoluntary. People's behavior will be influenced by their membership in either of these groupings. Groups serve as a reference in shaping attitudes and relationships, affecting group outcomes. Since a person's identity is closely related to membership in a group, a group label sets up both expectations and stereotypes. These become significant social forces in establishing interaction patterns in the group.

We also investigated how individuals are drawn to groups for biological, psychological, and social reasons. The fulfillment of interpersonal needs is a paramount concern. The need for affection, inclusion, and control will determine the extent of an individual's willingness to contribute to the group. Fulfilling interpersonal needs also affects the ability of a group to function. Groups are more likely to prosper when individuals express what they need and want, and receive what they need and want from others.

Standards for judging the worthiness of a group are based on how well the group serves an individual and by comparing the group with other group experiences. Individuals will continue to be a member of a group as long as the group continues to hold value for them.

We examined the roles that individual members undertake and perform in a group setting. Roles are not clearly delineated nor are they without conflicting expectations. Sometimes they are assigned, but, more often, they are worked out within a group as members communicate. Roles affect an individual's identity and status in the group and, in this way, help determine how groups work. In general, there are three basic types of roles: individuals working for their own agenda (personal roles); individuals helping with the task (task roles); and individuals helping maintain relationships (social-emotional roles). These roles are interdependent, but what is also important is that certain specialized roles must be present if groups are to prosper. These include a leader, a tension releaser, an information giver, and a central negative. Other roles that shape a group are a questioner, a silent observer, and an active listener. While most roles contribute positively to a group if performed when needed, an individual with a personal agenda—a self-centered follower—has a negative effect.

In the final section, we explored ways to be a valued member of a group. One way is by reinforcing productive norms. Groups also value members who help them to define and redefine goals so that they become doable yet challenging. Members will be treasured for bringing certain personal qualities to a group—credibility, competence, trustworthiness, and sensitivity. If there is one motto that group members can adopt, it is the commitment to do their very best for the group.

REFERENCES

Back, K. 1951. "Influence Through Social Communication." *Journal of Abnormal and Social Psychology* 46: 9–23.

Baird, J. E., Jr., and S. B. Weinberg. 1981. *Group Communication: The Essence of Synergy.* Dubuque, Ia.: Wm. C. Brown.

Bales, R. F. 1950. *Interaction Process Analysis: A Method for the Study of Small Groups.* Reading, Mass.: Addison-Wesley.

Barker, L., K. Wahlers, K. Watson, and R. Kibler. 1987. *Groups in Process: An Introduction to Small Group Communication* (3rd ed.). Englewood Cliffs, N.J.: Prentice-Hall.

Benne, K. and P. Sheats. 1948. "Functional Roles of Group Members." *Journal of Social Issues* 4:41–49.

Berne, E. 1963. *The Structure and Dynamics of Organizations and Groups.* New York: Grove Press.

Bormann, E. 1972. "Fantasy and Rhetorical Vision: The Rhetorical Criticism of Social Reality." *Quarterly Journal of Speech* 58:396–407.

Cragan, J. F., and D. W. Wright. 1986. *Communication in Small Group Discussions: An Integrated Approach* (2nd ed.). St. Paul, Minn.: West.

Festinger, L. 1957. *A Theory of Cognitive Dissonance.* Evanston, Ill.: Row, Peterson.

Forsyth, D. R. 1983. *An Introduction to Group Dynamics.* Monterey, Calif.: Brooks/Cole.

Goffman, E. 1959. *The Presentation of Self in Everyday Life.* Garden City, N.Y.: Doubleday Anchor.

Hyman, H. 1960. "Reflections on Reference Groups." *Public Opinion Quarterly* 24:303–396.

Kelley, H. 1952. "Two Functions of Reference Groups." In G. Swanson, T. Newcomb, and E. Hartley (eds.), *Readings in Social Psychology.* New York: Holt, pp. 410–414.

Kesey, K. 1964. *Sometimes a Great Notion.* New York: Viking Press.

Lewin, K., T. Dembo, L. Festinger, and P. S. Sears. 1944. "Level of Aspiration." In J. McV. Hunt (ed.), *Personality and the Behavioral Disorders.* New York: Ronald.

Lindesmith, A. R., and A. Strauss. 1968. *Social Psychology* (3rd ed.). New York: Holt.

Maslow, A. H. 1954. *Motivation and Personality.* New York: Harper & Row.

McTaggart, L. 1983. *Kathleen Kennedy: Her Life and Times.* New York: Dial.

Mortensen, C. D. 1972. *Communication: The Study of Human Interaction.* New York: McGraw-Hill.

Napier, R. W., and M. K. Gershenfeld. 1985. *Groups: Theory and Experience* (3rd ed.). Boston: Houghton Mifflin.

Patton, B. R., and K. Giffin. 1978. *Decision-Making Group Interaction.* New York: Harper & Row.

Phillips, G., and E. Erikson. 1970. *Interpersonal Dynamics in the Small Group.* New York: Random House.

Quey, R. L. 1971. "Function and Dynamics of Work Groups." *American Psychologist* 26:1077–1082.

Schutz, W. C. 1958. *Firo: A Three-Dimensional Theory of Interpersonal Behavior.* New York: Rinehart.

Schutz, W. C. 1966. *The Interpersonal Underworld.* Palo Alto, Calif.: Science and Behavior Books.

Shaw, M. E. 1981. *Group Dynamics: The Psychology of Small Group Behavior.* (3rd ed.). New York: McGraw-Hill.

Thibaut, J. W., and H. H. Kelley. 1959. *The Social Psychology of Groups.* New York: Wiley.

Wofford, J. C., E. A. Gerloff, and R. C. Cummins. 1977. "Group Behavior and the Communication Process." In J. C. Wofford et al. (eds.), *Organizational Communication: A Key to Managerial Effectiveness.* New York: McGraw-Hill, pp. 239–248.

Zander, A. 1971. *Motives and Goals in Groups.* New York: Academic Press.

Zander, A., and H. Medow. 1963. "Individual and Group Levels of Aspiration." *Human Relations* 16:89–105.

chapter 3

Participating in the Small Group

Understanding how people in groups interact is fundamental to understanding how groups work. How do people exchange ideas, process information, solve problems, accomplish a task? The members talk! What do they talk about? Is their talk planned? Does it follow a pattern? What can we learn about what is going on in a group from an analysis of how members talk? And if some members are talking, what are other members doing? Are they listening or responding? And how do these acts affect what is going on in the group?

Communication scholars and other experts in group behavior have found, after observing thousands of groups, that "talk" is clearly important. Who talks to whom and how frequently, what one person says to another, and how one person responds to others are major factors in distinguishing the effective from the ineffective group. This chapter explores the role of communication in a small group setting. First we will look at the way participation affects the proposing and nurturing of ideas. Second, we will address the question of how to listen and respond. For each of these processes, we will illustrate how you can become a more effective participant.

INEFFECTIVE AND EFFECTIVE COMMUNICATION

Scenario for an Ineffective Group Discussion

Suppose you were asked to write a scenario for an *ineffective group discussion.* What communicative procedures would you prescribe? Could you describe the key elements of the process that would lead group members to feel that their needs were unmet, their problems unresolved or resolved inadequately, and their communicative climate defensive and unsupportive?

We can create such a scenario by analyzing how an idea was actually processed in a small problem-solving group. This was a classroom group of five women members. They had chosen for discussion the issue of sex in advertising and its impact on the image of women in society. After some preliminary exploration of the nature of the problem, they began to consider possible ways of reducing what they perceived to be negative imagery about women. They were seeking ways to offset the portrayal of women as inept, silly, unintelligent, or merely sexual creatures. One of the women, Diane, suggested that the group come up with an educational plan as a counter to the impact of TV advertising. The other members then responded to her proposal.

> DIANE: I think it would be useful to work on a plan for educating young children. Perhaps we could even use advertising to do the job.
>
> PAULA: Advertising! That sounds overwhelming. We can't do anything that big.
>
> JEAN: Children are bombarded with too much advertising anyway.
>
> ANN: Also, we don't have the power to do anything anyway. Women are given so little credit.
>
> PAULA: I agree. Most advertising is handled by men, and they're incapable of learning.
>
> JEAN: Also, education sounds so unreal, as if it would take forever, and I don't think that's the kind of plan we're supposed to be coming up with.
>
> PAULA: You know, just thinking about this issue makes me angry. How can we overcome such negative stereotypes?
>
> ANN: Yeah! Especially our powerlessness.
>
> LINDA: Well, Diane, maybe it would be good if you could tell us more about what you had in mind.
>
> DIANE: Well, I'm not so sure; it was just a thought. I've always thought that one way to change people was to educate them. But I'm not so sure now.

What happened in this exchange? An idea was brought up, and, in what seems to be a rather common approach, the other group members looked for reasons to reject Diane's ideas. The sharpest criticism was directed at the inherent idealism of the idea. Their criticism was justified in the name of realism—"We can't do it" or "It won't work."

The scenario for ineffective group communication highlights some of the types of group interaction you will want to avoid. In the next section, we'll examine techniques that are more likely to lead to positive results.

Effective Communication and the Nurturing of Ideas

A study by Amarjit Chopra (1973), a vice president of Synectics, Inc., an organization that has studied groups to learn what made some of them more successful than others, suggests that effective groups respond to an idea differently from the way the members of Diane's group responded. In an effective group, an idea will be nurtured. Instead of immediately responding with some remark that makes the suggester feel foolish, group members ask questions or make some comments about the idea. The assumption underlying the nurturing process is that ideas do not come into the marketplace fully developed. Rather, ideas need help. Sometimes this help is given in the form of attention being paid so that the questioner can comprehend the issue more fully, such as: "I hear your idea, but I would like more information so that I can understand it better." Others may contribute to an idea and in this elaboration make the idea both more understandable and more acceptable. There could also be a proposal for modification, such as: "The idea of education is important, but could we deal with educating the adult public as a first priority?"

Efforts at *attention, comprehension, elaboration,* or *modification* are used to help a person develop his or her ideas. A significant difference between the effective and the ineffective group has to do with the way members are permitted to "own" their own ideas. In more effective groups, more statements are made that reflect a sensitivity to other members. There are more expressions of agreement, more paraphrasing, and more efforts at clarification. In an effective group, Chopra observes, members will put a good deal of energy into the framing of an idea, long before they look for possible solutions to a problem. Members question the proposer of an idea because they want to understand more clearly what the proposer meant before they criticize. They will make statements, ask questions, explore consequences, suggest other ways to think about the problem—in this way they are participating in an active search for possible solutions. Thus in an effective group, members try to assist the

person suggesting an idea in strengthening it, rather than first looking at flaws it may contain.

INDIVIDUAL NEEDS AS A BARRIER TO GROUP GOALS

Focusing on flaws is one mark of an ineffective group. Another, and
clearly related, cause for a group's inability to function at full potential may be that members are not contributing to the group's work—
they may even be sabotaging it—because their own needs are not
being met. Understanding the significance of these issues will help
you become a more useful group member.

Why the Focus on Flaws?

The question is, Why do ineffective groups focus on flaws? Does such
a tactic serve some kind of purpose? If not, then why is it that a focus
on flaws is so often the first response when an idea is introduced? We
will explore several reasons why group members look first at the
negative side of a proposal.

Opposition to New Ideas   One explanation is that we tend to view more
harshly ideas that are new. As Robert Zajonc (1965) has illustrated,
in a series of experiments in which subjects were shown unfamiliar
works of art in repeated trials, the repetition had a positive influence on their responses. The more the subjects saw a particular
work, the more they liked it, a phenomenon that led Zajonc to quip:
"We may not know what we like, but we like what we know." It is
probably easier to dismiss the new and unfamiliar than to admit
that we do not understand it. It is probably easier to tell what's
wrong with an idea than to put forth the energy to learn about what
we do not know.

Insufficient Time   Another factor seems to be time. As the size of a
group grows, the time for overt communication decreases, when, in
fact, what is needed is more time to examine ideas. If groups have
time constraints placed on them, they will likely hurry through the
beginning phases of their discussion. Therefore they may not devote
the necessary time to explore the value of an idea when it is offered.
The result may be the offhand dismissal of ideas that, if examined
in more depth, might have proved useful. Thomas Scheidel and
Laura Crowell (1964) reported, in a study analyzing the interaction
patterns in five small groups assigned to evaluate a metropolitan
newsletter, that members spent a relatively small amount of time
initiating ideas about how to analyze a newsletter. Scheidel and
Crowell had anticipated that activities such as proposing an idea
and then enlarging or modifying it, or perhaps synthesizing it with

other ideas formulated by the group, would have comprised the essence of the group's development of an idea. The reverse was found. The group devoted very little effort to any of these activities. Rather, it devoted more time substantiating ideas that had already been presented.

The Defense of Self A more compelling explanation for members' negative response is one provided by K. D. Benne (personal communication). Benne believes that people bring with them to any group an operating "psychology," "sociology," and "anthropology." According to Benne, we have been compiling "personal books" in these subjects throughout our lives. We have come to possess and use these notions of who we are, what we stand for, and what ways of dealing with other people are right and effective for us. In other words, we have developed characteristic ways of classifying other people in order to respond appropriately and economically to them. In this process we have acquired and formulated working "hypotheses" about what responses are appropriate in dealing with different kinds of people in varied situations.

These operating hypotheses are implicit as well as explicit. Our responses are shaped by the personal investment each of us has in who we are. If proposed ideas seem to be at variance with what we believe, we are inclined to reject them. Since we all seek an inner integrity, a way to uphold our self-worth, we will defend our beliefs against any likely disapproval from others. If we perceive that our concept of ourselves, our ideas, or our beliefs are somehow being called into question, then we begin to devote our energies to protecting and defending ourselves.

To understand why we first think of defending ourselves, it is necessary to understand our concept of self and how that concept has developed. A significant factor in shaping who we are is the important "others" in our lives and the messages they have given us. We are dependent on the reactions of others to tell us how we are doing. Understanding self-concept also involves understanding the "upper" and "downer" messages that we have received (Adler and Towne 1981). If we have been fortunate, the preponderance of messages have helped to enhance our self-concept by making us feel loved and appreciated. If we are unlucky, we have had too many messages that lower our self-esteem. And although not everyone may realize how threatening it is to have our worth called into question, we are all participants in the giving and receiving of "upper" and "downer" messages.

According to Adler and Towne, our behavior is influenced not only by the need to protect our image of self but also by the expectations of a society that demands too much of its members. Much of the conditioning we receive in our early years implies that anything less than perfection is unsatisfactory. Most of us have experienced a plethora of put-downs; some of us may have had to deal with uncaring teachers, critical parents, and overly demanding employ-ers. We are primed for uncertainty about about how we are doing. And although most of us assume we will not behave so critically ourselves, the combination of uncertainty and the myth of perfec-tion have had devastating effects on how we view ourselves and react to others.

Self-Defensiveness in a Group Setting

The concept of self-defensiveness has important applications to the study of effective group communication. In fact, we are especially likely to become defensive when we participate in a group setting. It is as if whole chapters of the personal "social science books" we have been compiling have not been published, even to ourselves, and only begin to be deciphered when we interact with others (Benne, personal communication). When the ideas of others appear to challenge what we believe—even though we may not be aware of our beliefs until we hear other people express theirs—our immedi-ate reaction tends to be a negative one.

Understanding group behavior means looking at the ways par-ticipants can satisfy their mutual needs and at the same time pre-serve the vital elements of their self-image. Each of us is deeply concerned about our own personal needs and goals. Indeed, a pri-mary motivation for the individual, unless he or she is extraor-dinarily selfless, is to survive without the loss of personal integrity. Thus in a group working on a problem, most of us look for confirma-tion of our own ideas. At the very least, we would like to hear that our ideas have some merit.

Closely related to the issues of personal needs is the question of identity. Every group member has to contemplate who he or she is and what role each is going to play in the group. Members are concerned that their participation in the group will ensure recogni-tion and acceptance. It is understandable that they should seek ac-ceptance in the best possible light, even though some people will go to extraordinary lengths to project a negative image because they fear a possible rejection. As Erving Goffman has depicted in his sociological perspective *The Presentation of Self in Everyday Life* (1959), individuals continuously examine how they will present themselves and their activities to others, even in an ordinary work situation. They will, to a large extent, control and guide the impres-sions others will form of them. This in turn influences what they say or do to sustain their performance. The larger implication of this effort at impression management is that individuals may be able to create their own world.

This is an awesome responsibility. Timothy Leary (1957) expressed this responsibility in a more profound way when he stated: "You are mainly responsible for your life situation. . . . Your own personal behavior has, more than any other factor, determined the reception you get from others. . . . You are the manager of your own destiny." Understandably, there is a great deal at stake when we enter into a communicative interaction in the small group.

In our interaction with others, we tend to seek corroboration of our ideas, seeing them as an extension of our personal image. Although this is not the group goal, unless the group can provide responses that will lead to the personal recognition of our contribution and to our personal fulfillment, we may either block a group's deliberations or withdraw physically or psychologically. Chopra (1973) found that when group members did not reinforce one another, there emerged subtle (and not so subtle) forms of defensive behavior—retaliation, passivity, and withdrawal.

This type of behavior is not necessarily conscious and intentional. Group members as a rule do not actively set out to undermine each other's work or ideas. Benne and Sheats (1948) have observed that negative reactions stem from the investment people have in their own ideas and the recurring need they have to protect themselves. Cattell (1955) and his associates have demonstrated that if the personal needs of group members are not met, then the ability of group members to resolve the issues before them will be reduced. It is for this reason, the need to protect the self, that individuals appear not to be working for a common group goal.

Personal Objectives Versus Group-Motivated Behavior   Benne and Sheats have given the label *individual roles* to behavior that is motivated by personal needs. These personal needs are at variance with the group's needs for accomplishing task and social-emotional fulfillment. Some of the more common forms of personal needs are the following:

Individual roles

Blocker:	Interfering with the group's goal by raising objections, telling the group, "It can't be done," or insisting on reintroducing an idea the group has thoroughly considered and rejected.
Aggressor:	Telling people that they do not know what they are doing; calling them names; joking at the expense of others.

Recognition-seeker: Proclaiming one's own expertise in a boasting manner or telling of an experience irrelevant to the group's task.

Dominator: Insisting on one's own point of view; telling people what to do; interrupting and cutting others off.

Special interest pleader: Serving as a representative of another group's view; opposing the interests of the current group; holding to a position regardless of the views of others.

Playboy: Joking around, taking neither oneself nor the group seriously; diverting the group from its task.

Avoider: Showing a lack of interest; hiding feelings; giving no response to others; refusing to get involved in the business of the group.

In contrast, Benne and Sheats offer a list of behaviors that group members use when they are aiding the group.

Group task behaviors

1. *Initiator.* Helps the group to understand the complex nature of a problem. Helps the group to define its goals. Contributes new ideas. Suggests ways of looking at an issue or of tackling a problem when the group is unable to proceed.
2. *Elaborator.* Supports an idea by providing illustrations. Extends the meaning of an idea. Helps a group to imagine how an idea might work or to anticipate the consequences of an idea that won't work.
3. *Coordinator.* Shows the relationship between members' suggestions, ideas, and proposals. Enables members to see the interdependencies of their ideas and the contributions of all the members.
4. *Evaluator.* Tells members how well their proposals match their stated goals. Measures and evaluates the group's achievement by giving feedback to the group.
5. *Summarizer.* Helps the group to understand what it has accomplished and what remains to be done. Gives the group a sense of how much progress it has made and how close it is to finishing.

In addition to these task-related behaviors, effective groups have members who reinforce one another by using group-building behaviors.

Group maintenance behaviors

1. *Encourager.* Is sensitive to the contributions of others and to the morale of the group. Praises members individually. Helps to build the group's cohesiveness and satisfaction.
2. *Harmonizer.* Encourages the group to confront personal issues that interfere with the group's work. Helps the group to focus on the issues rather than on members' personal antagonisms.
3. *Gatekeeper.* Helps regulate the participation of members. Asks for opinions and suggestions from those who do not typically contribute, thus ensuring that the group uses more of its resources.
4. *Standard setter.* Functions as the group's ego. Holds up the ideal for which the group is striving. Helps the group to determine how well it is functioning and whether or not it will succeed in reaching its goal.
5. *Tension releaser.* Eases the tension in the group when members are under stress. Reduces members' anxiety and helps to improve group productivity by suggesting a break, telling a joke, and so on, but without disrupting the essential work of the group.

Understanding group behavior means looking at the ways participants can achieve their mutual needs.

Questions for the Individual   Little wonder that interaction is fundamental to the understanding of group behavior; our identity, acceptance, and impression on others is greatly determined by our willingness to participate in the group. The poignant question for each
individual becomes, "To what extent am I willing to expose my
vulnerability to the group?" Much depends, of course, on how meaningful the group is, and how much each person wishes to be a member of it. It is not mere participation that is demanded, however. It
is participation that includes a willingness to risk intellectually and
emotionally. It is a willingness to adopt new ideas and to propose
actions as well as to be silent. Commitment to a group may require
answers to other questions: "What kind of interaction is needed for
meeting my goals and the group's goals? How do I ensure that members of my group will gain acceptance and recognition? How do I
encourage appropriate responses to suggested ideas? How do I make
certain that people with information to share get the opportunity to
participate?"

CONFIRMING AND DISCONFIRMING RESPONSES

One of the most troublesome aspects of group interaction is that
often the communication does not seem to lead anywhere. Group
members frequently complain that their remarks are not given attention and that they tend to feel disregarded. It seems that not too
many people provide clues as to how they are receiving and reacting
to the ideas of others, nor do they ask for information about the
effect they are having. Sieberg and Larson (1971), in their investigation of communication in effective and ineffective groups, found
that the types of responses members provided either encouraged or
discouraged the willingness of members to present ideas. Their
analysis of *confirming responses* and *disconfirming responses* provides us with important insights about how communication affects
the group's climate.

How do you offer confirmation? Sieberg and Larson suggest the
following ways to encourage effective communication:

1. *Responding.* You react to group members' comments. You
   tell members verbally that you have heard them.
2. *Agreeing.* You reinforce members' ideas by expressing
   agreement.
3. Supporting. You offer assistance in developing members'
   ideas.
4. Reassuring. You express understanding of other members or
   reassure them that you value them.
5. Clarifying. You help the other members clarify an idea, en-

couraging them to say more or to say it differently so that you can get a better understanding of the idea.

Disconfirming responses, on the other hand, go beyond the norms of acceptable criticism. The most damaging are comments by participants who ignore another member's communication, either by not acknowledging that the person was heard or by immediately introducing a topic unrelated to the other's communication. At other times a member may interrupt or cut off a group member while he or she is still speaking. Other discomforting responses include impersonal conversation, long monologues, use of language that is more abstract than necessary, or incoherent, rambling speech full of hard-to-follow ideas.

Obviously a group will prosper if confirming responses are the predominant mode. Using confirming responses rather than disconfirming responses helps develop a more beneficial group climate. If you can communicate in this way, it will undoubtedly help promote more effective group discussions and greater individual satisfaction. The remainder of this chapter will focus on two variables that significantly affect this process—patterns of participation and the way you listen and respond to others.

Patterns of Participation

Accomplishing tasks and meeting personal needs are of concern to any problem-solving group. Understanding how you communicate in the group is an important component of your understanding both of these needs. The exercise "High Talkers and Low Talkers" (page 66), which has been used in classes and in consultations with task groups in organizations (Lewin 1947, Napier and Gershenfeld 1973), illustrates the role of participation in the group.

Observations of the Action

One of the results of participating in the activity may be an increased sensitivity to the reciprocal relationship of the two patterns of interaction. Observations have been made of groups participating in this exercises, and behavior patterns have been noted. Your group may want to discuss whether its members' observations were similar to the following findings.

The low talkers display frequent pauses and have little direct eye contact with other group members; their voices are soft. Sometimes one hears defensive statements directed at high talkers, such as: "I don't like to blab," "I see no reason just to talk for the sake of talking," "I think it is more important to listen than to talk," "I don't like to interrupt, which is what high talkers do."

HIGH TALKERS AND LOW TALKERS

Identifying the Groups

Assemble a group of individuals and ask them to identify themselves as either "high talkers" or "low talkers." The assumption underlying this identification is that people generally are not aware of, or are insensitive to, their characteristic style of participating in a group. High talkers in this context are defined as those who engage in talk for the sheer joy of it, for the necessity of it; within a group they show an eagerness to initiate conversation. Indeed, they find it necessary to talk because silence is not comfortable.

To be a low talker means to be hesitant about starting a conversation in a group. Low talkers tend to hold back their comments, to wait until others have spoken before participating. They will take time to size up a situation and will generally to be more comfortable as a "listener." (As we will be discussing in the next section, listening is much more than merely not talking).

If you are unsure which of these "forced choice" categories you belong to, ask someone who knows you well which category more accurately describes your participation in groups. Once all the individuals have identified their pattern of participation, the exercise can proceed.

The Activity

1. A "fishbowl" structure is set up with low talkers assuming the role of Actors. They are seated in the center; the high talkers are seated around the outside of the circle as Observers. Actors and Observers will reverse roles in the second round.
2. The low talkers are asked to discuss, for approximately five minutes, any problems they have encountered as low talkers. The Observers make notes about the verbal and nonverbal communication of the Actors.
3. This procedure is then reversed. The high talkers are now the Actors in the center of the fishbowl. The low talkers are the Observers. The high talkers discuss any problems they have had as high talkers.
4. After completing both parts, the groups share their observations and reactions and discuss the implications of their findings.

On the other hand, some statements reveal that this was an area of sensitivity for low talkers: "I don't talk a lot because I don't want to make a fool of myself," "I'm uncertain of the reaction I will get, so I wait to get a sense of what is going on from others," "I feel overwhelmed by high talkers, because I can't say what I want to as fast."

When high talkers take their turn, the effect is dramatic. They sit forward, watching the eyes and mouths of other speakers, waiting for an opportunity to come into the conversation. There are few, if any, pauses. There is a high energy, and voices overlap as each person tries to enter the conversation. But they, too, reveal a certain defensiveness with such statements as, "I talk a lot to hold up my own end," "It's hard to be with low talkers; they make me feel uncomfortable," "I wouldn't talk so much if others would do their share," "I'm uncomfortable with silence, so I guess I fill in the blank space." At the same time, they show an appreciation for being high talkers: "I talk because it's fun to get to know people that way," "I enjoy being at the center of the action," "I do my best thinking when I can express myself to others."

Comments on the Exercise

One of the findings from this exercise is that both high talkers and low talkers realize that each style has advantages and limitations; they become aware of how different their patterns are, but are able, after going through the exercise, to appreciate each other's needs. They also realize that both styles are necessary for a discussion group. Indeed, when asked, "If you could be with either all high talkers or all low talkers, which would you pick?" participants overwhelmingly stress the advantage of a mixed group.

Since a group is advantaged by being able to tap the resources of all its members, it is important to learn how to enable all members who wish to contribute to be able to do so. Indeed, an important lesson is that all members should have the opportunity to be heard, and that all should be able to respond to the exchange of ideas in a group without being either suppressed or overwhelmed.

We can draw some insights about the communicative behavior of a group from this exercise. It highlights such issues as personal and self-oriented needs. We can contrast personal needs with the task and maintenance needs of the group. As Norton (1983) reports in his work on communicator style, "The way one communicates affects the perception and assessment of social reality." Being sensitive to whether one is talkative, overtalkative, or undertalkative will clearly have an impact on the group. Our communication pattern will affect who is willing to talk, who is talking to whom, and such interpersonal dimensions as susceptibility to patterns of dominance and submissiveness. In subsequent chapters we will examine other factors that influence communicative interaction in small groups—such issues as status, group size, cohesiveness, power structure, leadership, decision making, and conflict.

Listening and Responding to Others

This chapter began with a scenario that illustrated how a proposal tends to be rejected by others. We indicated that, typically, members of small groups put forth little effort to modify or extend an idea or even to examine whether there is any value in what has been suggested. We also noted that this tendency to reject appears to be imbedded in our image of ourselves, societal demands for perfection, and our own fears of rejection.

The problem this represents for a group is a difficult one, for often the behavioral patterns of members are hidden in highly ritualized group interaction. A group may be operating according to well-defined rules of procedure. A tight agenda, rigid leadership, or a competitive atmosphere may move a group along without the members having a chance to clarify their ideas, their attitudes, their feelings—or to alter their typical responses to each other.

Passive and Active, Hard and Soft Listening   To overcome this problem, everyone has to learn how to listen and how to respond. In any interactive group, individuals spend a great deal of time listening, although not all listening is helpful either to members or to the group. Specialists in listening have distinguished two forms of listening, one labeled *passive listening* and the other called *active listening.* In passive listening, we may hear the sounds but we are not necessarily using the type of mental activity that would help us understand the message. In active listening, on the other hand, we make a conscious effort to hear and to understand the message.

What often keeps people from understanding the meaning of a message is what Paul Friedman (1978) has labeled *hard listening.* This is the type of listening that occurs when a speaker is talking, relaying information, or providing a view, but the listeners are not really focusing on what is being said; they are probably too wrapped up thinking about their response. If you, as a listener, are concentrating on figuring out what your response will be, then you are probably missing some of what is being said to you. In contrast, Friedman describes *soft listening* as the attempt to listen to a message without attributing a motive either to the messenger or to the message. When you are a "soft listener," you are focusing on what the speaker is saying; you are not formulating your response.

Preparing to Listen   Getting ready to listen means becoming prepared psychologically. It's somewhat like thinking, "O.K. Another person is taking a turn, and I need to get ready to hear." When you are with just one other person, you are much more likely to listen because you know that the other person expects you to respond. In a group, though, you may find that your attention is not so concentrated, because you believe that, with other people around, you won't have to respond. But if everybody reacted in this way, a speaker would feel ignored. It is important for the health of a group that every member find useful ways to listen. Perhaps it will help if you take notes, or at least try to repeat mentally what each person is saying. Most important of all is to try not to let your thoughts wander.

Improving Your Listening   Carl Rogers (1970) has described the many barriers that prevent us from listening and understanding. The major barrier appears to be the tendency to *evaluate* what another person is saying before it is fully understood (Chopra 1973). This is particularly true if we are inclined to disagree with the person's philosophy or belief system. Often we may think we know what the person means before he or she has finished speaking. We decide the meaning or intent behind a statement and react without checking it out, without asking for clarification. When this happens, we are engaging in what George Bach (1968) has called *mind raping.* It may be surprising, if and when we do check, how often the person had something different in mind from our interpretation (Chopra 1973).

Charles Kelly (1984) has provided a number of ways to become a better listener. He sees a reciprocal relationship between our desire to get favorable responses to our ideas and the sensitivity with which we listen to someone else. A sensitive or empathic listener is someone who works very hard to get the sense of what a speaker is saying. You can improve your listening habits by learning to treat listening as a skill.

1. *Prepare yourself to listen.* Even though you find the speaker boring, you should not be deterred from a commitment to listen. When you don't listen well, you may be missing valuable information. It is only by learning to listen and accepting that it is your responsibility to listen that you can improve your participation in the group.
2. *Concentrate on what the speaker is saying.* If note taking helps, use that technique. If asking a question or paraphrasing what the speaker has said will help you understand more clearly, then try it. Concentrating on listening also means discarding the extraneous, random thoughts that may preoccupy you and prevent you from giving the other person your full attention.
3. *Treat each person as a unique individual.* If you accept

the fact that every person has special talents and contributions to make, then you will be more responsive. If you refrain from interrupting, you will be more open to what others are saying—to think about it, to probe a little, rather than dismissing their ideas before it has been examined.

The Technique of Itemized Response   An approach that can create an awareness of the choices we have in the way we listen and respond to others is an exercise called "Itemized Response" (Chopra 1973) that incorporates a fundamental concept of listening, that of feedback. *Feedback* represents an effort on the part of participants to communicate with the least possible distortion between a speaker's intent and the message actually received by others (Miles 1967). At one level, it is a process geared to making certain that the content is understood (soft listening). Beyond this level, feedback is the attempt to communicate the feeling or expressive domains of the message. It is fundamental to being a good listener.

ITEMIZED RESPONSE

Ground Rules

This exercise involves learning one assumption and two forms of response. The assumption is that whatever anyone proposes has in it at least a little bit of good, if we are willing to listen for it. One form of response is to state specifically what you as a listener heard that was good or useful. The response has to be more than, "That's a good idea." It must be an itemized one—that is, you should state the particular positive elements of the idea presented. The second form of response is critical and analytical; you indicate what you think is not good or workable in the proposed idea. This is not meant to be an easy way to "let the other shoe drop." On the contrary, this is a response that offers a specific accounting of where you perceive some problems.

The Activity

1. A small group (up to 12) is seated in a circle. One person begins the activity by offering a suggestion or a proposal about how a problem (any that the group might choose) could be remedied.
2. After hearing this suggestion, the person to the right of the speaker gives a critique, telling first what he or she liked about the idea and then what was not liked.

3. The group continues in this manner until all members have had a chance to suggest ideas and receive two forms of response.

Sample Discussion

The following discussion, on raising the drinking age from 18 to 20, will illustrate the form of this training exercise:

John: What I think we should do is license everyone the way we do drivers. In that way we can take care of those who abuse their drinking privilege. If they do something wrong, they get demerits. So many demerits, and they lose their license to buy drinks.

Debbie: I like what you said, John. It's an idea I never would have thought of. It's really unusual and a very good approach. It would take the burden off everyone and put it only on those who abuse the system. That sounds good to me. On the other hand, I am troubled about enforcing it. This means another layer of bureaucratic management, a police force or something like it. I just don't know if that's a good thing to do.

This is the first stage. After Debbie has given her critique, she turns to the person on her right and suggests an idea of her own. Lou, who is sitting on Debbie's right, responds to Debbie as she did to John. This process is illustrated in the following exchange:

Debbie: What I would like to propose is that 18- to 20-year-olds be permitted to drink in certain locations, or when accompanying their family, like when they go out to eat. I don't think it's fair to cut off an adult from taking part in pleasurable activities. My proposal means some limitations but also some freedom.

Lou: Well, I think you have a good point there. A family would certainly like to be together for a special occasion. But the whole proposal sounds impossible. It would be difficult to enforce, I think. You say that 18-year-olds are adults, on one hand. But, on the other hand, you want to supervise them. This doesn't make sense to me. Yet I understand what you are saying—don't be so hard on the mature 18- to 20-year-old.

And so on, until everyone's ideas have been heard and critiqued.

Comments on the Exercise

Clearly, this training module is a contrived form. Group members do not typically speak only to members on their right. Nor do other members usually offer first a positive and then a negative response, with no chance of rebuttal from the person being addressed. For purposes of training, however, the exercise provides many insights.

During the exercise, a group becomes aware of how many more ideas will be contributed if the atmosphere—the climate of the group—encourages responses from more rather than fewer members. And although the format is artificial, participants report that in trying to find something good to say about an idea, they listened with more attention and understanding than they had felt compelled to do before.

Those members presenting ideas said that knowing they were going to get a response gave them a reward they had not anticipated—the pleasure of being listened to. While it is sometimes difficult to find positive and negative things to say in a specific way, the process of itemizing encourages the participants to find responses that satisfy both the needs of the group—the presentation of a number of ideas—and the personal needs of members—the recognition of their worth.

This exercise demonstrates that *listening* and *feedback* are process skills. Group members can learn to use them to encourage others to share their ideas, suggestions, and opinions. When we take on the responsibility of providing feedback, we are helping ourselves develop better listening skills. And listening increases the group's likelihood of success. It allows information to flow among members and ensures that their ideas are heard and understood before they are evaluated. Listening and responding using itemized response is a way to undo our characteristic form of negative response. When we engage in itemized response, we are letting the speaker know that he or she is being heard. What we are communicating is that we value both the speaker and the message.

Your responses to others are likely to be different when you perceive that they are disagreeing with you because they do not accept your ideas rather than because they do not accept you. It is also the case that a careful and responsive listener need not suggest only positive comments. It is true, of course, that positive statements represent nonthreatening comments and clearly reinforce that the speaker has been heard. Nevertheless, if speakers know that they have been heard, then being told what is not liked is more apt to be accepted as a criticism of the idea and not one directed at the person.

Using Itemized Responses to Become Nondefensive By using the techniques illustrated in the exercise, you as a participant in the small group can learn how to evaluate the ideas of others in a nonthreatening communicative interaction. By separating the useful elements of an idea from its potential drawbacks, you can modify ideas, retain the advantages, and eliminate the disadvantages. By recognizing the useful aspects, you are telling the other members that they are valued.

In this way, you are learning to be nonjudgmental, a skill that Jack Gibb (1961) identified as essential for counteracting defensiveness. It is the ability to separate the evaluation of an idea from the judgment of a person. Instead of feeling compelled to protect your investment in an idea because you assume you are under attack, you are motivated and encouraged by the techniques of itemized responses to learn and to participate.

A question that participants in this training exercise often ask is, "What if I can't find anything useful in someone's proposal?" (Chopra 1973). One answer is that the form of responses you are learning does not mean that there will always be something worthy in a proposal or that merit should be falsely stated. The premise underlying the training is that this form of responding overcomes an initial tendency to see new ideas in negative terms. Although there will be times when you will be unable to find anything worthwhile, a single instance of inability to state usefulness—or nonusefulness, for that matter—will not necessarily be detrimental to the person or the group (Chopra 1973). It is more important that the positive statements address the task needs of the group, and not be merely a way to say something pleasant before you let the other person have it.

A group that is oriented toward assisting in the development of ideas is likely to find workable solutions. Fewer ideas are discarded because of premature rejection. When members of a group do not have to spend their energy and resources defending themselves or their ideas, they will be able to use their time and energy more constructively. They will have the opportunity to build on the suggestions and ideas of other members. The final product may reflect a portion of what was recommended by several group members or by all (Chopra 1973). With such identification and commitment, and with the expectation that ideas will be nurtured, higher-quality solutions are the likely outcome.

A FINAL COMMENT

We have suggested in this chapter that participative patterns within the small group are greatly influenced by who talks and how much, and with what frequency, as well as the type of response given to such talk. We presented a scenario that showed how a suggested idea was processed in a way that was defeating to the presenter. This pattern is not untypical of what goes on in many groups, and it is not very effective.

Let us contrast, now, some of the rules that distinguish the ineffective from the effective group.

For the ineffective group, a first step would be to keep people from expressing their ideas. If responsiveness begets responsiveness, then members can limit communication by such simple procedures as not recognizing the merit in an idea or, even better, by providing no response to a suggested idea.

A second step in furthering deterioration of interaction is to have individuals respond to ideas with such vehemence and certainty that others in the group pull back. By this action we may induce some members to go along with an idea even though they know it is a weak one, or they may reject an idea they believe is worthwhile, to avoid the pressure of the group. We can allow only a few individuals to speak, to dominate, and to let others be passive or withdraw. Without the sharing of perceptions and ideas, without the freedom to speak openly and responsively, we can help produce an ineffective group (Benne, personal communication).

In the opening scenario you can see some of these detrimental effects. Diane's idea was rejected as unrealistic. Only Linda offered Diane a chance to explain further, but the damage was already done: Diane was hedging and moving toward withdrawal of her idea. And as became apparent later in the session, Diane did not venture forth with other ideas, having had the initial experience of nonnurturing responses.

Let's rewrite the dialogue so that the rules for good communicative interaction may be applied.

DIANE: I think it would be useful to work on a plan for educating young children. Perhaps we could even use advertising to do the job.

ANN: I'm not sure what you have in mind. Could you spell it out a little more?

DIANE: Well, I was thinking that we are all unsophisticated in evaluating what goes on in television. We need to develop a program that will teach children to be critical of what they see. Sort of help them to understand that not everything they see is to be accepted.

ANN: Do you mean something like art or music appreciation?

DIANE: I hadn't thought of it that way until you mentioned it, but that is sort of what I had in mind. I do think we need to have some ongoing programs that will help us all develop a critical ability. Putting it that way makes it seem possible to learn new behavior.

JEAN: That sounds very interesting. At first, when I heard the term *education,* I thought, "Oh, no! Not that again!" It seems to be the old reliable standard for how to solve anything. But what you are suggesting sounds worthwhile.

PAULA: I like what you are saying about teaching children critical skills, but I am having trouble seeing the relationship between your idea and our need as women to overcome the hostile effects of television advertising on women.

LINDA: Let me try to get at that. What I sense from Diane's proposal is that if we as a people are sensitized to the methods of advertisers, then the way they present material won't influence us. If what they are doing did not have so much influence, then they might have to change. Is that it?

ANN: I would like to add something to that. Not only should we have a program for children's education about television, but we should offer it as part of adult education.

This discussion may continue for several hours. The group will explore Diane's proposal, and only after much elaboration and modification will members be able to decide if it is a feasible solution. There will be other suggestions and proposals. With an examination of alternatives, the group will sort out the ideas that could work.

Members can go a long way toward improving their participation in a group by making messages clear, by repeating them when necessary, by asking for feedback, and by communicating feelings. And in responding to messages, members can paraphrase accurately, can ask for clarification, and can express support and give assistance to the development of an idea. In the final analysis, we can evaluate all messages by asking to what extent they help the group prosper—that is, allow the group to reach its goals and complete its task—or to what extent the messages hinder the group's performance (Johnson and Johnson 1975).

It will not be easy to decide which messages are valuable. Since all groups will have disagreements about what is useful and important, there will be misunderstandings. However, the willingness to participate and respond in a facilitating way will clearly help the group achieve its goals in the long run. The willingness to talk—that is, to participate—and the willingness to listen and to respond with sensitivity, produces interactions that increase the probability of the group's accomplishing its task. What is at issue is to understand how patterns of communication and styles of responding affect participants' identity and acceptance in a group and impact on the group's ability to accomplish its aims.

SUMMARY

This chapter has examined what you should know about participation patterns in the small group. A fundamental premise is that the way you interact with others is a function of the way you communicate in groups. Participation means understanding some fundamental processes of communication.

Effective groups assist members in developing ideas. They do this by giving an idea attention, comprehension, elaboration, and modification. Members will devote their time and energy to helping each other explore the implications of an idea or suggest ways for offsetting the limitations of an idea.

Ineffective groups, in contrast, have a tendency to reject new or unfamiliar ideas. Our discussion has shown how a concern with identity and acceptance, as well as the need for favorable recognition, influences individuals to think first of protecting their self-concept. This encourages members to push ahead with what are called *individual roles,* rather than focusing on the task and maintenance behaviors that would benefit the group.

Group participation is affected by members' patterns of participation. Learning to identify whether you are a "high talker" or "low talker" is a way of helping you understand how individuals can achieve their mutual needs while at the same time working for the needs of the group. Although there are both advantages and limitations to each pattern of participation, an effective group will give both high talkers and low talkers the chance to participate.

Since communication involves giving a response to a message, the chapter presented the processes that affect the exchange of information and ideas. Learning to listen, using an active rather than a passive style, encourages more participation. Using a style of response that first states what is good about an idea, followed by what may be problematic, is a way to let a speaker know that he or she has been heard.

Finally, the replay of the opening scenario in the chapter showed how an appropriate response style can help participants develop their ideas so that they may work effectively on a problem.

REFERENCES

Adler, R. B., and N. Towne. 1981. *Looking Out/Looking In: Interpersonal Communication.* (3rd ed.). New York: Holt, Rinehart and Winston, pp. 58–59.

Bach, G. R., and P. Wyden. 1968. *The Intimate Enemy.* New York: Avon.

Benne, K. D. Personal communication. "Group Dynamics and Education in Human Relations." Working paper prepared for the Human Relations Workshop Evaluation Study Conference of Social Scientists and Educators.

Benne, K. D., and P. Sheats. 1948. "Functional Roles of Group Members." *Journal of Social Issues* 4:41–49.

Cattell, R. B. 1955. "Concepts and Methods in the Measurement of Group Syntality." In A. P. Hare, E. F. Borgatta, and R. F. Bales (eds.), *Small Groups: Studies in Social Interaction.* New York: Knopf, pp. 107–126.

Chopra, A. 1973. "Motivation in Task-Oriented Groups." *Journal of Nursing Administration* 21:55–60.

Friedman, P. G. 1978. *Interpersonal Communication: Innovations in Instruction.* Washington, D.C.: National Education Association.

Gibb, J. 1961. "Defensive Communication." *Journal of Communication* 11:-141–148.

Goffman, E. 1959. *The Presentation of Self in Everyday Life.* Garden City, N.Y.: Doubleday Anchor.

Johnson, D. W., and F. P. Johnson. 1975. *Joining Together: Group Theory and Group Skills.* Englewood Cliffs, N.J.: Prentice-Hall, pp. 112–117.

Kelly, C. M. 1984. "Empathic Listening." In R. S. Cathcart and L. A. Samavar (eds.), *Small Group Communication: A Reader* (4th ed.). Dubuque, Ia.: Wm. C. Brown, pp. 296–312.

Leary, T. 1957. *Interpersonal Diagnosis of Personality.* New York: Ronald Press, pp. 116–117.

Leavitt, H. J., and R. Mueller. 1951. "Some Effects of Feedback on Communication." *Human Relations* 4:401.

Lewin, K. 1947. "Frontiers in Group Dynamics." *Human Relations* 1.

Miles, M. B. 1967. *Learning to Work in Groups.* New York: Teacher's College Press, Columbia University.

Napier, R. W., and M. K. Gershenfeld. 1973. *Groups: Theory and Experience.* Boston: Houghton Mifflin, pp. 72–73.

Norton, R. 1983. *Communicator Style: Theory, Applications, and Measures.* Beverly Hills, Calif.: Sage Publications, p. 187.

Rogers, C. 1970. *On Becoming a Person* Boston: Houghton Mifflin.

Scheidel, T. M., and L. Crowell. 1964. "Idea Development in Small Group Discussion Groups." *Quarterly Journal of Speech* 50:140–145.

Sieberg, E., and C. Larson. 1971. "Dimensions of Interpersonal Response." Paper presented to annual conference of the International Communication Association, Phoenix, April.

Zajonc, R. B. 1965. "Social Facilitation." *Science* 149:269–274.

chapter *4*

The Communicative Environment of the Small Group

Imagine the following scene. The Hall Director has called a special meeting of your dormitory's residence assistants. Perhaps ten people will attend the meeting scheduled for a small conference room in your dormitory. You are the first one to enter the room. As you walk in, you see a long rectangular table with eight chairs placed around the table—one at each end and three chairs along each side. A few chairs are scattered around the room, and in a corner of the room you see a sofa and an upholstered arm chair. Where would you sit? Some people, eyeing the sofa, might take a seat there. But suppose you have an important issue you would like to discuss with your director. Should you sit on the sofa, if what you want is good interaction with the director?

The question of where to sit is not a frivolous one. An instance of how a choice of seating created an international dilemma occurred in 1968 at the Paris peace talks between the parties involved in the Vietnam conflict. Newspapers featured headlines such as, "Peace Talks Postponed—Negotiators Quibble over Seating." The controversy over seating was cast as "ridiculous."

More was at stake than was apparent from the initial story. The United States and South Vietnam, not wishing to award status to the National Liberation Front (N.L.F.), which had been fighting in the south in support of North Vietnam, argued for a two-sided arrangement—the United States and South Vietnam on one side, and North Vietnam on the other. In contrast, North Vietnam and the N.L.F., seeking equal status with the United States and South Vietnam, proposed a four-sided table. The relationship of seating arrangement and perceived status was important to all parties. Indeed, it took eight months for them to agree to use a round table. Only then could the issue of status be put aside (Knapp 1978).

The choice of where to sit is only one of the factors affecting a group's environment. The next time you meet with your group, ask yourself if noise outside the meeting room affects your group's interactions. If you are meeting during classtime, does the sound of other students' activities intrude on your group's work? Do you notice the color of the walls or how close someone is sitting next to you? Do you smell the candy bar being unwrapped? What about the chair you are sitting in—how comfortable are you in it? You might also be thinking about how much time your group will take to complete its project, or whether participants will get bogged down without ever arriving at solutions. If you are like most people, you probably tend to take the world for granted until some discomfort makes you pay attention. However, learning to become more sensitive to the way ecological issues influence group interactions will certainly make you a more effective group member. With increasing awareness of your group's environment, you will be able to alter those components that interfere with your group's performance (Forsyth 1983).

This chapter is about the ecology of small group behavior. *Ecology* refers to the relations that groups have with their environment, whether it is the structure of the group and its influence on communicative interaction or the spacing of people and the resulting interdependence among them. First we will analyze the relationship of the nonverbal environment to group communication. We will discuss some important dimensions of nonverbal communication: personal appearance, the use of space, bodily movement and facial expression, and the tone and sound of the human voice. Following this discussion, we will propose an exercise that can help you understand how much information is available from nonverbal messages. The concluding section will examine additional factors affecting a group's communicative environment: the size of a group, the time a group spends in interacting, and the phases that groups go through in their development.

THE EFFECT OF NONVERBAL CUES

Nonverbal Versus Verbal Messages

Nonverbal messages are usually more believable than verbal messages. They are more believable because they are more difficult to fake (Mehrabian 1972). When words and actions do not agree, we are more likely to pay attention to the actions than to the words. An unenthusiastic "Yes, I'll do it" suggests to the hearer, "I would rather not." Despite the affirmative words, we tend to focus on the negative tone of the message. For example, suppose your group is discussing a time to meet and one of the members says, "I can't do it at that time." If another member asks, "Why not?" and the answer begins, "Uh, well, . . . (pause) I've got to be somewhere else," chances are that that message will not be believed.

Nonverbal communication functions in a notably different way from verbal communication (Anderson 1984). For one thing, regardless of the diverse spoken languages people use, we all seem to share certain similar nonverbal gestures. Also, we use many more channels for delivering nonverbal messages than verbal ones—a smile, a frown, a clenched fist, a nod of the head, the raising of an eyebrow, the movement of a leg—and all of these are open to interpretation. Although nonverbal messages are often very subtle, and indeed ambiguous, they are delivered continuously, without a precise beginning or ending. Verbal codes, in contrast, are more consciously learned and delivered through a single channel, with each word having a discrete beginning and ending. Moreover, we spend years studying our native language, developing a vocabulary, learning to articulate what we mean. Rarely do we devote that kind of energy learning to interpret nonverbal codes (Burgoon 1978).

Although nonverbal messages are often very subtle, they are delivered continuously.

Nonverbal messages seem to have a greater impact on us, whether it is through the raising of an eyebrow, a wink, a pat on the shoulder, a comforting smile, or an agreeing nod (Anderson 1984). As one group member wrote in her diary:

> When I helped the group solve a problem, everyone turned to me as if I were the leader. I felt embarrassed, even though the solution I offered turned out to be the right one. Then Maria put her hand on my shoulder and patted me. This made me feel so good.

Nonverbal Communication in the Small Group

Most research in nonverbal communication has not focused directly on small group interaction; nonetheless, the data are appropriately applicable to the small group setting and valuable for the insights they provide. There are benefits to be gained by paying close attention to nonverbal cues:

You can become more sensitive to messages. You will learn to be sensitive to the emotional impact of the messages, yours and others. The Japanese, for example, are known to appoint a "watcher" during negotiation sessions. "Watchers" look for people willing to compromise as well as for the "unyielding." They want to learn the habits of their opposition, to be able to assess the emotional needs, as well as the substantive demands, of the people they are confronting. While it would be too great a task to process all the nonverbal cues going on in a group, you can learn to watch for those cues that do provide important information.

You will learn how to observe interaction patterns. When you enter a group, you undoubtedly seek information that will help you understand how other people are interacting with you. By focusing on nonverbal messages, you can learn to be more attuned to the feelings and attitudes of group members. As you look around at the other group members, you can appraise the scene, the actors, and the action. Here is an example.

It is probably a norm of most groups that only one person talks at a time while a problem is being discussed. What else goes on, then? Although you cannot know what the other people may be thinking, you may observe their interactions. If Judy looks at her watch, this may be a sign that she would like the meeting to be over. When two people smile at each other, though you may not know the circumstances, you can assume that they have a friendly relationship.

You will learn more about the way you are being received by others. While there is much to observe about what others are communicating, you may not realize that you, too, are giving off messages. That we all send messages that we are not aware of is reinforced by the observations of Erving Goffman in his book *The*

Presentation of Self in Everyday Life (1959). Goffman states that although people have control over some of the messages they use to create an impression, there are other times when the messages they communicate are not in their control. For example, you may be sitting quietly in a group, unaware that a powerful impression has been created about you—your silence has permitted others to make a judgment about your willingness to participate. Some people may speculate about your interest in the group or your knowledge of the topic.

Watzlawick and his colleagues (1964), in a study of the communication of schizophrenic patients, used an expression that has become a standard descriptor of the impact of nonverbal communication: You cannot *not* communicate. Watzlawick found that even when patients were denying that they heard questions addressed to them, their body movement revealed that they were hearing the questions anyway. Their nonverbal response was to turn their heads away from the speaker. This led Watzlawick to declare that, although we may be trying not to communicate, we are still sending messages—messages that others are interpreting.

In a small group, you may be surrounded by activities that are open to interpretation. Some members may be looking directly at the person talking, while others are not making eye contact with the speaker. Some may be head-nodding; others seem to be sitting passively. Someone else may be writing, perhaps catching up on another assignment. Two members may be off to the side talking to each other. "What is going on?" you may wonder. Without understanding how nonverbal messages contribute to the establishment of rules that govern the exchange of ideas and the development of a supportive climate within your group, you would be missing important clues for working effectively in a group.

DIMENSIONS OF NONVERBAL COMMUNICATION

When you first join a group, you may form an immediate impression of the other members. You are likely to evaluate the scene—the clothes people are wearing, the expressions on their faces, their physical characteristics, the sounds of their voices, the way they are sitting, and, probably, the social relationships among the participants. Most researchers typically include the following dimensions as significant to understanding the impact of nonverbal communication (Knapp 1978):

Artifacts include such factors as how people dress—the styles of their clothing and hair, their physical features, and their overall personal appearances.

Physical environment refers to the color, lighting, and shape of a room, the layout of furniture, and the overall attractiveness and comfort (or absence of those qualities) in a room.

Proxemics refers to the way people arrange themselves in a space—how close or how far apart they sit and what postures they assume.

Kinesics refers to all bodily movement, from head to toe, from shoulders to hands, and to the use of eye contact and facial expression.

Paralanguage refers to the tone of voice, the way words are accented, and how messages are to be interpreted.

We can learn more about how to observe nonverbal interaction by examining these dimensions more closely.

Artifacts

Nonverbal cues included in the term *artifacts* provide much of the emotional meaning of a message. Your choice of clothing, the way in which you present yourself to others, your physical appearance, your hair style, and even the kind of wrist watch you wear can lead to judgments and attributions. First impressions are often determined by personal appearance. For instance, you probably would treat a well-dressed person differently from a poorly dressed person. Attorneys know this, and when their poorer clients appear before a jury, they are dressed in a well-fitting outfit. Researchers have found that attractive, well-dressed people have more credibility than those judged not as attractive (Napier and Gershenfeld 1985).

The general shape and size of a person's body affects how others will perceive that individual. The research data suggest that fat people are judged as less good-looking than thin people. Athletic figures are rated as more mature and adventurous, while tall and thin body types are seen as tenser than others. Although you cannot control, for the most part, the basic shape of your body, you can take responsibility for your personal appearance. Artifacts not only affect your judgments of others and their judgment of you; they influence your behavior. Since personal appearance and the artifacts you choose in your presentation of self help form lasting first impressions, you will need to take this knowledge into consideration. It will be your choice to decide how you want to present yourself—to seek confirmation for the self you wish to represent.

Physical Environment

The physical attractiveness of the environment is also an important issue for you and your group. You are doubtless aware of how a particular setting will affect your mood. That a full moon will inspire lovers is expressed in many songs. The environment that a group works in will have an effect as well. If a room is too small to hold the number of people expected, too cold or unattractive, these conditions may interfere with a group's work.

A now classic experiment performed by Mintz (1956) showed the remarkable effect of environment on judgment. Subjects were placed in one of three different settings—a messy janitor's closet (the ugly room), a professor's office (the average room), and a living room decorated with attractive furniture (the beautiful room)—and were asked to evaluate some photographs. They rated the photographs viewed in the beautiful room most positively. Subjects in the beautiful room liked the task better and were willing to continue working on the project, whereas subjects in the janitor's closet complained that they felt irritated and did nor want to continue working.

What are the implications of these data for understanding group work? Poor surroundings can negatively affect how you feel as well as the decisions you make. An unsatisfying environment can cause you to transfer your feelings to the people who are meeting with you. When you are with a group, it is wise to consider whether you are in a reasonably good location. If the room is not conducive to pleasant feelings, then perhaps a change of location would be a useful step. Providing people with an attractive room, good lighting, and comfortable chairs is advantageous both for building group spirit and inspiring productive work.

Proxemics

The term *proxemics* was coined by E. T. Hall (1966), an anthropologist, who used the word to describe the distance people establish between themselves and others, whether in the workplace or at home (for instance, the arrangement of furniture). The term also refers to the way particular spatial arrangements affect people's feelings about relationships. Even more important than the actual physical arrangement of people and objects, Hall observed that spatial arrangements have *symbolic* meaning. As humans we tend to attach meaning to the distance, location, shape, and size of objects we encounter in our environment.

Space and the Group Environment   You can think of your group environment as a space that allows you to be distant from other people or to be completely involved. If you have spent any time in an airport waiting room, you can appreciate the extent to which the seating arrangements constrain interaction. Rows of immobile plastic chairs, which cannot be turned around, seem to have been especially designed to discourage "loitering." They clearly make it hard for families to sit together and talk. Many areas in school are also set up in such a way that it is difficult for students to interact. Classroom desks lined up in a row, fixed-seat auditoriums—these arrangements discourage interaction. And so will any obstacles in a room that keep group members from interacting face to face.

Within a group you can determine where you will sit and how close you will be to others in the group. The concept of space extends beyond the physical arrangement of chairs, however. Two contrasting needs influence how you will use space: (1) your need to be close, to affiliate, to socialize, and (2) your need for privacy, to have some measure of control over your space (Burgoon and Saine 1978). Which of these needs will predominate will be decided by the kind of person you are and your feelings about other people. Those you like you will sit closer to. In unfamiliar settings, you will probably choose to sit farther apart.

Small group experiments have shown that highly cohesive groups occupy smaller spaces than noncohesive groups (Patterson et al. 1979). Factors such as sex, race, and age also influence spatial choices within the group. People of the same age, race, and sex usually sit closer together than people of different ages, races, and sex. Individuals who are cooperating with one another sit significantly closer together than those who are competing. Sommer (1965) found, however, that men and women will occupy space differently within their groups. When men were asked to form a circle, they were more apt to sit somewhat farther apart than were women when asked to do the same thing. When women are placed in a small room, they tend to increase their interactions, but men often show discomfort in small spaces. However, if both men and women are under stress, and if the discussion is considered to be a tense one, then they both prefer greater personal space.

There is some evidence that distance between people is related to whether they are extroverted or introverted, with introverts showing a preference for more distance between themselves and others (Patterson et al. 1979). As Hall (1966) explains, when people interact with one another, they tend to shift the amount of space between them. They will use different distance patterns, depending on the situation: for intimate conversation, people will stand fairly close together, anywhere from touching to 18 inches apart; but for social and public occasions, there may be a distance of anywhere from 3 to 7 feet.

Another influence on the way people occupy space is their need to lay claim to some territory (Birdwhistell 1970). *Territoriality* is a term used to describe the way animals stake out and defend a particular space. Human beings also seem inclined to stake out a particular area (Sommer 1965). When you are in the library studying, for instance, do you place books around you on the table and your coat on the next chair? Or when riding on a train, do you load up the seat adjacent to you with your belongings? This approach to space conveys the message "Don't bother to sit at this table or in the seat next to me." But how quickly you would remove all those belongings if a friend appeared!

Within a group you can also see that people leave their markers—a coat on a chair, papers or a book bag on the table. Some individuals like to spread out in such a way that they take over a larger area of the available territory. This seems to be the case for higher-status individuals. Lower-status individuals usually take over less space or are more willing to allow greater intrusion into their space. Thus the way people occupy the space around them can be an indicator of patterns of dominance and submissiveness, as well as of the desires for closeness and privacy (Lott and Sommer 1967).

Where members choose to sit can also help determine the perception that others will have of their status. A study by Strodtbeck and Hook (1973) examining jury deliberations found that a person taking a seat at the head of the table was more often chosen to be jury foreman.

Another environmental effect on the small group comes from the way people structure their groups. They may be organized into particular configurations that researchers have labeled *communication nets.* Leavitt (1951) reports on a classic study in which groups were formed according to the following patterns: a circle, a wheel, a chain, and a Y (Figure 4.1).

Leavitt learned that network patterns influence the number of messages a group can send, the errors the members make, and the length of time it will take to complete a task. Efficiency and satisfaction, however, are interdependent. Although the wheel is more efficient than the Y, the Y more efficient than the chain, and the circle

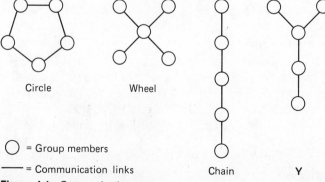

Circle   Wheel

○ = Group members

—— = Communication links

Chain   Y

Figure 4.1 Communication nets.

the least efficient, people are less satisfied when they participate in the wheel, the **Y**, or the chain patterns. They derive more satisfaction when they communicate in a circle.

While you are not likely to find yourself working in patterns such as the **Y** or the chain, you can appreciate the fact that structure affects not only the speed with which information is exchanged but also the satisfaction and morale of group members (Shaw 1981). Research data suggest that the way members arrange themselves in a group can encourage or discourage good interpersonal relationships—a finding that is important for you as a group member.

You can be aware that more visible members receive more communication, and that more centrally located members usually initiate more conversation (Leavitt 1951). When you participate more actively, you are given more leadership credit. This relationship was tested in an experimental study involving five-person decision-making groups (Howells and Becker 1962). Three people were placed on one side of a rectangular table and two on the other side. Leadership was more often attributed to the side with two people. They apparently had more opportunities to talk across the table, since more communication seemed to be directed at them. Thus they were judged more influential and emerged more often as group leaders.

While your assumptions about what is going on in the nonverbal domain of your group will need to be tested, one application of the data we have examined is that you can make choices about your own nonverbal behavior. When you want to show that you are cooperative and friendly, you can move your chair fairly close to others in the group. If you would like to participate actively, to have influence in the group—to be perceived as a leader—then choosing to sit in a more prominent place may facilitate this kind of involvement. When you want more interaction with a particular person, you can sit across from that person, unless the distance is so great that it makes conversation difficult. When you want less interaction, sitting adjacent to that person will diminish your opportunity to interact.

Kinesics

How do you know when it is all right for you to take a turn to speak in your group? Are you aware of the cues that tell you, "Go ahead." The answer is that you typically respond "kinesically." *Kinesics* is a Greek term meaning movement. Birdwhistell (1970) was probably the first to use the term to depict the study of bodily movement as communication.

Kinesics refers to the messages we express with your body. It includes posture—the way we orient our body to others when we are speaking. It is the degree to which we face toward or away from someone. Kinesics refers, also, to the way we sit—slumped in a chair or rigidly upright, leaning forward or turned away from a speaker. It includes facial expressions and the gestures we use to emphasize a point or elaborate on a thought.

When you are being observant of kinesic behavior, you are watching carefully while someone is speaking. Researchers suggest that, although you may not be aware of the cues you are paying attention to, you have learned to look for certain nonverbal signals. For example, if you want to know when to take a turn, you are probably watching the speaker's hands. Why? When the hands seem to relax, the speaker is probably signaling that he or she is through speaking. As you observe the nonverbal signals others are sending, you may be conveying nonverbal messages of your own. When you do not agree with an idea, for instance, you can express your feelings in several ways—by rubbing your nose, by turning your thumbs down, or by crossing your arms and looking straight at the speaker (Burgoon and Saine 1978).

The face is one of the most expressive channels for nonverbal messages.

In their study of gestures, Ekman, Friesen, and Ellsworth (1972) found that the use of gestures is influenced by people's emotional state. Although many people have learned to hide their feelings by controlling their facial expressions, they tend to be less aware of what their hands, legs, and feet are doing when they feel anger, boredom, tension, or stress. Those who have learned to become especially observant of gestural use may be able to discern from someone's clenched fist or fidgeting hand whether that person is experiencing anger or discomfort. Even more revealing is what the feet are doing. As you are describing a proposal to Tom, for instance, he may not realize that his negative reaction is being expressed in his kicking the chair in front of him. On the other hand, when two people are attuned to each other, they exhibit what is called *body synchrony,* a moving together in tandem. So when one crosses the left leg over the right, the other does the same. They are maintaining the same parallel positions (Knapp 1978).

The Functions of Gestures   The gestures you use—postural positions, movements of your arms, legs, hands, fingers, and face—can provide information about how you are responding to what is going on in the group. Some gestures facilitate group communication—direct eye contact, in particular, and a posture that is relaxed but indicates interest (Knowles 1973). The opposite effect comes from the absence of direct eye contact, a posture that is closed or turned away from the other party, and what appear to be nervous or distracting movements.

In general, researchers have found that gestures can accomplish the following functions (Knapp 1978):

Repeating. This occurs when you restate nonverbally what you have said verbally. It could be the expression on your face which conveys your joy as you say, "Thank you."

Substituting. You can use certain gestures to take the place of some of your verbal messages. Former President Nixon was famous for his A-OK sign, as was Winston Churchill for his V for Victory sign. In your group, you may see signs that tell you the discussion is not moving along very well: someone yawning, people looking at their watches, or members doodling on a notebook.

Complementing. When you express your feelings, you are much more likely to accompany your words with gestures and facial expressions that indicate the intensity of your feelings. In describing a meeting to a friend, you can illustrate how people were sitting: "There was hardly any room, so people were sitting like . . ." As you are speaking, your hands turn into fists squeezed tightly together.

Accenting. On the written page, accenting would appear as underlining or italics. Group members accent their words by raising their voices, setting off particular phrases with their hands shaping quotation marks, or indicating the importance of a message by slowing their rate of speaking.

Regulating. Regulating gestures help you start and stop conversations. You can indicate that you want to talk by extending your hand into the center of your group. In more formal settings, you would raise your hand to get recognition.

Contradicting. When someone says, "This is so exciting," but neither the voice nor the face reflects the excitement, listeners may be uncertain about the speaker's true feelings. Their uncertainty comes from the incongruity between the verbal and the nonverbal messages. Erving Goffman (1959) illustrates this concept with an example from his studies of people living in the Shetland Isles.

When a guest in one of the households is eating dinner, the housewife is not listening to the words the guest offers about how delicious the food is. Rather, she is watching how rapidly, and with what gusto, the guest is eating the food on the plate. The nonverbal clues are considered more indicative of the real feelings.

Adapting. Adaptors include those acts that gratify personal needs. Generally we are not aware when we use behavioral adaptations to cope with some bodily need, whether it is to scratch, rub, pull, or pick. We tend to use more of these self-adaptors when we are anxious or under increasing tension.

Two components of kinesic study are worth emphasizing for their implications for the small group.

Posture Posture communicates information about a person's well-being. According to Albert Mehrabian (1972), we are more apt to take relaxed positions when we are in nonthreatening situations and more likely to tighten up when we feel threatened. We tend to display symptoms of tension in ever-so-slightly moving fingers or in the tapping of a foot. The degree of relaxation we exhibit appears to be very high or very low when we are with people we dislike and moderate for people we like. In one study, subjects were asked to take on the posture they would use if they were talking to a friend, a person of high status, a male, a female, and a person they did not like. The results of this study showed that there are differences in the way people lean, stand, and use eye contact, depending on whether they are among those of high or low status—they stand straighter and taller, and use more eye contact, for higher-status people (Argyle and Dean 1965).

Facial expression   The face is the most expressive and most complex channel for nonverbal messages. Most people can make a fairly accurate judgment of what emotion is being expressed on another person's face, although we are influenced in our judgments by our past experiences and our stereotypes. There is also a cultural factor. Americans have learned to pay attention to even the slightest change in facial expression. Other cultures tend to pay more attention to the explicit statements. A particular context also affects how we interpret other people's facial expressions. When a glum face is shown next to a smiling face, it is typically characterized as "defeated" or "embarrassed," but when a glum face is paired with a frowning face, it is described as "cool" and "aloof" (Shaw 1981).

We have learned some valuable information about nonverbal interaction from research on eye contact. Eyes can communicate positive and negative feelings, as well as dominance and submissiveness. They can send any number of interesting messages, from "We agree, don't we?" to "I don't want to deal with you." Listeners judge speakers who gaze more directly at them as more persuasive, truthful, and sincere (Knapp 1978). Mutual gazing reveals something about the nature of the relationship between two people. In the small group, eye contact lets people know when it is their turn: "Go ahead and give me your idea." Or the eyes can tell you, "Please answer me. I need a response."

Eye contact can also be used as a measure of a person's status. As noted above, high-status individuals typically receive more eye contact from group members than do low-status members. When you accompany your message with direct eye contact, your message tends to be more favorably interpreted. Leathers (1969), in his review of the literature on facial expression, found that the face can communicate an individual's degree of involvement, interest or lack of interest, understanding or lack of understanding, and such evaluative judgments as good and bad. Although facial expressions are rich in cues, they are not always easy to interpret. You will probably do very well in diagnosing some basic emotions reflected on faces—surprise, fear, anger, happiness, and sadness—but other emotions such as boredom and adoration are not as easy to read. Your accuracy increases when you know the person and understand the circumstances that produced the expression.

You should also be aware that kinesic behavior is interdependent. Your behavior may influence subsequent behavior. A smile may beget a smile. Your willingness to pay attention to the kinesic behavior of group members has implications for both your behavior and the behavior of others toward you. Your use of eye contact may contribute to the perception of you as a potential leader. It can certainly help decrease the psychological distance among members. Your directness and warmth may help reduce tension within the group. Your sense of ease in the group may help other members to relax. In this way, appropriate facial and eye behavior contributes to the group's ability to accomplish its work.

Paralanguage

"I'm not upset. Why should you think so?" Janice asked, after Mike apologized for something he had said. But there were cues in Janice's voice that belied her statement. It was not the words she uttered that gave the group a cue to her feelings. It was the low pitch and the tension in her voice that allowed the group to infer how Janice really felt.

When you participate in the exchange of verbal messages, you are hearing more than the speaker's words. As you listen to a message, you are being influenced by the paralanguage as well. *Paralanguage* is a term used to describe the style in which words are spoken, the phrasing used, the tone of voice, the emphasis, the pronunciation, and the clarity of the message (Baird and Weinberg 1981). When you listen to a message, you react to the whole message. You are being influenced by the totality of the communication—the speaker's educational level, ethnic background, personality, anxiety or other emotional states—rather than by any single factor.

You acknowledge the importance of paralanguage when you say, "I wasn't upset by what she said, but by the way she said it," or "Say it as if you mean it." A key factor in interpreting paralinguistic cues is to know the context in which you hear the message. You will need to recognize changes in the quality (the rate or pitch) of a speaker's voice, as well as knowing who the speaker is and the situation as the speaker sees it, before you are able to understand a speaker's meaning.

Style   The term *style* refers to the words we choose and the particular phrasing and emphasis we give to our words. Some people have a style that encourages group members to feel wanted. Others somehow manage to antagonize group members. The research by Norton (1983) on communicator style indicates that an individual's style of interacting with others affects the extent to which others will view that person as someone they can trust and respect. A pleasant style produces a climate allowing a group to spend more time on its tasks, while an obnoxious style may be deteriorating of the group's efforts.

Articulation   Being understood is also important. Learning to articulate, to phrase your ideas so that they flow, can help other members grasp your ideas. You can highlight certain points by tone of voice. For example, if you are strongly committed to a position, you can express more emotion in your voice. You may not always be conscious of the tone you are using, but you will show your sensitivity to group needs if you learn to be clear in your pronunciation and speak at a level that others can hear. The important point is that paralinguistic cues are always available for interpretation. Do you know how you sound to others? It might be useful to record a group session so that you can have some sense of what others are hearing when you present your ideas.

Interpreting Nonverbal Cues—An Exercise

Although you probably are not usually aware of the nonverbal clues you display—the way you sit or stand, your gestures and bodily movements, your vocal tones—all nonverbal cues that reveal your thoughts and feelings should be of special interest to you and your group. If you can learn to be aware of your own nonverbal messages and to make an effort to understand the nonverbal messages of others, you will contribute to the making of a communicative environment that stimulates a high level of interaction and satisfaction. The exercise "Nonverbal Charades" will test your ability to interpret emotions as expressed by "actors" through the use of their voices only, facial expressions only, bodily gestures only, and voice and bodily gestures combined.

NONVERBAL CHARADES*

Here is a chance for you to discover how much information you can derive from nonverbal cues. A group of six to ten Actors will portray a variety of emotions. An audience (of any number) can serve as Judges. You will also need to prepare ten cards with the name of one emotion on each card as listed on the form on page 96. These cards are placed on a table or chair in front of the Actors, face down. Each Judge is given a copy of the form shown on page 96.

Instructions for Actors

1. The Actors decide who will go first, second, third, and so on and arrange themselves in a seated or standing line. Actors should identify themselves by number—1, 2, 3, and so on.

*This exercise was suggested by Professor Judith Anderson, University of Rhode Island. It is adapted from the research of Paul Ekman. 1985. *Telling Lies* (New York: W. W. Norton).

2. The first Actor draws a card from the pile and portrays the emotion named on the card. The card is put back into the pile. Then the second Actor draws a card and enacts the designated emotion. This procedure continues until each player has had a turn for each Condition, and so on for all Conditions.

3. The Conditions are as follows and must be performed in order:

Condition I: Voice Only. Actors turn their back to the audience and count to ten aloud. The way they count is the way they think they can best use their voices to portray the emotion named on the card they have drawn.

Condition II: Face Only. Actors stand behind a prop so that only their face is revealed to the audience. They use only their face to portray the emotion named on the card they have drawn.

Condition III: Whole Body. Actors use their whole body to portray the emotion designated on the card.

Condition IV: Body and Voice. Actors use their whole body and count to ten aloud to portray the emotion on the card they have drawn.

Instructions for Judges

The Actors are seated (or standing) as a panel before the audience of Judges. Actors are given numbers (1, 2, 3, and so on) to identify them. As each Actor selects a card from the pile of cards, he or she decides quickly how to express the designated emotion. When the first player has enacted an emotion, the Judges place a "1" under Condition I next to the emotion they think was being expressed by that Actor. Judges place a "2" beside the emotion they think is being expressed by Actor number 2 under Condition I, and so on, until all Actors have completed Condition I. The Actors will continue this procedure for conditions II, II, and IV. Judges should understand that, under each Condition, an emotion may be portrayed more than once, or some emotions not portrayed at all. Note, too, that Judges do not ask questions; they simply indicate the emotion they believe is being portrayed by each Actor.

(Exercise continues)

Emotions	Condition I Voice Only	Condition II Face Only	Condition III Whole Body	Condition IV Body and Voice
Admiration				
Affection				
Anger				
Anxiety				
Boredom				
Cheerfulness				
Despair				
Impatience				
Sadness				
Surprise				

Comments on the Exercise

From a poll of the audience, participants can determine how realistically each Actor portrayed the emotion, as well as which Condition seemed to provide the most accurate information. Did you find that some people were better at interpreting cues than others? Were some Actors more adept at providing cues? Were some emotions too ambiguous to interpret? And were some Conditions easier to interpret than others?

Paul Ekman (1985) found, in his experiments with Conditions I, II, III, and IV, that those who saw just the face or heard just the words did the worst in making judgments about whether subjects on video were lying to an interviewer. Suspicious people did not do much better. Those who saw subjects using their whole body (Condition III) did the best, but they were right only 65 percent of the time. A few people did very well. They correctly identified 85 percent of liars. Some of these accurate Judges were highly experienced psychotherapists with reputations for being expert clinicians. Other accurate Judges were just extraordinary sensitive people in other professions.

Overall, the best documented vocal sign of emotion is pitch.

Pitch becomes higher when an individual is upset, especially under conditions of anger and fear. There is also some evidence that pitch drops with sadness or sorrow. But, Ekman warns, the failure to show emotion is not necessarily a sign of truthfulness. These data reinforce the point that we all have to be careful when attempting to interpret nonverbal cues. We cannot know with certainty what is going on within a person simply by reading nonverbal cues. As this exercise demonstrates, nonverbal cues are often ambiguous. Nevertheless, as the research data suggest, it is wise to be continually aware of your nonverbal environment, since it has such an impact on your reactions and interactions.

OTHER INFLUENCES ON THE COMMUNICATIVE ENVIRONMENT—SIZE, TIME, AND PHASES OF DEVELOPMENT

Size of Group

Is there a right size for a problem-solving group? Although there may not be one appropriate size for all situations, we do know that the size of a group affects the amount and quality of communication within the group. There are data that suggest that when a group is larger than five, members tend to claim it is too large. As Kephart (1950) reports, with only three members, a group has the possibility of six relationships.* But if the group doubles in size, the number of possible relationships increases to 301, an astronomical rise. Moreover, as a group's size is altered, the structure within the group changes. With each additional member, the group will experience a different dimension of communication.

Size affects not only communication but the extent to which members are motivated to carry out tasks. There appears to be more satisfaction and cohesiveness with smaller groups. As size increases, members tend to show greater disagreement and greater antagonism toward others; at the same time, there is more opportunity for tension release (Rosenfeld 1973). Although, for many group projects, the saying "Many hands make light the work" should depict the additive strength of a group, yet individual effort decreases when members believe that others will do the work (Latane, Williams, and Harkins (1979). One reason for this reaction is that, generally, people in groups participate unequally. Typically a few members take part most actively, but as the size of a group increases, inequality becomes even more pronounced (Rosenfeld 1973).

Undoubtedly, the large group has more resources to help work on a problem. The available knowledge, skills, and abilities is greater. Yet when people find themselves in a large group, they often feel intimidated and unable to participate. With diminished com-

---

*In a group with members A, B, and C, the following relationships are possible: A→B; B→A; A→C; C→A; B→C; and C→B.

munication between members, the morale of the group often suffers. In addition, the larger the group, the more likelihood that members will form subgroups or cliques. Rather than relating on a one-to-one basis, participants may find that they are a member of a subgroup that must deal with other subgroups.

When a group gets too large, it affects participation. The dominant members become the most talkative. This effect was reported in a study by Riecken. He investigated the impact of talkative members on group problem solving. The solution to a problem was given to group members identified as either the most talkative or least talkative. When the most talkative member gave a hint of the solution to the group, it was accepted, but when the least talkative member gave essential information, it was rejected.

In contrast, a small group allows more opportunity for participation. It has the potential for developing the greatest degree of intimacy. But smallness also produces tension. With fewer individuals in the group, there is a tendency to hold to and argue positions. With fewer individuals, a small group may not have sufficient resources to be able to engage in a discussion of every prudent alternative. They may lack the ability to evaluate potential solutions.

The question posed at the beginning of this discussion was whether there is an appropriate size for a group. From some of our laboratory studies, we learn that a group of five will work best in a greater number of situations (Napier and Gershenfeld 1985). A five-person group is large enough to allow a variety of ideas to be considered, and yet small enough for everyone to participate. The better answer, however, is that much depends on such contingencies as the topic to be discussed, the personalities of the members, the way members like to work, and the goal they want to accomplish. What we do know is that size should be factored into your plans before you assemble your group. You can help determine what is an appropriate size by considering such questions as

What are the group's goals?

How complex is the problem?

What resources will be needed?

How will the different personalities interact?

Will the location of the meeting be adequate for the group's size?

How long will the group have for discussion?

Chronemics

The use of time and the meaning that we have for time is the focus of the study of *chronemics* (Anderson 1984). In the United States we talk about time as something precious—not to be wasted. In contrast with some other cultures, we appear to be very concerned about punctuality, about meeting deadlines, seemingly always to be in a hurry. From the study of chronemics we learn that while we are a time-conscious society, individuals reflect different rhythms. While some people are always in a hurry, others are slower paced, taking more time to reflect and respond. Group members need to be aware of the different attitudes that people have toward time.

Time, like size, plays a role in determining how well a group functions. In fact, one element in deciding how many people to include in a group is the amount of available time. In addition, groups must learn how to allocate their time, so that the group can accomplish its goals without creating unnecessary tension among members. This section will take a look at each of these elements.

One of the paradoxes in determining an appropriate size for a group is the tradeoff between having a useful number of perspectives represented and having the time to be able to hear each point of view. In a large group a greater proportion of members may feel that they have been given less than their fair share of participation time. Thus one aspect of time that is important to a group is the perception that members will be able to participate. If time is limited, group members should be discouraged against monopolizing the group and against not speaking up before the time runs out. People who dominate by talking too much are considered rude, yet minimal participation is not positively valued either. Finding a balanced way to share talking time is essential for positive group interaction.

Another way that time imposes demands on a group is over the question of how much time a group should devote to a discussion. This question becomes a problem in two ways. First, difficulties can arise when a meeting is scheduled to begin at a specified time, but the starting time is delayed. Even though the reasons for the delay may be rational, people resent being kept waiting. They may have given up other important tasks to come to the meeting. The delay may also impose time constraints, leaving insufficient time for a good discussion to take place. Frequently, when group members realize that they do not have enough time, they try to push for a decision prematurely. The constraints of time surely affect how well a group will perform.

Second, members are equally frustrated when a meeting seems to go on without end. If people expect to be at a meeting for an hour, they become uneasy when the hour has passed and no end is in sight. Groups need to consider both starting and finishing on time. If they have to continue beyond the scheduled meeting time, then members should be consulted about extending the time. Since many people find it difficult to maintain a high level of participation for much longer than an hour (concerts, lectures, and classes acknowledge this fact by including intermissions or break times), a short break may alleviate some of the uneasiness expressed. If a break is suggested, it is important to specify how much time should be taken. Group members working on a task need to understand how assumptions about time influence participation.

Phases in Group Development

In addition to understanding how nonverbal cues affect group performance, it is useful to recognize that groups go through developmental phases independent of where members are seated, what gestures they use, or what their social status may be. Yet the group's environment is dependent on where in their discussion the group is. Developmental phases occur in most groups, although the content and length of the phases will vary with the group and the task. Even though the passage through these phases may not be clear-cut, knowing that there are phases, and being able to identify them, should help you better understand why people communicate as they do.

If you think about the changes that have occurred in you as you have matured from your early years, through elementary school, high school, and now college, you can surmise that groups, like individuals, will change over time. At least that is what a number of theorists have suggested. Several studies in group development, using experimental groups, show that groups typically begin their work in an atmosphere of uncertainty. They go through a period of conflict and, if the conflict is resolved successfully, reach a stage at which members interact with each other comfortably.

Bales and Strodtbeck (1951) were probably the earliest investigators of developmental processes in groups. They found three phases in a group's development: *orientation, evaluation,* and *control.* When a group first meets, the emphasis is on what the situation is like. Orientation refers to a group's effort to understand its task and the information necessary for making a decision. When a group decides what attitudes it should take toward the situation, then problems of evaluation become the focus. In this phase, groups discuss differences in values and judgments. In the third phase, the group deals with problems of control. Control refers to the process in which the group examines what it is going to do about the situation. It is a time for choosing among decision alternatives.

Tuckman (1965) dramatizes these stages using catchy titles—*forming, storming, norming,* and *performing.* Forming implies orientation, a time for getting information about what is expected of group members. Storming refers to the conflicts that develop as groups work on the task. Members take more definite stands, and issues tend to become more polarized. Norming occurs as members come closer to making their decision. During this phase they will likely experience a feeling of harmony and cohesion. When a solution does emerge, groups are in the last phase, performing. Then the group functions in ways that allows members to feel they have contributed to the group's accomplishment of goals.

Aubrey Fisher (1970) analyzed the verbal interactions of task-oriented groups and also found a four-phase development. Although his stages are expressed in somewhat different terminology—*orientation, conflict, emergence,* and *reinforcement*—the phases are analogous to those of the other theorists. But because Fisher's category system focused only on the task dimension and the communication expressed in each phase, his analysis has been very important for understanding the communicative environment.

In the first phase, members' communication is geared to "breaking the ice," a time when members try to learn more about each other and about the task. They try to form opinions about the trustworthiness and competence of other members. In this phase, talk begins slowly. Participants do not jump into the discussion with fully developed ideas. Rather, their inclination is to be cautious, to use polite conversation, and to explore the climate of the group.

Communication during the second phase is focused on argument and persuasion. Members express different points of view. Although there will likely be conflict—and effective groups will allow conflict to surface—members have to learn to grapple with real issues. They are also learning to understand their own and others' contributions.

How a group handles the conflict phase characterizes the emergence phase. It is at this point that skilled communication can help reconcile divergent positions. If members express their views with some ambiguity, they can more easily alter their positions. For example, you may disagree with another participant, but if you do so with moderation, such communication can help your group reach consensus. Fisher suggests that when decisions are close at hand, people dissent less frequently. They find ways to soften strongly expressed positions by using such processes as mediation and consensus building.

As the group emerges from its prior struggles, realizing that it has accomplished something worthwhile, it is then at the final stage, reinforcement. Members communicate with each other by expressing their satisfaction. They show positive support by complimenting one another and by reinforcing the group's decision.

What can be learned from examining the theories of group development? A reasonable conclusion is that the developmental phases affect the communicative environment of the group. Groups do not automatically progress from one stage to another, however. Developmental phases are not readily predictable, nor does one phase necessarily follow another in a sequential development

(Poole 1983). What is important for your understanding of group ecology is that relationships in the group, as well as group interaction, will be shaped by whether the group needs to obtain more information, discuss procedures, evaluate decision proposals, or come to a conclusion. By being aware of developmental phases, you will be better able to identify group needs and more likely to take steps to deal with them.

The following excerpt from a diary of a group member illustrates how her awareness of developmental processes helped her understand what was happening in the group.

> We passed through the forming stage without much difficulty as we got together and exchanged a bit about ourselves, and our wants and needs at the present time. I felt that our group would get along well while it was in the forming stage, and, for a brief period, I didn't even think that we would hit the storming stage. But, alas, at the next meeting we did. To my great surprise, our group felt the impact of the storming stage much more than any of the other groups!

> We ran into a great big conflict over a decision to choose, out of a list of several different organizations, an organization to observe. Soon the discussion became heated, and we lost track of our original purpose for meeting. The storming process turned into a debate about individual desires; we progressed nowhere. Finally, we decided to talk about the way we were communicating.

> Our perceptions about each other and the perceptions that we felt others had about us were becoming distorted. As we talked about this, things began to change slowly and we got back to the topic at hand. For the good of the group, we decided by consensus to pick a new organization (one not originally on our list). We began to move toward the norming stage in which acceptable codes of behavior were established. We began to look at ourselves as a group. But at our next meeting the member who had so inflamed us didn't show up and this moved us into the storming stage again. Knowing that these stages of development are normal for the group made it easier for me to accept them, flow with them, and let them take a natural course.

> As we really begin to establish our norms, most of which are based on group informality, I know that we will ease our way toward the performing stage. I will really be an active participator in this stage; I will give the group my all, since I know that this stage is crucial for our group to reach our goal. I also know that we will have to enter the "reforming" stage. We will have to change when necessary. We all cannot be perfect.

> In summing up, I feel that just being aware of the stages of group development will be enough to help me improve the group. I can understand that all groups go through these stages—even having several at the same time. And by being familiar with them, it helps me go through the process.

A FINAL COMMENT

As a member of a group, or as a leader, you have an opportunity to help the group accomplish its goals. With your knowledge of how ecological issues affect the impressions you make, leadership choices, group interactions, and the group's well-being, you will be in a better position to diagnose what specific measures you can undertake to help your group. Knowing that spatial arrangements affect group interaction should make you more alert to the way people are seated in your group. Observing whether distances between people interfere with their communication and understanding that people need to feel they are central to the group are ways to apply your knowledge of proxemics to facilitate group communication. Your use of eye contact and a relaxed posture reflect how the study of kinesics may help group members feel more at ease.

How you sit or stand, your gestures and bodily movement, your vocal tones—all nonverbal cues that reveal your wants and needs should be of special interest to you as a participant in the group process. If you can learn to be in control of your own nonverbal messages and make an effort to understand the nonverbal messages of others, you will be better able to contribute to a communicative environment that stimulates a high level of interaction and satisfaction.

Similarly, your knowledge of how size, time, and phases of developmental affect the group's discussion of issues should give you some valuable insights about group processes. Seeing a group as a developing unit, one that will need time to accomplish a project, should help you feel less disturbed about the group's progress. You can also take definite steps to improve the workings of your group. For example, when a group has just begun to meet and the first communication is about who the members are, you can ensure that such comments as, "Let's move on" do not sway the group from the need to take time for orientation. You can reinforce the point that groups need time to sort out roles and functions, and that a group's consideration of ideas also takes time. Development cannot be forced. A normal part of a group's development is taking the time to become oriented to its tasks and to its members.

When a group is examining decision proposals, you can anticipate that there will be some conflict. Rather than squelching the conflicting views, it would be helpful to reinforce the group by supporting a full discussion of differing viewpoints. (Chapter 8 discusses the effect of conflict on group processes.) Your knowledge of how the group is structured and whether it is in an earlier or later phase of development will help you understand the types of communication that can facilitate the group's discussions. You can be influential in the early phases by helping to relieve the initial anxiety that members feel, and you can help the group feel a sense of achievement in the later phases by complimenting and thanking members for the contributions they have made. Knowing that a significant impact on a group's environment comes from its phase of development will help you understand why and how your group is functioning the way that it is.

SUMMARY

This chapter has examined the ecology of a group—the relations that participants have with their environment. The chapter first considered the way nonverbal cues provide much of the emotional meaning of a message. Physical appearance, style of dress, age, sex, eye contact, and tone of voice are some of the elements that contribute to the impressions people make on a group. Despite the lack of accuracy in nonverbal messages, they are important to the student of small group communication because they are more believable than verbal messages, they provide information about the group's environment, and they indicate what rules group members are using for conducting their exchange of messages.

Researchers of nonverbal communication typically divide the subject into five subtopics: artifacts, physical environment, proxemics, kinesics, and paralanguage. Of these five components, the latter three have the most significant impact on the small group, although the attractiveness and the comfort of the physical environment (or lack of these qualities) and members' personal appearance clearly influence how people feel toward each other and the judgments they make.

Proxemics—the arrangement of people and furniture in a room and the symbolic meaning of different spatial relationships—both influence and reflect patterns of intimacy and group cohesiveness. The data from experiments on communication nets show the effect of structure on group interaction. Members are more satisfied, though less efficient, in a circle pattern. The converse is true in the wheel, **Y,** or chain patterns. Good interpersonal relationships, as well as a more comfortable communicative climate for discussion, will depend on whether participants are in a central or a peripheral position in the group.

The messages people express by their posture, gestures, and facial expression—what has been labeled kinesics—provide information on what individuals are feeling about themselves and others. Routinely, people use gestures for repeating, substituting, complementing, accenting, regulating, contradicting, and adapting their verbal messages. How they sit, stand, and use gestures and bodily movements reveals feelings. People can express boredom, relaxation, tension, and stress through kinesic behavior, with the face as the most complex channel for conveying emotion, and the eyes the most influential in communicating positive and negative feelings.

Paralanguage, the style and articulation of a message, reveals something about the emotional state of an individual. Individuals who speak pleasantly and use their voice well increase their own credibility in the group; a person using a sarcastic tone can infuriate other members. Members can use paralanguage to influence the group by being considerate of the needs of other members to understand them clearly, and by matching their words with their facial expression so that the other members will find them trustworthy.

Other factors that shape a group's environment include size, time, and the phases of group development. Determining the size of a group will be dependent on the needs of group members, the complexity of the task, and the time available for the project. Chronemics, the use of time, is important for recognizing both different attitudes toward time and the different ways that people will use time.

Whether participants employ the three-dimension category of Bales and Strodtbeck (orientation, evaluation, and control), the four-stage system of Tuckman (forming, storming, norming, and performing), or Fisher's dimensions (orientation, conflict, emergence, and reinforcement), these studies suggest that groups communicate differently in their different phases. Understanding these differences provides valuable data about a group's communicative environment.

REFERENCES

Anderson, P. 1984. "Nonverbal Communication in the Small Group." In R. S. Cathcart and L. A. Samavar (eds.), *Small Group Communication: A Reader.* (4th ed.) Dubuque, Ia.: Wm. C. Brown, pp. 258–273.

Argyle, M., and J. Dean. 1965. "Eye Contact, Distance, and Affiliation." *Sociometry* 28: 289–304.

Baird, J. E., Jr., and S. Weinberg. 1981. *Group Communication.* Dubuque, Ia.: Wm. C. Brown.

Bales, R. F., and F. L. Strodtbeck. 1951. "Phases in Group Problem-Solving." *Journal of Abnormal and Social Psychology* 46: 485–495.

Birdwhistell, R. L. 1970. *Kinesics and Context.* Philadelphia: University of Pennsylvania Press.

Burgoon, J. K., and T. Saine. 1978. *The Unspoken Dialogue: An Introduction to Nonverbal Communication.* Boston: Houghton Mifflin.

Ekman, P. 1985. *Telling Lies.* New York: W. W. Norton.

Ekman, P., W. V. Friesen, and P. Ellsworth. 1972. *Emotion in the Human Face.* New York: Pergamon Press.

Fisher, B. A. 1970. "Decision Emergence: Phases in Group Decision-Making." *Speech Monographs* 37:53–66.

Forsyth, D. R. 1983. *An Introduction to Group Dynamics.* Monterey, Calif.: Brooks/Cole, pp. 274–286.

Goffman, E., 1959. *The Presentation of Self in Everyday Life.* New York: Doubleday Anchor.

Hall, E. T., 1966. *The Hidden Dimension.* New York: Doubleday, 1966.

Howells, L. T., and S. W. Becker. 1962. "Seating Arrangement and Leadership Emergence." *Journal of Abnormal and Social Psychology* 64:148–150.

Kephart, W. M., 1950. "A Quantitative Analysis of Intragroup Relationships." *American Journal of Sociology* 60:544–549.

Knapp, M. L. 1978. *Nonverbal Communication in Human Interaction.* New York: Holt, Rinehart & Winston.

Knowles, E. S., 1973. "Boundaries Around Group Interaction: The Effect of Group Size and Member Status on Boundary Permeability." *Journal of Personality and Social Psychology* 26:327–331.

Latane, B. K. Williams, and S. Harkins. 1979. "Many Hands Make Light the Work: The Causes and Consequences of Social Loafing." *Journal of Personality and Social Psychology* 37:1531–1535.

Leathers, D. G., 1969. "Process Disruption and Measurement in Group Communication." *Quarterly Journal of Speech* 55:288–298.

Leavitt, H. J., 1951. "Some Effects of Certain Communication Patterns on Group Performance." *Journal of Abnormal and Social Psychology* 46:38–50.

Lott, D. F., and R. Sommer. 1967. "Seating Arrangements and Status." *Journal of Personality and Social Psychology* 7:90–95.

Mehrabian, A., 1972. *Nonverbal Communication.* Chicago: Aldine-Atherton.

Mintz, N., 1956. "Effects of Esthetic Surroundings: II. Prolonged and Repeated Experience in a 'Beautiful' and an 'Ugly' Room." *Journal of Psychology* 41:459–466.

Napier, R. W. and M. K. Gershenfeld. 1985. *Groups: Theory and Experience.* Boston: Houghton Mifflin.

Norton, R., 1983. *Communicator Style: Theory, Applications, and Measures.* Beverly Hills, Calif: Sage Publications.

Patterson, M. L., C. E. Kelley, B. A. Kondracki, and L. J. Wulf. 1979. "Effects of Seating Arrangement on Small Group Behavior." *Social Psychology Quarterly* 42:180–185.

Poole, M. S., 1983. "Decision Development in Small Groups: III. A Multiple Sequence Model of Group Decision Development." *Communication Monographs* 50:321–341.

Riecken, H. W. 1958. "The Effect of Talkativeness on Ability to Influence Group Solutions of Problems." *Sociometry* 21:309–321.

Rosenfeld, L. B. 1973. *Human Interaction in the Small Group Setting.* Columbus, Ohio: Charles E. Merrill.

Shaw, M. E., 1981. *Group Dynamics: The Psychology of Small Group Behavior* (3rd ed.). New York: McGraw-Hill.

Sommer, R., 1965. "Further Studies of Small Group Ecology." *Sociometry* 28:337–348.

Strodtbeck, F. L. and L. Hook. 1973. "The Social Dimensions of a Twelve Man Jury Table." *Sociometry* 36:424–429.

Tuckman, B. W. 1965. "Developmental Sequences in Small Groups." *Psychological Bulletin* 63:384–399.

Watzlawick, P., J. H. Beavin, and D. D. Jackson. 1964. *Pragmatics of Human Communication: A Study of Interactional Patterns, Pathologies, and Paradoxes.* New York: W. W. Norton.

chapter 5

Leadership in the Small Group

There is an aura that surrounds the individual perceived as "leader." We tend to associate a leader with fame, influence, power, and, indeed, the "good life." Moreover, when we hear the term *leader,* we are not likely to picture our friends. Rather, we tend to name famous people: presidents, generals, corporate chiefs, millionaires. Nonetheless, there may be the desire among many of us to become some type of leader—if not the ambition to become a world-class political leader, then a desire to achieve recognition as a leader in the workplace, or in social and political groups and organizations. The desire to influence, to be able to give direction, to count as somebody, is a strong one, at least for some people.

Ideas about leadership are numerous and various. But most explanations of leadership suggest, as James MacGregor Burns remarked, that "leadership is one of the most observed and misunderstood phenomena on earth" (1978). Some people explain leadership as power over others—power to force, to manipulate, to mold, and to shape. Others believe that a leader has authority over others, a legitimate dominance among the less organized people and groups of people. Some people believe that one is born a leader; it is a talent one either has or does not have. Other views hold that once a leader, always a leader, and that the ability to lead in one situation is transferable to other situations. It is also believed that a leader must be well liked to inspire followers. A corollary of this view is that few individuals have leadership qualities. From the perspective of current research, however, all of these views are questionable.

This chapter addresses issues important to an understanding of leaders and leadership in the small group. First, we will examine the various approaches to the study of leadership, including perceptions of and misperceptions about leaders. We will also discuss the specific leadership functions that help a group accomplish its goals. The last section will deal with how you can use leadership behaviors to become a more effective participant or leader in your group.

ATTRIBUTES OF LEADERS AND LEADERSHIP

Throughout our history, people have had an interest in and concern with what makes a leader and the attributes of leadership. Leaders and leadership have been the focus of study by scholars from many disciplines: psychology, communication, history, political science, anthropology, and sociology. Although there is a fair amount of overlap between the two terms, they are not synonymous. The term *leader* refers to the person occupying the position. It refers, too, to the leader as a role, a set of behaviors *expected* of a person in the position of directing the activities of others. *Leader* refers to that person who assumes the responsibility for making decisions for others. On the other hand, *leadership* represents the behaviors *displayed* by a person who is given responsibility as leader. It refers to such activities as organizing a group, delegating assignments, coordinating information, supporting the contributions of others—tasks which many individuals can perform.

Researchers have used many approaches to understand who becomes a leader and how leadership is displayed. The following section contains a brief history of their efforts. We will also discuss why individuals with certain types of attributes are likely to be chosen as leaders from among members of a group.

Approaches to the Study of Leadership

1. Trait Approach The earliest approach to identifying leaders focused on personality characteristics and traits, with the hope of discovering some way of testing or predicting who would be or who should be a leader. Psychologists and social psychologists were particularly interested, as were many organizations and the military, in finding tests that would distinguish leaders from nonleaders. But, after 30-plus years invested in such research, scholars were unable to find the magic scale for predicting who should be a leader. It was not that some personality traits did not correlate with leadership— indeed, leaders were found to share certain traits. Rather, the traits that were found to be in common—intelligence, attractiveness, tallness, age, verbal abilities, social skills, self-confidence, and a sense of responsibility—are well distributed throughout the population.

For example, leaders were found to be taller than nonleaders, although the correlation was not high. Yet, as we know from our examination of leaders—from Napoleon to Mussolini, from Harry Truman to Jimmy Carter—tallness, per se, cannot be said to have been a prerequisite for leadership. Wisdom and experiences are clearly criteria taken into account, especially when choosing political leaders, but this is not always the case. And as a study by Archer (1974) demonstrates, even the belief that attractive people are more likely to be chosen leaders is open to question. In his study, individuals who were perceived as relatively unattractive were rated as more influential. The correlation with intelligence is also not high. While groups look for leaders who are more intelligent than the average group member, the research data indicate that members do not seek a leader who is too different from them (Stogdill 1948).

Whether traits were examined singly or in combination, they simply lacked distinctiveness; they could not be used to forecast who would emerge as a leader and were not useful in selecting potential leaders. As R. D. Mann (1959) reported in his examination of more than 100 leadership studies, there appeared to be no consistency among the personality traits which each study had described as significantly related to leadership.

Another weakness of the trait approach is that it disallows the role of learning or training in becoming a leader. If you accept the fact that leadership traits are attributes that you either have or do not have, then it would appear fruitless for anyone to try to become a leader. Further, a belief in inborn traits diverts attention from what leaders actually do when they are leading. Nor does a belief in inborn traits help to distinguish between leaders who are effective and those who are ineffective. Because of contradictory findings, as well as the inability to predict potential leaders, the trait approach has been largely abandoned, although there will probably always be some people who will continue to believe that leaders are born that way.

2. Leadership Style Approach In a classic study of leadership behavior, Lewin, Lippitt, and White (1939) conducted an experiment with groups of young boys meeting in after-school clubs. Their study found that the way a leader relates to followers affects the group's process and outcome. In their experiment, the researchers examined three styles of leaders, which they labeled "democratic," "autocratic," and "laissez-faire" (from the French for "let [people] do [as they choose]"). The leader exhibiting the democratic style was trained to encourage participatory decision making, whereas the autocratic leader took complete charge of all activities. The "laissez-faire" leader represented a neutral approach, willing to help but taking no initiative in doing so.

Before discussing the results of the experiment by Lewin and his colleagues, it would be useful for you to discover whether you have one of these characteristic styles of leading. The "Sargent and Miller Leadership Scale" will help you do that. As you go through each set of questions, try to imagine yourself as a leader and think about how you might act.

SARGENT AND MILLER LEADERSHIP SCALE (1971)

Directions

Listed below are several pairs of statements. Read each pair of statements and place a mark next to the one you believe best represents your behavior when you are leading a group discussion. As you react to the statements, observe the following rules:

1. Check only one of the items for each statement.
2. Do not omit any of the items.
3. Do not look back and forth through the items; make each item a separate and independent judgment.
4. Record your first impression, your immediate reaction to each statement.

(To score your self-test, turn to page 133.)

1. a.——To give everyone a chance to express an opinion.
   b.——To know what the group and its members are doing.

2. a.——To assign members to tasks so that more can be accomplished.
   b.——To let members reach decisions by themselves.

3. a.——To know what the group and its members are doing.
   b.——To help members see how the discussion is related to the purposes of the group.

4. a.——To assist the group in getting along well together.
   b.——To help the group get to what you think is the best answer.

5. a.——To get the job done.
   b.——To assist the group in getting along well together.

6. a.——To know what the group and its members are doing.
   b.——To let members reach decisions by themselves.

7. a.——To get the job done.
   b.——To assist the group in getting along well together.

8. a.——To help members see how the discussion is related to the purposes of the group.
   b.——To assign members to tasks so that more can be accomplished.

9. a.——To ask questions that will cause members to do more thinking.
   b.——To get the job done.

10. a.——To let members reach decisions by themselves.
    b.——To give new information when you feel the members are ready for it.

Comments on the Exercise

In the experiment run by Lewin and his associates, all groups experienced each leadership style. The results—not surprisingly, considering that the experiments were conducted during the late 1930s and early 1940s—showed that groups with democratic leaders were more satisfied and functioned in a more lively, positive manner. Groups working under authoritarian leaders showed either very high levels of aggressiveness or of apathy, depending on the group. The least effective leadership style occurred in groups led by laissez-faire leaders. Lewin concluded that this type of leader did not represent leadership and, in future experiments, the laissez-faire category was dropped.

Films of this experiment revealed a dramatic finding: groups with an authoritarian leader spent more time in productive work, but only if the leader was present. In the absence of the leader (a part of the experimental manipulation), there was chaos: spit balls were thrown, scuffling and fist fights took place. In contrast, groups working with a democratic leader continued to work even when the leader was not in the room. In many cases, the groups seemed unaware that the leader was not present.

Implications of Leadership Styles   Current research confirms the general findings of Lewin and his colleagues that the democratic style appears to be the most effective for producing satisfied participants and desirable group outcomes. But more recent studies have also added to our knowledge of the impact of leadership styles. Studies by Sargent and Miller (1971) and Rosenfeld and Plax (1975) indicate that there are communicative as well as stylistic differences between democratic and authoritarian leaders. In the democratic condition the leader encourages group discussion and policies are determined by the group. In the authoritarian style the leader gives orders to group members and sets all policies.

Most research shows that the democratic style is preferred, but what is also evident is that different styles are effective under different conditions. Even in Lewin's experiment, some of the boys showed more satisfaction with an authoritarian leader. Thus the more important question is, Which style or which combination of styles will be most effective for which circumstances? In times of crisis, a group may survive better with a take-charge, authoritarian leader. When decisions of an immediate nature must be made, then a directive by an authoritarian leader would be appropriate. If you are dealing with a highly skilled technical group, then laissez-faire leadership would probably be welcomed. When crucial decisions affecting group members in future actions must be made, then participatory decisions work best.

Another result of current thinking about leadership is that the leader is not the sole determiner of which style is appropriate. As David Korten (1962) has found in his research, under certain conditions there is pressure from within the group for variance in leadership style. Factors such as changing membership and a changing task can affect a leader's style. When group members seek high goal attainment and are under stress, they may need a more authoritarian leader. Under conditions of less stress and uncertainty, they would look for a more democratic leader.

Two Types of Leaders   What we learn from the research on leadership styles is that there are essentially two types of leaders—those who focus more on getting a task completed, and those who show more interest in the relationships of people in the group. Which style should dominate or which style is more suitable for a given situation will have to be analyzed. For example, when you first learned to ride a bike, it was doubtless a three-wheeler. Your parents probably encouraged you, watched over you, until you began to show the confidence and mastery to ride by yourself. Then came your graduation to a two-wheeler. Here, again, somebody had to help, direct you, encourage you, until you could say, "I can do it by myself." There will always be individuals and groups who will require assistance, as well as individuals and groups who work out their own procedures and tasks (Napier and Gershenfeld 1985). The challenge for a leader is to discern when more, or less, assistance should be given.

The challenge for a leader is to discern when more, or less, assistance should be given.

Robert Bales (1958), in his research at Harvard, found that effective groups seemed to have two leaders—a task specialist concerned with getting a project completed, and a social-emotional specialist, concerned with the maintenance of good relationships. The concept of two leaders as necessary to a group's effective functioning has led other researchers to propose a "Great Man" theory of leadership (Borgatta, Couch, and Bales 1954). According to this theory, leaders face a dilemma between getting the task completed and, at the same time, maintaining good relations with and among group members. Why the dilemma? Leaders who are motivated by the need to get a task done may not want to spend a great deal of time on relationship issues. In contrast, leaders who are concerned about fostering good relations may not wish to prod their groups if their positions were to be put in jeopardy. There is doubtless an inherent contradiction between prodding people to work and also remaining on good terms with them. On the other hand, an individual who can combine the two specialties would surely fit the description of the "Great Man" theory of leadership.

Other Types of Leaders The data on leadership styles have led to some interesting spin-off research directed at understanding leadership in an organization. Douglas McGregor (1960), using the categories "Theory X" and "Theory Y," examined the relationship between leadership style and the assumptions that a leader has about people in general. With a Theory X perspective, a leader assumes that people are fundamentally lazy and, unless they are supervised closely, nothing will be accomplished. Leaders who operate from this premise supply direction, often using methods of control and coercion. Theory Y leaders, on the other hand, believe that people try to work to the best of their ability. Such leaders do not believe it is necessary to control every move. Rather, they look for ways to empower people to do their best work.

How a leader relates to followers can influence their productivity and satisfaction.

Current thinking indicates that leader effectiveness cannot be determined by style alone. Rather, it depends upon a variety of interrelated factors, such as the group's composition, the complexity of the project as well as the group's desire to get on with the task, the compatibility among participants, interaction patterns, and time constraints.

3. Situational Approach The situational approach to leadership is closely related to the stylistic approach and incorporates some of the features of the trait approach as well. Researchers using the situational approach looked for a match between a leader's personal style and a given situation (Hollander 1978). In a particular situation, then, the goal would be to find the person who would most successfully meet the demands of a particular situation. The situational approach assumes a relationship between a leader's style and the context in which that style will be used. The following example illustrates the situational perspective.

The chairman of the Board of Directors of a chemical firm known for its rapid rise to success in a short period of time announced that the company's president, one of the company's founders as well as the largest shareholder, was being removed from office. The reason for this unexpected action, reported the chairman, was that the president's participation on the Board had "fostered an atmosphere of contention."

Although the chairman praised the president for his early contributions to the company, his concluding remarks illustrate a fundamental thesis of situational determinates of leadership: different situations may require different types of leaders. As the chairman put it, "Leadership means different things at different times in a company's life cycle. We felt that the company had to move forward in a slightly different style." He indicated that the former president would be replaced by another founder who was more of a "team player," one "who would heal divisions at the company and move the firm toward stronger earnings."

Understanding how different situations necessitate different styles of leadership is at the heart of the situational approach. The emphasis is on the nature of the task—what needs to be done? It is an emphasis on environmental factors. It is also the recognition that different situations will create different demands on the leader. When examining a situation, a leader will have to look at such variables as the physical setting, the size of the group, the complexity of the task, the composition of the group, as well as the needs of the larger organization.

In its emphasis on the demands of the task, the situational approach has provided a needed corrective to the more traditional emphasis on traits. But this approach is not without its problems or critics. The data show that we should be cautious about choosing leaders on the basis of a situational analysis. For one thing, some personal characteristics do seem to affect leadership choice. In addition, choosing a leader on the basis of what the situation presumably demands implies that we can generate a countless number of situations in which the individual would be able or not able to lead on any given day. The difficulty of conceiving of every possible condition has made the situational approach somewhat flawed.

4. Contingency Model   An outgrowth of the situational and trait approaches was the contingency model developed by Fred Fiedler (1967). Fiedler assumed that a leader's effectiveness depended both on the personal qualities of the individual and on the nature of the group situation. His definition of personal traits, however, veered from the traditional explanation of personality characteristics to a concern with the way a leader interacts with followers.

Fiedler assumed that some leaders are motivated to create good working relations while others are more concerned with completing a task. To investigate his theory, Fiedler asked leaders to complete a scale, known as the Least Preferred Co-Worker Scale (LPC Scale). The scale measured how a leader would relate to a person whom the leader considered difficult to work with but did not necessarily dislike. Fiedler found that a person willing to tolerate an LPC was more apt to be a social-emotional leader. Individuals who were less willing to accept an LPC were more likely to be task leaders. Fiedler's research, while confirming other research that identified a dual structure of leadership, extended these findings to include three factors as significant to leadership effectiveness (Fiedler 1978).

Leader/follower relations. Fiedler considered the leader's acceptance by the group as the most important of the situational variables. A group's cohesiveness and willingness to cooperate give a leader confidence that his or her suggestions will be considered. Because there is less need for monitoring the interpersonal relationships in the group, more energy can be devoted to the task. The loyalty and respect both of the leader for the group and of the group for the leader also produce favorable leader/follower relations.

Task structure. Getting a task accomplished is the second most important situational factor. Some tasks are fairly routine and can be completed quickly and easily. Others are more ambiguous and require more structure and direction. But when group members realize that they have worked well together and can achieve their goals, then their task will bring satisfaction.

Position power. The power factor refers to the degree of power that a leader possesses in order to make something happen. In some groups, the power is low—that is, despite what the group and the leader may decide, others outside the group will make the final decision. In other situations, a leader has a high degree of power. He or she may control the rewards—bonuses, salaries, raises, task assignments—as well as the punishments.

Fiedler found that, depending on the contingencies, either a task-oriented or a relationship-oriented leader would be needed. Task-motivated leaders perform best in highly structured situations, whereas relationship-motivated leaders perform best in moderately unstructured situations. What Fiedler's contingency model shows us is the value of analyzing a group before choosing a leader. After you have examined your group's characteristics in detail, for instance, you could then ask such questions as: How well liked is this person? Is the task simple or complex? How much power does the person have? How well would the person satisfy the group's needs and expectations?

Suppose you determine, in answering the questions, that the task is not difficult, the structure is fairly routine, the group members are eager to work, and the leader has high power. This would be an extremely favorable situation for a task-oriented leader. On the other hand, if the task is complex, the structure is unclear, and members are not enthusiastic about working on the project, then a relationship-motivated leader would be a better choice.

Although the contingency model, with its fusion of leadership style, situation, and needs of followers, is an improvement over the trait approach or situational approach, it has also been criticized (Lombardo and McCall 1978). For one thing, the model assumes a beginning point for a group which leads to the selection of a particular type of leader. In so doing, the model ignores the dynamic quality of groups and situations. A leader chosen to meet one set of conditions may not be able to change and adapt to another set of conditions. And if a person is flexible enough to change with changing conditions, then knowing the predilection of a leader either for task motivation or for relationship motivation would not be important. Moreover, since groups in continuing interaction require that both leader and followers learn how to handle changing conditions, an awareness that the leader was selected according to certain contingencies still does not tell us what leaders actually do when they lead.

5. Studies of Power and Influence   The relationship of power and influence to a leader's function has been the subject of a number of studies. Researchers have explored how leaders use power, how they attain and hold onto power, and even whether perceived power is an essential condition for leadership. While the term *power* might correctly be defined as the ability to get something done, there seems to be a great deal of ambivalence about the word.

How would you respond if you were asked whether you had power? Perhaps your response would reflect what many people feel. They either do not believe that they have power or they would rather not accept that they have power over others—for to admit that one is powerful brings associations with such negative terms as *conniving, manipulative,* and *corrupt.* Yet if one truly has power and understands the many situations in which one is powerful, then power as a concept can be more readily appreciated as the ability to influence, to persuade, and to get something done.

There are advantages to being perceived as having power. A study by Hurwitz, Zander, and Hymovitch (1968) demonstrates that having power correlates with positive regard for the person perceived as powerful, and that an individual so perceived is more highly valued than an individual who appears to be less powerful. The perception that we are powerful can affect our self-satisfaction as well as our mental health. Dr. Bertram Brown (1982), a counselor and president of Hahneman Hospital in Philadelphia, says that in his dealings with people who hold power in Washington, he has become convinced that exercising power "is the most effective short-range, antidepressant in the world." People feel good about being in control.

Whether you view power as negative or positive, power is an important variable in the relationship between leaders and followers. For example, even in cases where an individual does not believe that he or she has power, there is a need to recognize that people have varying degrees of power. In student/teacher interactions, it is not only the teacher who wields power. Students have the power of rewarding the teacher by coming to class, by paying attention, and by evaluating the teacher positively. There is research indicating that people who have a high need for power also have a high need for being flattered. In a study, Fodor (1973) found that "flatterers" received noticeably higher ratings and pay raises than "non-flatterers" even though the two groups performed equally at assigned tasks.

Another perspective for exploring power is offered by French and Raven (1959). Their analysis of power encompasses five categories: legitimate, expert, reward, coercive, and referent.

Legitimate power refers to the authority given individuals through appointment, through traditional hierarchical structure, or through popular vote. Leaders with legitimate power can make decisions affecting lives and—as the example of the army sergeant telling the private to "jump," and the the private asking only, "How high?" reveals—a legitimate leader may be accepted without objection.

Expert power stems from the specialized knowledge that a person may possess. If you are perceived as knowledgeable, you will be asked more questions and sought out for your insight. This in turn will lead you to participate more actively, a factor that influences leadership perception. Although you may not have thought that being able to provide highly specialized information is power, expertise does indeed bring power.

Reward power refers to the ability to offer people what they desire. The reward could be something as simple as a pat on the back, or a verbal "good job," or salary increases, bonuses, and other "perks." Although some rewards may be perceived as bribes or attempts to manipulate someone, most of us comply with the conditions that bring forth a reward, especially if what is being asked appears to be reasonable.

Coercive power refers to the power to punish, used when a reward does not bring desired results. If you are rewarded in an organization, presumably it is because you have complied with what the organization expects of you. In a coercive system, you would obey because you would fear not to. When promotions are at stake, for instance, following the rules becomes an acceptable way to comply. Otherwise, the costs of noncompliance can be high. Unfortunately, while you may lose the promotion if you do not go along with the expectations of the people in power, the organization also loses when people with good reasons for noncompliance are not respected. When a scientist in a pharmaceutical company suggests that a drug should not be marketed until further tests are run, but sales and marketing people do not listen, there is likely to be trouble ahead within and outside the company.

Referent power refers to the personal qualities we admire or respect in a person. There is a tendency to identify with such individuals—to emulate them, seek their company, and be influenced by them. When Larry Bird walks into a room, it's not only his size that attracts attention. His skill in playing basketball wins him respect. Having referent power is the most pervasive of the powers of leadership. The term *charisma* is often used to identify the qualities that give a person referent power. Since we are all susceptible to the influence of the charismatic individual, we should be aware that an influence process has taken place.

What we learn from looking at leadership from the perspective of power and influence is that leaders usually display some combination of the five types of power. The more of these components that a leader has, the more influential the leader will be. While it is important to recognize that having power is an integral function of leadership, it is also important to know that having power is not absolute. In most situations leaders are dependent on factors other than their own individual efforts. The ability to get something done depends on the willingness of followers to carry out what the leader wishes. The amount of power a leader has also is influenced by the makeup and size of the group, the resources within the group, the demands of the task itself, and other organizational constraints.

6. Leadership Function Approach   Thus far, we have discussed five approaches to the study of leadership, representing an evolution in the theoretical perspectives of what makes a leader. From the early search for personality and stylistic characteristics that would determine who should be a leader, to an exploration of situations and contingencies affecting the role of leader, to the bases of leadership power, each approach provides valuable knowledge about the role of leader in a group.

We have also discussed the difficulties researchers have had in establishing a relationship between personality traits and the personal qualities of those who are chosen to lead, or in identifying successful leaders by their style of leadership or the contingencies they might face. The search for an understanding of the role of leader continues, albeit with a realization that no single theory can explain the complexities involved in the concepts of "leader" and "leadership."

Current researchers have reframed the questions being asked about the leadership role. Rather than focusing on the individual and his or her capacity for leadership—a person-centered theory of leadership, researchers now emphasize leader/member interaction as the unit of analysis. Using an approach called *leadership functions,* a number of theorists are exploring what a leader does, what makes a leader effective, and how leaders, followers, and the situation combine to produce particular outcomes.

A functions approach assumes that leadership is a process in which a leader engages in many behaviors, verbal and nonverbal, to help a group achieve a goal. But a key element in the group's effort consists of the interaction patterns of leaders and followers.

Rather than search for the special person who will be the leader, the functions approach posits that there are individuals within any group who contribute to group processes and who can aid the group. These premises rest on two assumptions: (1) members, as well as leaders, can perform the functions necessary to a group's achievement, and (2) members can learn behaviors to help the group become more effective. If, for example, a group is at a loss as to how to handle an interpersonal conflict, then it will look for people with skills in conciliation; or if members need help with interpreting data, they will make use of people with that special knowledge. In this sense, a group is seen as unique, having its own protocol, demands, and problem-solving abilities.

The early work examining the functions that either contribute to or hinder a group was carried out by Benne and Sheats (1948) and expanded on by Bales (1958). In Chapter 3, we discussed more fully their analysis of functions that facilitate or hinder group performance. Essentially, the functions approach delineates two types of functions: task functions, such as asking for and providing information, and suggesting, coordinating, and summarizing ideas; and maintenance functions, such as energizing a group, encouraging contributions, and relieving tensions. An additional assumption of the functions approach is that, as groups work, members may change, the purpose of the group may change, and, thus, leaders will have to change. Although this approach may sound like another "it depends" philosophy, similar to the situation approach and contingency model, the functions approach provides more assistance in understanding what leaders do.

The functions approach is preferred by this author both because of its emphasis on the role of learning and because of its focus on communicative behaviors involved in leadership acts. Individuals who wish to lead can analyze the functions that will be needed and learn to perform them when they are needed. By defining and specifying which leadership acts will help the group, it allows a group to determine what it needs and to call for those behaviors during any phase of its deliberations. When leadership is viewed as a dynamic process involving leaders and members, it cannot be thought of as only personal qualities that some members have and others do not.

Although an improvement over other perspectives, the functions approach is not without its flaws. By concentrating on the functions displayed by leaders and members, it has not given as much consideration to the impact of leader/member interactions as had been anticipated. Nor can lists of functions tell us which are more essential for group performance, or how the functions should be distributed within a group or how they may be interpreted within a group. Nevertheless, the functions approach allows us, more than other approaches, to focus more directly on the communicative behaviors that help a group work effectively.

The emergent leader   You can learn more about the functions valued by group members by considering the *emergent leader* condition. The question of who becomes a leader has been an important stimulus for researchers exploring the functions of leadership. In many groups—task forces, juries, committees, business meetings—a leader is formally appointed. Yet, in groups with no prescribed leader, a person emerges as leader with a great degree of regularity. The questions to consider are, Why do certain individuals emerge as leaders? What behaviors do individuals display that group members value? The answers to these questions—to why some people are perceived as leaders, even when they are not the official leaders— can be explained in terms of group behavior.

a. *Groups try to reach a goal, and the activities they select are designed to move them along a path toward that goal.* Researchers have labeled this process the *path-goal* theory of group development (House 1971). The concept underlying path-goal theory is that followers have task requirements and will seek guidance as to which activities will produce satisfying outcomes. The more that group members are committed to reaching a desired goal, the more apt they are to seek the help of a person who can assist them in achieving that aim.

b. *Group members would like to believe that they are contributing to getting the group's work accomplished.* It is only when members feel that they are participating usefully that they can be productive and satisfied. Thus a member who can coordinate individual contributions and assist members in their movement toward a goal will likely be rewarded leadership status (Hollander 1978).

c. *The interactions of leaders and followers stimulate individual and group accomplishment.* The reasons for the interdependence of leaders and followers can be explained by the theory of *social exchange* (Blau 1964). The theory suggests that since the ability to contribute to the accomplishment of the group's goal is both desired and valued, members will accept the direction of the most capable performer in "exchange" for such assistance. In other words, leadership in the group is an exchange process in which leaders and followers give and receive benefits. Hollander (1958) called this process a transactional" view of leadership. He considered the leader/follower relationship as dynamic, a situation in which benefits are continually traded.

Another theoretical view, *reinforcement theory,* is also applicable. The assumption of this theory is that behaviors leading to rewards will increase, while behaviors not rewarded will be extinguished. From this perspective, if you are rewarded for behaviors that assist a group, then you will continue to perform those behaviors (Sorrentino and Boutillier 1980). The questions to consider, then, are, What behaviors are rewarded? What is a "fair exchange" between leaders and followers?

Why Leaders Are Chosen

1. Verbal Activity.   The person who speaks the most, or perhaps takes the lead in speaking up first, has an edge in gaining leadership status. Of all the variables associated with leadership, none stands out more clearly than participation (Burke 1974; Stein and Heller 1979). Communication is a key, both in providing talk and in enabling others to talk. It is the means for exchanging information, establishing a common purpose, and achieving a goal.

The correlation between rate of participation and leadership perception is quite high. The sheer magnitude of participation outweighs even the quality of the contributions. An experiment in which a confederate was trained to provide either high-quality remarks (those that moved the task forward) or low-quality remarks (those that interfered with the task) demonstrated that although participants viewed the confederate as more competent when he contributed high- rather than low-quality comments, leadership perception was more strongly related to the quantity rather than to the quality of the remarks (Sorrentino and Boutillier 1975).

While it may seem puzzling that quality should not matter as much as quantity, an explanation of this finding is that an individual's motivation, involvement, and desire to work for the group is more valued than the particular contribution. Leadership perception adheres to the person willing to take the risks involved in "sticking out." Thus the person who emerges as leader is the one most willing to be in the forefront of the group's discussions. One qualification should be added, however. The work of Geier (1967) shows that if a person is too glib, talks incessantly, is overly directive, holds rigid beliefs, or uses stilted or offensive language, that person may be eliminated from leadership consideration.

2. Task Competence Ability to direct others in doing the group's work is the second significant variable in leadership perception. Competence has been evaluated by a number of researchers. Hollander (1958) suggested the theory of *idiosyncracy credit* to explain that leaders initially perceived as competent in directing the group's tasks earn enough credits to be given the status of leader; with these credits, they are able to take innovative actions necessary for the group's achievement. Indeed, a leader who fails to use such credits may be seen as not fulfilling the role of leader. And in a complementary finding, Burke (1966) reported that a leader's lack of competence in providing goal-oriented activity led to a process breakdown within a group, resulting in the group's inability to accomplish its goals.

The Ohio State leadership studies, evaluating leaders in organizations, identified leader competence as the following: supporting others, stressing goals, and facilitating work and interaction. Evans (1968), building on the work of the Ohio State researchers, found that a leader who showed "consideration" toward followers, and "initiated" a structure in which members could work together, influenced the motivation of members to work productively. Subsequent studies have confirmed that these two basic competencies, that of "consideration" and "initiation," are significant to group performance.

3. Communicative Competence Studies by Schultz (1974, 1982), examining the characteristics of emergent leaders in initially leaderless problem-solving groups, found a correspondence between some few communicative functions and members' perceptions of leaders. Individuals identified as leaders were seen as more self-assured, but they were also rated as more competent than nonleaders in providing goal orientation, procedural direction, and summaries. Leadership was also attributed to more argumentatively competent persons.

The research of Gouran (1969) singles out *orientation behavior*—letting people know what is expected of them and of the task—as important communicative activity for reaching consensus and effective decision making. People who provide orientation help group members use their resources and therefore are more likely to be perceived as leaders. Gouran indicates that several other leadership acts contribute to group performance.

Procedural sensitivity—helping the group understand contributions that are relevant.

Substantiveness—keeping the group on track, moving the participants toward constructive ends.

Agreeableness—smoothing over potentially damaging situations.

Skepticism—helping the group avoid premature judgments.

Pondy (1978) found that the way a leader uses language is an important factor in determining who is valued as a leader. Leaders are known to contribute more ideas to their groups. What is more significant is that leaders give members a vision, a sense of what they are doing and what needs to be done. As an example, Pondy relates that the "real power of Martin Luther King, Jr. was not only that he had a dream, but that he could describe it, that it became public, and therefore accessible to millions of people."

Among the other attributes of leader competence is a willingness to understand the limitations, defects, and strengths of ideas, themes, or visions the group is considering. It is not only that a perceived leader can help a group discuss critically the ideas being considered; it is also that a person who emerges as a leader provides the group with more than a single frame of reference. By considering other frames of reference, a group can improve the quality of its decision making, a subject discussed in Chapter 7; for now, we can illustrate with a favorite "Peanuts" story what it means to have another "frame of reference."

Charlie Brown was telling Linus about a great football game he had just seen. Charlie said that the visiting team was ahead 6 to 0 until the last minute of the game, when the home team scored a touchdown and the extra point to win, 7 to 6. "You should have seen the excitement!" Charlie exclaimed. "Everyone was so happy."

Linus answered, "Yeah, but I wonder how the other team felt."

In sum, the studies we have mentioned point to a group's need for direction, both procedural and substantive. They also point to the significance of talking and facilitating talk as a leadership act. Potential leaders are more likely to be chosen from among "high" talkers. By providing more ideas, information, themes—a sense of reality for the group, as well as frames of reference—the leader functions as a relevant and sensitive communicator.

In addition to making a number of important contributions themselves, emergent leaders facilitate interaction. They engage in turn-taking. They ask for opinions, and solicit ideas and suggestions from others. They recognize the individuality of members and their need to contribute to the overall work of the group. By letting the group participants know how they are doing, where they are going, and how to get there, the emergent leader functions as an essential communicator in the group.

BECOMING AN EFFECTIVE LEADER

In our discussion of the emergent leader condition, it has become reasonably clear that potential leaders are recognized because they help groups achieve their aims. Also, the qualities that allow a person to be perceived as leader are typically the qualities that allow a leader to be judged effective. For example, leaders are considered effective when they let people know what is expected of them and solicit group reactions before going ahead. As the evidence for emergent leaders has shown, providing a group with directions is highly valued.

Research by Wood (1977) on actual small groups indicates that effective leaders learn how to adapt their contributions to the needs and expectations of members. To be adaptive means to be able to diagnose and interpret what is going on in the group. (Diagnosing and intervening in the group is the subject of Chapter 10.) Thus to be effective, leaders will need to learn how to analyze such factors as the issues before the group, the strengths and weaknesses of members, the physical situation in which the group will meet, and the choice of an appropriate leader style.

Effective leaders also recognize that, as a group works for task completion, an entire interpersonal communicative system is also involved. Leaders cannot overstep the bounds of what individuals are able or willing to do. Even while working on getting a task completed, an effective leader establishes a relationship with members, communicating credibility, trustworthiness, and good intentions. In this sense, they take responsibility for the quality and maintenance of an effective group climate.

Effective leaders must also be prepared to face continuing challenges. As Gouran (1982) has expressed it, effective leaders help their groups counteract forces that interfere with their ability to make the quality decision. To move the group on its goal path, leaders need to be aware of the effect of such obstacles as ambiguous terms, issues that are not clarified, faulty or missing evidence, hidden agendas, misunderstandings, personality problems, and the like—obstacles that, if left unattended, will prevent the group from accomplishing its goals.

From the data we have gathered as to why certain individuals emerge as leaders and what makes for leader effectiveness, it is obvious that no single individual can provide all the leadership functions that a group needs to succeed. So if every member can provide some leadership contribution, what does a potential leader have to know to be effective? We'll examine some answers to this question.

1. *Groups need direction.* Groups perform more effectively when they know what they are supposed to do. Studies of groups without designated leaders show that members will search for a direction and choose people to lead who will help them determine how to proceed. As Gouran (1969) has illustrated in his studies, providing statements of orientation helps a group both to structure its discussion and to conclude its work more successfully. Lewis Carroll's *Alice's Adventures in Wonderland* delightfully engages this issue.

"Would you tell me, please, which way I ought to go from here?"

"That depends a good deal on where you want to get to," said the Cat.

"I don't much care where—" said Alice.

"Then it doesn't matter which way you go," said the Cat.

"—so long as I get somewhere," Alice added as an explanation.

2. *Groups do not progress in an orderly manner.* From the initial definition of a problem to its solution, there will be both order and disorder—differences between members, conflicts over procedures and goals. A leader reflects an understanding of group process by allowing various views to be heard, by seeking and providing information, by clarifying a point or probing for more information, and by summarizing the progress the group is making toward its goals.

Although group members probably differ in their tolerance of uncertainty, continuing uncertainty about where the group is going is, for most people, disorienting. Therefore, an effective leader will provide summaries of the group's progress. Leaders can make such statements as, "I think what we have to do now is . . ." "We've been discussing this issue for quite some time and my sense is that we understand it. Now, what we have to do is . . ." But leaders have to provide balanced summaries, showing no favoritism for a particular view. The group is more advantaged when leaders discuss the strengths and weaknesses of all proposals.

3. *Groups alternate between task needs and social needs.* All groups have a tendency to digress, to get off the track. In any group there will be tangential remarks, stories, and informal social interaction—and appropriately so, if the interpersonal needs of members are to be met. Yet, while it is inappropriate to follow a predetermined agenda too closely, leaders will have to recognize when a group has wandered off and bring the participants back to the issue at hand. Leaders can learn to use such statements as, "I wonder if we can take that issue up after we complete this point," or "I think we need more discussion of this issue before we look for solutions," or even simply, "I think we have wandered off the topic. Could we go back to our discussion?"

4. *Issues will need clarification.* An important phase of group deliberations is the discussion of issues relevant to solving a problem. To judge the importance of an issue means to recognize when a contribution is of value and when it might lead the group astray. Raising questions about the relative importance and relevant of a topic should help a group distinguish between more important and less important issues. Seeking supporting evidence for opinions, as well as questioning the validity of evidence offered, also ensures that a group will give more careful consideration to its discussion of issues (Gouran 1982).

A leader has to discover when a group has reached a consensus on an issue. Checking on the sense of the group as to whether participants have had sufficient time to discuss an issue, yet, at the same time, keeping the group moving along so that members feel they are accomplishing their task, will promote satisfaction with the group's progress. One clue that a group has spent enough time on an issue is to note whether the same ideas are repeated. Leaders can ask if the group is ready to make a decision or whether more discussion would be fruitful. Evaluating proposals for solution is also important. Leaders can check on whether solutions proposed will bring the change the group believes is necessary. They can say, "In terms of what we regard as important, will these proposed solutions help us get there? Are there any unexpected consequences that we haven't discussed?"

5. *The impact of social-emotional relations must be* understood. Members in groups will, from time to time, experience frustration, tension, anger, and disappointment. In these situations, leaders need to display sensitivity and tolerance for ambiguity, for disagreement, and for conflict within the group. It is also a time for providing support for individual members, especially for their substantive contributions. "Stroking" people for their efforts on behalf of the group, supporting them in times of stress, can go a long way

toward building a group climate that is generally supportive of the many paths groups take before they complete a task.

If an idea offered is disregarded by the group, a leader can paraphrase it and compliment the person offering it. If a negative, personally damaging comment is made, a leader can indicate that personal remarks denigrating an individual are inappropriate. At the same time that the leader is offering support for substantive contributions, there is also a recognition of the right, and even the necessity, of members to express dissenting and divergent views, and to see this expression as a positive effort toward reaching an effective decision.

The "Behavioral Description Questionnaire" (Morris and Hackman 1969) will allow you to evaluate the leadership activities in your group. You can fill in the questionnaire with greater understanding after you have worked with a group on a task over a period of time. The exercise will let you know how leadership behaviors are distributed in the group, and how your perception of your contri-

---

BEHAVIORAL DESCRIPTION QUESTIONNAIRE

Directions

Each person in the group fills out questionnaires to rate every member of the group, including himself or herself. At the top of the form, write the name of the person you are evaluating. For each question, circle the number that you believe applies to the person you are rating.

1. He/She prodded the group to complete the task.

1	2	3	4	5
Not true				Very true

2. He/She was the real idea person in the group, suggesting new ways of handling the group's problems.

1	2	3	4	5
Not true				Very true

3. He/She is a creative person.

1	2	3	4	5
Not true				Very true

4. He/She was concerned only with his/her own ideas and viewpoint.

1	2	3	4	5
Not true				Very true

5. He/She influenced the opinions of others.

1	2	3	4	5
Not true				Very true

6. He/She interrupted others when they were speaking.

1	2	3	4	5
Not true				Very true

7. He/She criticized those with whom he/she disagreed.

1	2	3	4	5
Not true				Very true

8. He/She was an aloof sort of person.

1	2	3	4	5
Not true				Very true

9. He/She was the real leader of the group.

1	2	3	4	5
Not true				Very true

10. He/She worked well with others in the group.

1	2	3	4	5
Not true				Very true

11. He/She was disruptive to the group.

1	2	3	4	5
Not true				Very true

12. He/She was in the forefront of the group's discussion.

1	2	3	4	5
Not true				Very true

13. He/She kept the group from straying too far from the topic.

1	2	3	4	5
Not true				Very true

14. His/her attitudes hurt the group's chances of success.

1	2	3	4	5
Not true				Very true

15. He/She seemed to be a tense, nervous person.

1	2	3	4	5
Not true				Very true

Scoring: The ratings that members receive from other members of the group and from themselves are summed for each question. Then a mean score for each question is derived.

   Suggestion: An easy way to score the data is to have one person collect all the sheets for another person in the group. He or she then sums the scores, computes the mean score, and, with members of the group, compares and contrasts the different ratings members received. After this discussion, the questionnaires for each person are returned (Napier and Gershenfeld 1981, pp. 282–286). Members then discuss their reactions to the exercise.

bution matches the perception group members have of you. After you complete the exercise, you can both give and receive valuable feedback about the special leadership needs of groups.

Comments on the Exercise

After completing and analyzing the questionnaires, you will have a better idea of how both the composition of a group and the contributions of individuals will vary. Using mean scores to evaluate group responses can provide a good indication of how characteristic each of the statements was of each person's behavior. It will also allow the group to generalize about which behaviors were valued, the roles that corresponded with the perceived leader or leaders, the influence and impact that different members of the group had, and the differences between individual perceptions and group perceptions about role behavior in the group.

Although there may be disagreement among members' perceptions, and sometimes disappointment with the results, especially if they do not conform with your expectations, nevertheless you can find out whether your view is consistent with the views of others. This experience can be insightful for becoming both a more effective participant and a leader.

A FINAL COMMENT

Sometimes it is easier to describe what keeps people from becoming leaders than why certain individuals are chosen as leaders. Fisher (1980) has proposed a set of principles that, if followed, would keep people from being a leader in a group.

Rule 1. Stay away from as many meetings as possible.

Rule 2. Contribute to the interaction as little as possible.

Rule 3. Volunteer to be the secretary or recorder of your group's discussion. While this is often a valuable role, it will help eliminate you from leadership contention.

Rule 4. Indicate that you are willing to do what you are told. And when accompanied by a lack of interest, this will even be better.

Rule 5. Come on strongly early in the discussion and show that you are unwilling to compromise.

Rule 6. Try to assume the role of joker. In that way you will not be taken seriously.

Rule 7. Demonstrate your knowledge of everything, including your extensive vocabulary of big words and technical jargon.

Rule 8. Demonstrate a contempt for leadership.

While these are tongue-in-cheek recommendations for avoiding leadership, they are behaviors that will keep you from being a leader. Understandably, most of us do not intentially use behaviors to avoid being chosen as leader; yet, without being aware of which behaviors contribute to or limit a group's performance, you may not know what effect you are having.

From the discussion of the many different approaches to the study of leadership, one significant learning comes through: leadership behavior cannot be evaluated by examining individual traits alone. Leadership is a multifaceted concept. While no single theory can explain who should be a leader, we have learned something from all perspectives. Perhaps the most important lesson is that we cannot separate the leader from the needs of and expectations from followers.

A second learning is that all members contribute to group effectiveness. All members can add to the leadership necessary for a group, though they will offer different specialties. Some individuals are more adept at asking questions, while others can provide information. Some people know how to clarify issues, while others can respond to emotional needs, and so on. Members who perform acts that help a group counteract obstacles in its path and further the group's movement toward achievable goals will receive the gratitude of their group.

The individual who is perceived as leader plays a vital role in pulling the group together as a collectivity. A better way to understand the leadership role in your group will come from understanding the mixture of leader activities, group needs, and group processes. As the comments from an emergent leader's diary illustrates, performing as a leader can be an important and fulfilling role:

The reason I was perceived as a leader was that I enjoyed starting conversations, and the group recognized this enthusiasm in my attitude and in my behavior. I especially enjoyed starting the conversation when my initiating led to further communication among the other group members. I felt at ease taking risks—initiating conversation, expressing my opinions, and directing the group toward a goal. The reason I felt so at ease was mainly that the other group members reinforced my actions. They never objected to my leads, they never criticized by ideas, and they always added to my opinions.

I would describe myself as a socio-emotional leader. But I was also a task leader, in some situations. When Gary or Theresa were not directing the group and their interaction did not include any task-oriented behavior, I intervened and tried to direct the conversation. Sometimes I was influential, other times I was not. When the group needed no directing, and we were working on the task, I considered myself more of a participant. In this situation no leadership was necessary. The only thing we needed was resources and most of the time I did my best to provide the group with any knowledge I possessed. I will admit that at times my mind was not on the task and I just sat back and let the other group members do the work.

Now that I have had this experience, I have gained some insight as to why in some other groups I was unsuccessful in my leadership attempts. I used to try to dominate the group, trying to be the leader. I have learned that everyone has important contributions to make and that domineering behavior stifles contribution. Not only that, but a leader is not as necessary as leadership. A group can be successful without a specific leader, but cannot accomplish much without the qualities of leadership—initiating, giving directions, mediating, and all-around supporter. In other words, I have learned to refrain from dominating the conversation and forcing my opinions on others.

A fine understanding of leader behavior!

SUMMARY

This chapter has addressed the phenomenon of leadership in the small group. Although there has been widespread interest in learning about and choosing appropriate leaders, no single theory can explain either how leaders should be chosen or what makes leaders effective. Through the years, various assumptions have guided research about leadership. A major premise, that leadership traits are inborn, was discarded after too many inconsistencies about leaders and personality traits were found.

Other theories—the leadership style, situational, contingency, and power approaches—have added considerably to our knowledge about leadership. But none of these person-centered approaches explains leadership acts sufficiently to be without flaws. What has been learned, however, is that some leaders are motivated by a need to complete a task and some by a need to build good relationships. On the other hand, the study of leadership styles, motivation, situational constraints, and degree of power and influence points to the fact that leadership is a multifaceted concept.

By acknowledging the evolutionary development in theoretical explanations, we have learned how to employ leadership behaviors in the group. In particular, the functions approach, with its examination of leadership activity and the emergent leader condition—focusing on follower expectations—provides the most information about what leaders do. The essential behaviors of leaders revolve around their active participation; their ability to offer orientation and a structure for the group to follow; their sensitivity to, and consideration of, the social and emotional needs of members; and their overall task competence.

A major learning from leadership research is that we cannot separate leader behavior from the expectations of followers. No one person can offer a group all that is needed to help members accomplish their goals. Rather, all members can learn to employ behaviors that assist the group when they are needed. A questionnaire is provided that can help you learn how you are perceived by other group members and which of your contributions are perceived as leadership acts. Finally, a list of "negative behaviors" describes how people can act if they do not want to be perceived as leaders—either they can remain silent and generally uninvolved or they can behave insensitively to the needs of group members.

Scoring the Sargent and Miller Leadership Scale

Put a (1) after each item you checked that corresponds to the responses listed for each question below. Total your score. A maximum of 10 means that you are very likely a democratic leader. A minimum score of zero means that you are more likely an authoritarian leader. If your score falls in the middle range, then you may have a desirable degree of flexibility.

Key: 1. a; 2. b; 3. b; 4. a; 5. b; 6. b; 7. b; 8. a; 9. a; 10. a.

REFERENCES

Archer, D. 1974. "Power in Groups: Self-Concept Changes of Powerful and Powerless Group Members." *Journal of Applied Behavioral Science* 10: 208–220.

Bales, R. F. 1958. "Task Roles and Social Roles in Problem-Solving Groups." In E. E. Maccoby, T. M. Newcomb, and E. L. Harley (eds.), *Readings in Social Psychology*. (3rd ed.). New York: Holt, pp. 437–447.

Benne, K. D., and P. Sheats. 1948. "Functional Roles of Group Members." *Journal of Social Issues* 2:42–47.

Blau, P. 1964. *Exchange and Power in Social Life.* New York: Wiley.

Borgatta, E. F., A. R. Couch, and R. F. Bales. 1954. "Some Findings Relevant to the Great Man Theory of Leadership." *American Sociological Review* 19:755–759.

Brown, Dr. B., 1982. Quoted in news story, *New York Times,* November 8.

Burke, P. J. 1966. "Authority Relations and Disruptive Behavior in Small Discussion Groups." *Sociometry* 29:237–250.

Burke, P. J. 1974. "Participation and Leadership in Small Groups." *American Sociological Review* 39:832–842.

Burns, J. M. 1978. *Leadership.* New York: Harper & Row.

Evans, M. G. 1968. "The Effects of Supervisory Behavior upon Worker Perception of Their Path-Goal Relationships." Doctoral dissertation. Yale University, New Haven.

Fiedler, F. E. 1967. *A Theory of Leadership Effectiveness.* New York: McGraw-Hill.

Fiedler, F. E. 1978. "The Contingency Model and the Dynamics of the Leadership Process." In L. Berkowitz (ed.), *Advances in Experimental Social Psychology.* (vol. 12). New York: Academic Press.

Fisher, B. A. 1980. *Small Group Decision Making.* (2nd ed.) New York: McGraw-Hill.

Fodor, E. M. 1973. "Disparagement by a Subordinate, Ingratiation, and the Use of Power." *Journal of Psychology* 84:181–186.

French, J. R. P., Jr., and B. Raven. 1959. "The Bases of Social Power." In D. Cartwright (ed.), *Studies in Social Power.* Ann Arbor, Mich.: Institute for Social Research.

Geier, J. G. 1967. "A Trait Approach to the Study of Leadership in Small Groups." *Journal of Communication* 17:316–323.

Gouran, D. S. 1969. "Variables Related to Consensus in Group Discussions of Questions of Policy." *Speech Monographs* 36:387–391.

Gouran, D. S. 1982. *Making Decisions in Groups: Choices and Consequences.* Glenview, Ill.: Scott, Foresman, pp. 147–169.

Hollander, E. P. 1958. "Conformity, Status, and Idiosyncracy Credit." *Psychological Review* 65:117–127.

Hollander, E. P. 1978. *Leadership Dynamics: A Practical Guide to Effective Relationships.* New York: Free Press.

House, R. J. 1971. "A Path Goal Theory of Leader Effectiveness." *Administrative Science Quarterly* 16:321–338.

Hurwitz, J. I., A. F. Zander, and B. Hymovitch. 1968. "Some Effects of Power on the Relations of Group Members." In D. Cartwright and A. Zander (eds.), *Group Dynamics: Research and Theory.* (3rd ed.). New York: Harper & Row.

Korten, D. C. 1962. "Situational Determinants of Leadership Structure." *Journal of Conflict Resolution* 6:222–235.

Lewin, K., R. Lippitt, and R. White. 1939. "Patterns of Aggressive Behavior in Experimentally Created 'Social Climates.' " *Journal of Social Psychology* 10:271–299.

Pondy, L. R., 1978. "Leadership Is a Language Game." In Lombardo, M. M., and M. W. McCall, Jr. *Leadership Research: Where Else Can We Go?* Durham, N.C.: Duke University Press.

Mann, R. D., 1959. "A Review of the Relationship Between Personality and Performance in Small Groups." *Psyhcological Bulletin* 56: 1969. 241–270.

McGregor, D. 1960. *The Human Side of Enterprise.* New York: McGraw-Hill.

Morris, C. G., and J. R. Hackman. 1969. "Behavioral Correlates of Perceived Leadership." *Journal of Personality and Social Psychology* 13:350–369.

Napier, R. W., and M. K. Gershenfeld. 1981. *Groups: Theory and Experience.* Boston: Houghton Mifflin.

Rosenfeld, L. B., and T. G. Plax. 1975. "Personality Determinants of Autocratic and Democratic Leadership." *Speech Monographs* 42:203–208.

Sargent, F., and G. Miller. 1971. "Some Differences in Certain Communication Behavior of Autocratic and Democratic Group Leaders." *Journal of Communication* 21:233–252.

Schultz, B. 1974. "Characteristics of Emergent Leaders of Continuing Problem-Solving Groups." *Journal of Psychology* 88:167–173.

Schultz, B. 1982. "Argumentativeness: Its Effect in Group Decision-Making and Its Role in Leadership Perception." *Communication Quarterly* 30:-368–375.

Sorrentino, R. M., and R. G. Boutillier. 1975. "The Effect of Quantity and Quality of Verbal Interaction on Ratings of Leadership Ability." *Journal of Experimental Social Psychology* 11:403–411.

Stein, R. T., and T. Heller. 1979. "An Empirical Analysis of the Correlations Between Leadership Status and Participation Rates Reported in the Literature." *Journal of Personality and Social Psychology* 37:1993–2002.

Stogdill, R. M. 1948. "Personal Factors Associated with Leadership: A Survey of the Literature." *Journal of Psychology* 25: 35–71.

Stogdill, R. M., 1974. *Handbook of Leadership: A Survey of Theory and Research.* New York: Free Press.

Wood, J. T., 1977. "Leading in Purposive Discussions: A Study of Adaptive Behavior." *Communication Monographs* 44: 152–165.

chapter 6

Problem Solving in the Small Group

If you should ask how most people go about solving a problem, you would find that they tend to use similar processes. After determining that "something is not working," they then ask, "What should we do about it?"—a fairly rapid movement from problem to solution, with more of the discussion focused on solution than on the problem itself.

An example of this pattern occurred when a group of students discussed the issue "What can be done about the lack of participation in weekend activities by the student body?"

RICH: People are just not interested.

JEFF: Yeah, nobody cares.

CYNTHIA: I agree. There's a great deal of apathy.

AMY: You know what would help? If there were more things to do around here.

RICH: If we had a good football team, that might help. Other schools have really exciting things to do that go along with a football weekend.

SUSAN: I don't think that would help here. Most people would go home on weekends anyway. They have friends home or they have to work.

AMY: I think kids go home to be with their boyfriend or girlfriend and we can't change that.

CYNTHIA: Well, what can we do?

As the members of this group continue to discuss their feelings that the campus spirit is not as great as they would like, they are probably unaware that in their rapid movement from problem to solution, they have skipped some essential steps for effective problem solving.

A number of researchers have analyzed the problem-solving process. They suggest that the process involves several steps. For example, John Dewey (1933), in considering how people think, developed a model that has given us many insights into the problem-solving process. His approach, which he called *reflective thinking,* details a five-step procedure beginning with (1) an awareness of a problem, (2) a definition of the problem, and (3) a proposal of possible solutions, followed by (4) a discussion of implications, and (5) the adoption of the single best solution.

According to Dewey's analysis, the individual's awareness of a problem is probably a response to a "felt difficulty," a feeling that something is not right. This is a beginning point for analyzing a problem. The second step, defining a problem, means looking at the factors that make the present situation undesirable. Here is a place for examining the nature of the problem and its underlying causes. It is also a time to phrase clearly the problem to be investigated.

The third step consists of looking at alternatives, the many possible ways of dealing with the problem. This is the time for proposing solutions. Then the fourth step provides an opportunity to examine the implications for each proposed solution. The advantages and disadvantages of each alternative are compared, and some of the proposals may be changed or elaborated or even found to be unacceptable. Finally, the remaining ideas are scrutinized and a decision is made as to which proposal will achieve the desired outcome.

Most problem-solving methods rely on Dewey's reflective thinking method, whether they include all five steps or some modification of them. For example, L. Richard Hoffman (1965), a researcher of problem-solving methods, writes that groups will perform more effectively if their procedures reflect the following three steps:

1. Identify the problem facing the group and the criteria for a good solution.
2. Generate as many ideas for solutions as possible.
3. Evaluate each proposed solution, choosing the best alternative available.

The *agenda system* developed by Raymond Ross (1974) for solving problems uses a four-step instead of a five-step procedure:

1. **Definition and limitation**—a specific statement of felt difficulty, problem, or goal.
2. **Analysis**—an examination of the type and nature of the problem and its causes.
3. **Establishment of criteria**—a group consensus on standards of evaluation.
4. **Solutions**—decision and suggested implementation.

The assumptions and distinctive features of all problem-solving systems is that groups must devise methods to define and evaluate problems before they can begin to consider solutions. What we learn from Dewey and other scholars is that a more systematic approach to problem solving will probably help a group increase its effectiveness both in its analysis of a problem and in its choice of solution (Gouran 1976; Scheidel and Crowell 1964).

These data suggest that a careful consideration of problem-solving procedures should help produce higher-quality solutions to problems. What is troubling about these findings, however, is that there are also data suggesting that groups often do not reach good solutions, nor do they necessarily solve problems more effectively by using a step-by-step sequence (Poole 1981). One of the questions this discrepancy raises is why groups have not been able to apply the insights that scholars have provided about good problem-solving procedures.

One reason is that the assumption that people behave "rationally" when they are problem solving may not be valid. What is more likely is that people in groups, when confronted with multiple interactions, as well as their own needs, often do not use a rational approach. For example, in some groups, some individuals dominate, so that their agendas become the important ones. There is often a conflict of interest, coupled with annoyance at those members who disagree with the majority's view. These factors—as well as a desire for acceptance, the fear of talking, the lack of commitment, unproductive communicative patterns—can interfere with rational problem solving.

A second response is that what the experts prescribe may not relate to what a group actually does. Perhaps individuals in a group cannot adhere to an agenda because too many unanticipated events occur—the absence of key members, time constraints, the addition of new members. Such factors inhibit the use of a logical structure. In this sense, without learning and practicing problem solving, the recommendations of experts cannot be translated in any meaningful way by groups of individuals who have little or no practice in problem solving, and who, at the same time, have to to deal with their own tensions, biases, perspectives, and conflicts.

While we cannot know the multitude of reasons that keep

groups from applying good problem-solving procedures, we do know from observations and research of the last 40 years that a key to effective problem solving is an understanding of the functions of group problem solving. This chapter addresses the current data we have about problem solving. First, we will offer prescriptive information, combining the insights gained from Dewey and the more recent work of other theorists. Second, we will offer descriptive information, reporting the results of experiences people have had in groups, including an extended example of a problem-solving exercise that participants in your group can use to broaden their understanding of how to analyze a problem. If group problem solving is to be improved, members will need insights into how the process operates. That is the task of this chapter.

ANALYZING THE PROBLEM-SOLVING PROCESS

What is evident from recent research is that groups can and do use many paths to arrive at a solution (Poole 1981). Although the problem-solving process is depicted as an orderly procedure, in reality problem solving is not a step-by-step process. Learning about the process is important because it helps members learn that many factors must be considered before a problem can be resolved. But, rather than assuming that groups, as they work through a problem, take each step in order, sequentially, in a linear direction, let me offer an alternative proposal: *thinking through a problem means movement, back and forth, among issues and solutions* (Schein 1969). Problem solving is a *cyclical* process rather than a strictly sequential process.

Another way to examine problem solving is to think of it as comprising two phases: (1) a phase that takes place before a decision is made, and (2) a phase that begins after a decision has been made (Schein 1969). In the first phase are the following steps:

1. Identifying and defining the problem.
2. Suggesting proposals for solution.
3. Analyzing and evaluating proposed solutions.

The second phase includes the following:

4. Choosing a proposed course of action.
5. Implementing a proposed solution.
6. Evaluating the effectiveness and the consequences of the action taken.

The steps in each phase allows group participants to understand the demands of problem solving. At the same time, it is important to know that at any point in a group's discussions, members can move back and forth, from defining a problem to examining the consequences of various proposals. If, for example, group members find in their examination of solutions that they have erred in their analysis of the problem—either they have failed to consider some important factors, or the proposed solutions are undesirable in themselves—then the group can revert to the first step, and reformulate its definition of the problem.

The focus of this chapter is on the first phase of problem solving: defining the problem, proposing solutions, and evaluating proposed solutions. These steps are preliminary to making a decision or taking an action. Chapter 7 discusses decision making and how to make effective decisions.

THE FIRST PHASE OF PROBLEM SOLVING

Defining the Problem

Observers of problem-solving groups in organizations sometimes find that the most difficult step is in defining the problem. Why should this be so? One substantial reason is the confusion between the problem and its symptoms, a confusion that often makes problem solving a tortuous process. An example will indicate why.

You are a good student and spend hours in the library every day poring over your tomes. You get headaches (a symptom) and you take aspirin for the headaches. But the headaches don't go away, so you take more aspirin. The headaches hinder your studying so much that you drink a lot of coffee so that you can stay up and study into the night, in order to get your work done. As this procedure continues, you are becoming a "basket case." You still get horrible headaches when you study, and that aspirin–coffee 1–2 punch is getting you in the stomach. You're developing an ulcer.

If, on the other hand, you had probed further, perhaps had gone to see a doctor, you might have discovered that those study-only headaches meant that you needed glasses. That would have saved taking all that aspirin and coffee and would have kept the ulcer at bay. As happened in this case, treating only the symptoms of a problem only made it become worse. If you react only to the symptoms of a problem, you are likely to make a hasty diagnosis. A hasty diagnosis can be an inappropriate diagnosis, leading to inappropriate actions to alleviate or remedy the problem. What you need when defining a problem is a more careful consideration of possible causes as well as a more careful diagnosis.

The rules below offer help for the initial phase of problem solving.

> **Rule 1.** When defining a problem, confront the underlying tensions, concerns, and frustrations, and bring these tensions and concerns out into the open.
>
> **Rule 2.** When defining a problem, express the problem as a condition that exists because of many factors, and bring these factors out into the open.

The first rule is an aid to confronting the underlying tensions that brought the problem to the surface. For instance, a group might ask, "What is the problem? What is its nature? How do we all view it?" The second rule suggests that the group state the problem as a condition—something that is going on that is either harmful, unfortunate, damaging, or unwise. These rules prompt members to ask, "How large a problem is it? How many people are involved? What are the reasons the problem exists? How urgent are the conditions that have produced the problem? What evidence do we have or should we have to assist us in diagnosing the problem?"

In addition to confronting the underlying tensions, a group needs to discuss and comprehend the multiple factors that impinge on the problem. Consider what happened during the summer of 1981 in England as an example of an inadequate definition of a problem.

At the same time that Prince Charles was marrying Lady Diana, there were countless numbers of devastating riots in London and in other large cities. Government leaders, under severe pressure to get rid of the riots at this time, first identified the problem as one of "hooliganism" or "wanton greediness," indicating that they would take all measures necessary to halt the riots. No doubt, this posture was an initial strategy, and while we cannot know what deliberations led to this choice of tactics, we can look at the results of that diagnosis.

As the weeks went on, the riots did not calm down. Buildings were burned and scores of individuals were hurt. Of more significance, especially to government decision makers, were the injuries to hundreds of police who were attempting to bring the riots to an end—this in a country that took pride in its amiable relations between police and citizens. As the tensions and conflicts mounted, it became clear to all concerned—the government, the press, and the people—that unless a more careful definition of the problem and an accompanying solution were forthcoming, the conflicts and tensions would continue to worsen.

Because of the nature of the crisis, government leaders were forced to reconsider their definition of the problem. And in their revised definition we can see how advantageous it is to take into account the many factors that impinge on a problem. The revised definition included such factors as high unemployment, the deterioration of the cities, tension among the races, and a changing relationship between the population and the police. To address these issues, the government submitted a proposal designed to cope with some of these factors, especially the high unemployment among young people. It also led to what one writer called "the anguished re-evaluation of the British police as they operate in this traditionally calm and civilized society" (Borders 1981).

Before a problem can be solved, a group will need to discuss the many factors that impinge on the problem.

Proposing Solutions

The first two rules for more effective problem solving emphasized the need for an extensive diagnosis of the problem. Two additional rules are useful for discovering a good solution.

> **Rule 3.** When proposing solutions, consider a wide range of alternatives as potential solutions.
> **Rule 4.** When evaluating potential solutions, establish appropriate criteria.

We'll examine rule 3 here and, in the section on evaluating solutions, consider rule 4.

What turns out to be a hindrance to effective problem solving is a group's tendency to choose, from among a few proposed ideas, the one idea with which participants are most familiar. A group's problem-solving effort is limited not only by its choice of the familiar solution but by its having coalesced around one idea before other ideas have been explored. As a result, the possibility of finding the most beneficial solution is often lost.

Groups would profit from the principle underlying rule 3: Consider other proposals before choosing one, even though the first proposed solution seems like a good one. In this way groups can eliminate a weakness in their problem-solving methods—that of selecting a solution prematurely, before they have evaluated other potential proposals.

There are additional reasons for avoiding premature decision making. (1) A group gains insight into how a problem can be solved by examining several proposed solutions at the same time, and, (2) the process is a boost to individuals in the group. When members of a group are encouraged to discuss an issue at length, as well as to propose possible solutions, they are being recognized and rewarded, important factors for group morale and sense of accomplishment.

Brainstorming: An Aid to Generating Alternatives   One way of assisting a group in developing the skill of proposing alternatives is to use the technique of *brainstorming* (Osborn 1957). Brainstorming was developed by Alex F. Osborn, who, in his advertising agency, found himself always searching for creative ideas. Osborn's assumptions have been adapted by many groups and include the following rules:

1. *Express any ideas you have.* New, unique, or unexpected ideas are useful. The wilder the idea, the more likely a creative idea will come forward.
2. *Do not evaluate.* Criticism of ideas should be withheld until all ideas have been suggested.
3. *Keep your ideas coming.* The greater the number, the more likely you will find a good solution.
4. *Build.* Ideas can be combined or improved. One person's idea can trigger an idea from someone else. People learn from hearing ideas.

Osborn suggests that all ideas be recorded (on paper or on the blackboard) so everyone can see them. Open-ended questions can be used to stimulate even more ideas. Elaboration of ideas and critiques of ideas can follow after all ideas have been collected. The process of brainstorming, as outlined in these rules, encourages the flow of ideas and even more imaginative proposals for solving a problem. Although brainstorming allows "silly" and even "dumb" ideas to be presented, which some people may feel is time-wasting, many excellent solutions have come from so-called dumb ideas. When a group learns to use the technique of brainstorming, it is learning to reinforce valuable communicative processes for encouraging participation—the withholding of criticism so that ideas can be nurtured.

The exercise "Brainstorming" may seem "silly" to you at first, but try it with a group. You may enjoy the experience, and, even more, you may learn a great deal about how brainstorming works.

BRAINSTORMING

Getting Started

The following experience is designed for groups of five to seven members; several groups can participate at the same time.

Imagine that you have been shipwrecked and then awaken to find yourself nude on a deserted tropical island with a leather belt (and buckle) as your only possession. As a group, brainstorm about what you can do with this belt to help you survive. Have someone in the group take down all suggested ideas. It is important that there be no evaluation until all ideas have been recorded. The group can spend anywhere from 10 to 20 minutes on this task.

The Results

When you have finished, listen to the ideas that each group has discussed. Then the group can go through a process of evaluation. Careful evaluation, after all ideas have been contributed, is an important part of the brainstorming process.

You can take several approaches in this evaluation. Your evaluation or criticism can be directed toward choosing the best ideas from all the groups, using as a criterion those ideas that most promote survival. Or you can pull together the best ideas into a package labeled "most noteworthy." You can also discuss what you learned from going through this experience.

Source: J. W. Pfeiffer and J. E. Jones (eds.). 1974. *A Handbook of Structured Experiences fo Human Relations Training,* vol 3. La Jolla, Ca.: University Associates, pp. 14–15.

Comments on the Exercise

Now we can assess the results of this experiment. Did you feel that you had a sense of freedom because you knew you were not being evaluated at the start? Did your group come up with new and novel approaches and even some apparently strange proposals? Did even these ridiculous-sounding suggestions add to your enjoyment of the exercise? As a result of this experiment, did you feel closer to members of your group? If you answered "yes" to these questions, then you can appreciate why brainstorming has been so widely used in groups and organizations.

When used well, brainstorming can be both rewarding and profitable to a group. Brainstorming is not a panacea—some really hard thinking and diagnoses have to made if difficult problems are to be solved. What brainstorming does demonstrate is that a process of openness can contribute to a group's ability to solve problems. A variation on the brainstorming technique is that of the *nominal group technique* (groups of individuals work alone to generate ideas, and then their ideas are added together as if the individuals were an interacting group). The Appendix explains how to use nominal groups for generating ideas for long-existing problems.

Evaluating Solutions

This step can be troublesome because (1) of the need to develop criteria to aid in the evaluation of solutions, and (2) of the arduousness of the task of developing these criteria. If you participated in the brainstorming exercise, your evaluation of the best ideas would have been based on the *criterion* of what would most help you survive. But to make that determination required some familiarity with tropical islands, experience with survival techniques, imagination about the uses of a leather belt, among others.

You will need to understand your bases of judgment for every problem that is to be resolved. Hence, a search for solutions involves determining the criteria for testing the adequacy of proposed solutions. Groups can begin the search by relating their personal experiences or by summoning the testimony of experts. Groups with a great deal of resources could employ formal surveys or other forms of information gathering such as interviews, questionnaires, and experimental research. Although personal testimony or the opinions of experts are the easiest to gather, these may sometimes be unreliable, since they reflect the biases of specific individuals. Surveys and experimental research have more validity than personal experience or "expert opinion," but they are more difficult to gather and certainly more time-consuming (Schein 1969).

What is important is that problem-solving groups take the time to determine the criteria they will use to judge the appropriateness of a solution. They will also have to determine what resources they will need to assist their development of criteria. If, for example, a church group is trying to decide whether to convert from oil to gas for heating the church more economically, members could ask advice from energy experts or get assistance in preparing a cost analysis. If, however, the church group is trying to determine the best way to use a large donation, participants could take a survey of their membership to get some sense of what is best for the congregation.

As another example, if an entertainment committee at your school is charged with bringing a musical group to campus, the group would be more likely to attract a large turnout if members either surveyed or interviewed the various constituencies on campus about their preferences, rather than rely only on their own estimation of what people would like.

Here are some questions to ask as a guide in evaluating potential solutions.

1. Will the proposed solution bring about the desired change? Will it accomplish the objective?
2. Is the proposed solution feasible? Does the group have the wherewithal to carry out the proposed solution?
3. Would there be any serious disadvantages to the proposed solution? Would there be any unplanned repercussions?

The first question asks how probable it is that the proposed solution will accomplish the group's goal. The second question examines whether the group has the means to carry out its proposal. If not, then the group faces still another task. How can it influence other groups which could carry out the desired changes? The third question tests whether there are any risks that may be greater than the anticipated rewards of the proposed solution.

For example, suppose the student affairs committee has proposed that the library be kept open 24 hours during the school week. Some of the repercussions might be: the risk to women students walking home to their dormitories late at night; the need for, and the cost of, an escort system to offset the danger; and the cost of providing extra library personnel and cleaning services. If the costs of putting in such a system are judged to be unreasonable, then the benefits of keeping the library open 24 hours may not be large enough to offset the costs.

The Cyclical Process of Problem Solving

If the solution turns out to be inconsistent with the goals of the group, then the group should investigate different solutions. As we noted at the beginning of this section, a fundamental tenet of problem solving is that the process itself is not a sacred one. Each step may open up new points that can lead to a redefinition or reformulation of the problem. And the same is true for potential solutions.

Let me illustrate how a proposed solution can lead to a redefinition of a problem.

A consultant gave a workshop in "Problem Defining" for the staff of an agency dealing with teenagers in trouble with their families or the law. The staff had encountered a problem for which they could find no satisfactory solution. Their agency, somewhat like a "half-way" house, was mainly for clients who would stay for a few months. In a departure from this policy, the staff had decided to open their facility to teenagers with short-term needs. This meant allowing some clients to stay on a transient basis, overnight or for a few days. As a result of this decision, there was a split in groupings—the longer-term versus the short-term clients. And, to add to this rift, the long-term clients began reporting that some of their personal belongings were missing. They charged that the "transients" were responsible.

The staff accepted this diagnosis. The problem they discussed was, "How can we control the stealing by transients?" The solutions proposed were oriented to punishment and control, with such measures suggested as putting personal items in locked trunks, or locking bedroom doors, or reversing the new policy of admitting teenagers for short-term stays. It was while proposing these solutions that the staff became alarmed.

None of the solutions met the agency's goal of developing individual and group responsibility. The staff's *criteria* for a good solution had to include the freedom for their clients to come and go as well as security for themselves and their possessions. Nor did the staff relish having to mete out punishment when the purpose of their agency was to encourage a change of behavior based on internal motivation rather than external coercion.

The consultant asked them if they would reformulate their definition of the problem so that the criteria for a good solution could be stated as an "ideal" outcome. That is, could they state what behavior should be forthcoming from any solution they proposed? With an agreement as to what course of action was desirable, they could then plot the appropriate action to bring about this solution.

The suggestion the consultant gave is based on another approach to problem solving, called the *ideal-solution format* (Brilhart and Jochem 1964). As Goldberg and Larson (1975) point out, the format enables members to see the problem from several points of view and to search for the best, or ideal, solution. The group can accomplish this by asking the following questions:

1. Are we agreed on the nature of the problem?
2. What would be the ideal solution from the point of view of all the parties involved in the problem?

3. What conditions within the problem could be changed so that the ideal solution might be achieved?
4. Of the solutions available to us, which one approximates the ideal solution?

On this basis, the staff redefined the problem from "How can we stop the stealing?" to "How can we create the conditions that would promote respect for the property of others?" The rephrased question, which represented a new framing of their problem, led to a discussion of what programs had to be developed to serve the two populations of the agency. By redefining the problem, the staff could now engage in a productive search for solutions. In this process of redefinition, the staff engaged in a process of recycling—that is the staff learned that it was not a waste of time to review their understanding of the nature of the problem. They also learned that it was important to link their definition of a problem to the appropriateness, as well as the desirability, of the solutions suggested.

We have now examined three important steps of the first phase of problem solving: defining the problem, proposing solutions, and evaluating proposed solutions. Four rules have been suggested to help you with the overall analysis of a problem.

Rule 1. When defining a problem, confront the underlying tensions, concerns, and frustrations, and bring these tensions and concerns out into the open.
Rule 2. When defining a problem, express the problem as a condition that exists because of many factors, and bring these factors out into the open.
Rule 3. When proposing solutions, consider a wide range of alternatives as potential solutions.
Rule 4. When evaluating potential solutions, establish appropriate criteria.

If you have gone through these preliminary steps of problem analysis, then you are probably ready to choose a specific solution. At this point, you are in the second phase of the problem-solving process—deciding which solution from among the proposed solutions would be most effective. As noted earlier, the issue of choosing and implementing solutions is the subject of the next chapter. For the remainder of this chapter, we will discuss ways your group can practice defining and analyzing problems and proposing solutions.

IMPROVING GROUP PROBLEM SOLVING

We have stressed that group problem solving is a collective undertaking. It requires the collaboration of group members as well as a knowledge of the problem-solving process. One other issue remains: *practicing.* It would be useful for your group to choose a problem the members would like to resolve and use the "Force Field Analysis" exercise (page 153) to help them go through the problem-solving process.

Problem Solving Using Force Field Analysis

One of the more insightful approaches to problem solving, *force field analysis* (FFA), was developed by Kurt Lewin as a guide for improving group problem solving (1947). As you learned in Chapter 1, Lewin was influenced in his thinking about problem solving by the physical sciences. Using the concept of a field of forces, Lewin developed force field analysis as a method for dealing with social and psychological problems.

FFA uses steps that this chapter has emphasized, proposing alternatives and evaluating solutions, but adds something unique in its consideration of a problem. The method impels a group to state a problem as a *condition,* and in so doing, helps a group overcome one of the large issues in problem solving, getting members to agree on what is the specific problem they are discussing.

In addition, FFA assumes that any problem is the way it is because of a set of counterbalancing forces. An extended illustration will demonstrate how force field analysis can help a group define a problem and work for an effective solution.

As an example consider the issue of being overweight. Assume that you are aware of this problem and express your desire to change. If you are like many other people with a weight problem, you may believe that if only "I had more will power, then I could lose weight." If, on the other hand, you used FFA for your diagnosis, you would not be permitted to name only one factor as the cause of your problem. Rather, you would be encouraged to state your problem as a *condition* that exists, and then state what specifically you would like to change. Instead of merely saying, "I want to lose weight," you would be obliged to say something like, "I am 20 pounds overweight and I would like to lose those 20 pounds." Following this statement, you would then go to the next step, and list the many factors that keep you from losing weight. Lewin classifies these as *restraining forces* and *driving forces.*

Restraining Forces   The restraining forces are the forces that hold back a solution—do not allow the problem to be solved. In addition to citing "will power" as your reason for being overweight, you are asked to think about the many reasons that keep you from losing weight. As you think about it, you will discover that more than "will power" is involved. You eat not only because of life-sustaining needs. How else can one explain the consumption of soft drinks, candy, chips, and so forth—the ubiquitous junk food we all seem to consume so liberally. You eat these and other foods for a variety of reasons: taste pleasure, habit, business needs, socializing, relief from boredom, and so on. These and other factors become the *restraining forces.*

Driving Forces   Looking at the restraining forces, however, is looking at only one side of the identification of forces. There are also forces that can prod you in the direction of change: health, societal expectations, self-esteem, desire for romance, an awareness of fashion, a lover's request, pressure from friends and relatives. These are the *driving forces.* They could help move you to change.

A Counterbalance of Forces   A third assumption of FFA is that not all of the restraining and driving forces carry the same power or intensity. Some factors are more important than others. Your present condition, being 20 pounds overweight, can be thought of as a *state of equilibrium,* with the driving forces pushing against the restraining forces, a counterbalancing of forces, keeping your weight unchanged. Sometimes one set of forces will win out—as, for example, accepting your lover's request to pursue a diet plan. On the other hand, an invitation to a "posh" restaurant might throw the balance in the other direction. This concept is illustrated in Figure 6.1.

The important point is that a consideration of various forces in

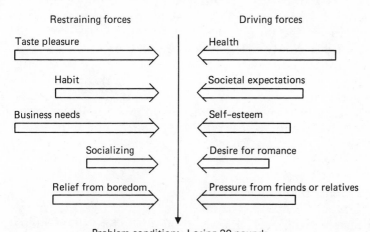

Figure 6.1   A force field analysis based on the problem condition of wanting to lose 20 pounds. Restraining forces are those that pull the individual away from the goal; driving forces are those that impel or motivate the person to seek the goal.

a problem can be very useful to a group's examination of possible solutions to the problem. When you examine these forces, you are then able to understand the complexity of the problem. No solution that fails to consider both sets of forces can resolve a problem for long. If we wish to change a condition, then we must either reduce the number of restraining forces or increase the number of driving forces. Lewin called this process an *unfreezing of the equilibrium* (1958).

Lewin believed that it is easier to change when we work on reducing the number of restraining forces before increasing the number of driving forces. Thus if you can find taste pleasure (reducing the impact of the restraining force of eating "because it is pleasurable") in less caloric food or if you can substitute other rewards for taste pleasure, then you may be able to curtail your food intake and accomplish a weight loss. If, on the other hand, pressures are put on you to lose weight—threat of loss of romance, or nagging from friends—then you may become more tense and unable to follow steps that would encourage weight loss.

You are more likely to respond to proposals that reduce the impact of restraining forces, because when you are being pushed by driving forces, you may feel you are being coerced. In responding to coercion, you may become defensive or use some other compensating reaction. If you are told to lose weight because you are endangering your health, you can respond, "My boyfriend (or girlfriend) likes me the way I am!" or "It's better to be too fat than too thin." These reactions are less likely to occur when more of the effort to change is directed at reducing the restraining forces. Still, understanding how driving forces can be used is important in any move toward change. It is from these forces that many of the innovative ideas for solving a problem will be found.

The "Force Field Analysis" exercise provides an outline of the steps of FFA. As was indicated earlier, groups do not necessarily move in a step-by-step sequence to solve a problem, nor is it necessarily desirable that groups move in this way. What FFA encourages is practice in a structured method. It will let your group learn more about problem solving and, in this way, help your group find better and more satisfying solutions.

Excerpts from a Group Diary It may be helpful to look at what our beginning five-member group (Group A: Jeff, Rich, Cynthia, Amy, and Susan) did when the participants applied the first seven steps of force field analysis to the troubling issue of apathy among students on their campus. Their comments, paraphrased below, are from their collective diary, in which they summarized their interactions over the course of their meetings.

FORCE FIELD ANALYSIS: A METHOD OF PROBLEM SOLVING*

General Outline of the Steps in Force Field Analysis

Step 1. The problem is defined as a condition that the group wants to change. The group does this by understanding how the problem is felt—its scope, its intensity. The discussion should include the reactions of members and their concerns. Members should state specifically what changes the group is seeking.

Step 2. The group identifies the restraining and driving forces impinging on the problem. Participants use brainstorming to assist them in listing both sets of forces. The rules of brainstorming are in effect. Hence, there should be no evaluation until all responses have been recorded. (The forces can be listed on a large sheet of paper—the restraining forces on the left and the driving forces on the right.) A member of the group writes down all responses and serves as a record keeper.

Step 3. Looking only at the restraining forces, the group assigns a priority to each force. Members are asked to consider how important each force is to the resolution of the problem. (They may at this time add to both the restraining and driving forces.) This is an important diagnostic process. It lets the group weight those forces that bear most heavily on the problem. With this step, the group recognizes that although many factors are important, some are not as important to solving the problem as the forces more that are highly ranked.

Step 4. With the restraining forces more clearly in focus, the group eliminates the restraining forces for which it does not have either the *time, energy,* or *resources* to deal. By eliminating forces that it cannot change, the group imposes a *reality* test. Thus, members can focus on those forces that are within their power to do something about. The remaining forces are those to which the group can devote its energies.

Step 5. Members develop specific proposals for reducing the impact of the restraining forces. Proposals are developed so that potential repercussions, or unintended "boomerang" consequences, are minimized. At this time, new driving forces can be added. (Driving forces

*Source: R. W. Napier and M. Gershenfeld. 1973. *Groups: Theory and Experience.* Boston: Houghton Mifflin, pp. 225–231.

often contain possible solutions.) Sometimes it is helpful if a group subdivides, with two or three people
working on proposals that will minimize the impact of
restraining forces. These proposals are then reported to
the larger group.

Step 6. The entire group considers how each of the proposals
might be implemented. (The implementation process
will be discussed in more depth in Chapter 7.) Members
focus on such matters as who will undertake which
activities, whether committees will be formed, whether
petitions need to be drawn up, and so on. This is a time
for determining who will be accountable for ensuring
that a recommended course of action will take place.

Step 7. The group considers all proposals and all plans for implementation. It designates which members will take
responsibility for seeing that specific proposals and
plans are implemented. This is an important discussion, for the group examines and discusses the proposals as a total package.

Step 8. This final step take place at a future date. As a follow-up process, the group agrees to meet at a specified
time to evaluate how well its proposals have done in
resolving the problem.

Step 1. In attempting to choose a problem, we considered many ideas, but our
feelings were with our university and the growing sense of apathy on our
campus. We asked ourselves what some of the causes of apathy were, and one
point emerged as a major factor: the lack of student involvement from Friday
to Monday. Students can only have a certain level of concern for their school
if they are here only four or five days a week. *The condition we want to change
is the lack of involvement of students in weekend activities.*

Step 2. We began to focus on the problem: Why do so many students leave
on weekends? This led us to examine the present situation on campus. As we
brainstormed, we found that there is usually a limited range of activities available to the student: movies, lectures, and an occasional concert. There are not
enough activities to keep students on campus.

In addition, we saw a "feast or famine" situation. Sometimes a weekend
is overcrowded with activities, and at other times, nothing is happening. Also,
there does not seem to be a consistent way to publicize events. Sometimes
there are banners, or flyers; other times, only a brief announcement in the
student paper.

Another major issue, outside of what is going on at the university, is the
need to go home—to see family, friends, and to work at a job.

On the other hand, there could be many good things to do on campus:
we have three large gyms, a fine arts complex, the Memorial Union, and large
dining halls. We also have a variety of clubs and organizations, which, if coor-
dinated, could offer plenty of activities.

The need for students to work and the availability of jobs is a serious issue, and perhaps would be very difficult to change, but it would be worth finding out whether more jobs were possible near this campus and whether students would then be interested in staying around (these are some of the driving forces—factors that would encourage change).

From this discussion of restraining and driving forces, the group then proceeded to assign a weight to each of the restraining forces (step 3) and to eliminate those forces for which they had neither the time, energy, or resources to change (step 4). The group eliminated the restraining forces of jobs and obligations to go home, and decided to work on the one force they thought they could influence—the development of a program of activities that might entice students to stay on campus on weekends.

Step 5. We divided ourselves into subgroups. Each smaller group worked on and developed several plans: a questionnaire to be filled out at freshman orientation and at registration. We could give students a sticker after they turned in their completed questionnaire, and only then would they fulfill the registration requirement. Then the university could compile the results. We would have a better idea of students' preferences for organizations and activities.

We thought we needed another proposal to deal with the "feast or famine" situation and also the lack of coordination among all the campus organizations and the types of events that were scheduled. We proposed the creation of a Student Activities Coordinating Committee (SACC) to serve as a repository for all the information about activities and sites, funds needed, scheduling, and so on, from which committee members would prepare a workable, conflict-free schedule, supported by the university.

In steps 6 and 7, the group continued to discuss the proposals. Members took up the issue of how each of their proposals would bring about the desired change. Each subgroup became accountable for a proposal and the reasoning in support of it. Members had to visualize how a particular proposal would operate, and whether any proposal had undesirable consequences. Their concern about the lack of publicity was handled by the following proposal:

We need a highly visible and well-maintained bulletin board system on campus—for enclosed signs to list all campus activities for a week prior to the event. We also need to use more direct appeals—letters to alumni and to parents notifying them of major events on campus, video presentations at the Memorial Union and other areas of the campus, appeals on the university radio.

And so on. Participants continued to discuss their proposals and how feasible each was for changing the existing problem.

Comments on the Exercise

Although there is nothing sacred in these steps, they do provide a structure for exploring the problem-solving process. Using a structure to work through problems you have identified can help you deal with a multitude of factors that impinge on a problem. No longer will you be able to move too quickly to the solution phase, if you have not thoroughly analyzed the problem.

As the diary showed, the group did not consider one of the suggestions raised early in its deliberations, before the group adopted the FFA method (page 153)—if the university had an exciting football team, that would encourage students to stay on campus on weekends. In using FFA, the group participants recognized that the issue was indeed more complex. Moreover, they accepted that while they could not deal with some of the issues, they were able to address and offer proposals for those issues they could do something about. That is the beauty of using force field analysis.

The problem-solving exercise allows groups to identify those forces responsible for an existing problem, to examine alternative solutions, and to estimate the potential consequences of proposed solutions. The steps are not meant to be adhered to with rigidity; they are tools for understanding how to address a problem. Although it may seem that this exercise calls merely for a listing of pros and cons, there is more to the activity than that. An important learning is that group members discover how to think about a problem in a more systematic way. By looking at a set of alternatives, and by practicing the various steps that can move a group to solution, a group is more likely to achieve a productive solution.

A FINAL COMMENT

The problems that most groups face are not simple. They are more likely to be complex and to have multiple restraining and driving components. Our research and experience indicate that groups willing to spend time identifying the nature and scope of a problem, defining or redefining the problem, and examining a number of possible solutions, is a group that can markedly improve its problem-solving ability.

A group profits from a willingness to engage in an analytic process in developing solutions for a problem. It is also helpful to realize that, although problem solving is not necessarily a step-by-step process, a group's work is enhanced if participants will be mindful of certain steps in working out a problem. It is also advantageous for a group to use a recycling process, a process in which the group moves back and forth between defining a problem and searching for solutions.

A structure can help, but other components of group dynamics must also be present. For example, if group members are to work well together, they will have to be personally involved with the task. With personal involvement, individuals will more likely take responsibility for their actions and commit themselves to participate meaningfully and actively.

Participants in a problem-solving group have to feel that they are in an emotionally supportive as well as task-oriented environment. When members can learn to accommodate individual styles of participating, then they are able to work together more productively. If the group has difficulty with interpersonal relations, it should take the time to establish roles, goals, and effective group behavior, rather than plow ahead with the task and ignore the unsatisfactory emotional climate.

Encouraging good interpersonal relations promotes cohesiveness in the group. Listening to people's ideas, bonding with other individuals, focusing on the priorities and needs of the group—all help foster group harmony. Being attuned to group needs also assists a group in developing the skills of gathering information and evaluating and incorporating new ideas into proposals made. When a problem has been analyzed with care, when participants understand what is happening, and why, and when they agree that the process has been reasonable, then it is time to move on to the second phase of problem solving, learning to make effective decisions, the subject of the next chapter.

SUMMARY

This chapter has focused on problem solving as a cyclical process that comprises two stages—one that takes place before a decision is made, and the other that occurs after the group reaches a decision. In the first stage the group defines the problem, proposes solutions, and evaluates the solutions. The second stage, to be discussed in Chapter 7, focuses on how a group can ensure that it is making effective decisions. Some groups will be effective in their problem solving if they adhere to a series of logical steps, but they will gain even more insight if they understand the cyclical nature of problem solving and practice some important steps in the problem-solving process.

Learning to analyze problems can be aided by understanding four basic rules. The first rule states that when defining a problem, a group pay attention to underlying tensions that brought about the problem. The second rule reinforces the need to examine carefully all of the factors related to the problem. The third rule encourages group members to consider a wide range of alternatives when they are proposing solutions, and the fourth rule emphasizes the importance of establishing criteria when a group is evaluating the adequacy of proposed solutions.

Learning about the processes that affect problem solving can have a positive outcome for a group. A group's willingness to spend time on the definition of a problem, on the generation of alternative solutions, and on the evaluation of those solutions, fosters the conditions for choosing a more effective solution. The evidence shows that a structured approach can be helpful even when hindering factors are present within a group. The structure can at least provide a clearer sense of mission around which the group can coalesce.

An exercise, "Force Field Analysis," provides practice in some of the necessary functions of problem solving. The exercise is based on the concept that a problem can be changed only if group members understand the complexity of forces that keep a problem the way it is. The exercise allows groups to work with a structure that encourages good problem-solving habits.

REFERENCES

Borders, W. 1981. *New York Times,* July 19.

Brilhart, J. K., and L. Mm. Jochem. 1964. "Effects of Different Patterns on Outcomes of Problem-Solving Discussion." *Journal of Applied Psychology* 48:175–179.

Dewey, J. 1933. *How We Think.* Boston: D. C. Heath.

Goldberg, A. A., and C. E. Larson. 1975. *Group Communication: Discussion Processes & Applications.* Englewood Cliffs, N.J.: Prentice-Hall, pp. 149–150.

Gouran, D. S. 1976. "The Watergate Cover-up: Its Dynamics and Its Implications." *Communication Monographs* 43:176–186.

Hoffman, L. R. 1965. "Group Problem-Solving." In L. Berkowitz (ed.), *Advances in Experimental Social Psychology* (vol. 2). New York: Academic Press, pp. 67–113.

Janis, I. L. 1972. *Victims of Groupthink: A Psychological Study of Foreign Policy Decision and Fiascoes.* Boston: Houghton Mifflin.

Lewin, K. 1947. "Frontiers in Group Dynamics." *Human Relations* 1. An expansion of this theme is provided in R. Lippitt, J. Watson, and B. Westley, 1958, *The Dynamics of Planned Change.* New York: Harcourt, Brace.

Napier, R. W., and M. Gershenfeld. 1973. *Groups: Theory and Experience.* Boston: Houghton Mifflin.

Osborn, A. F. 1957. *Applied Imagination* (rev. ed.). New York: Scribner.

Poole, M. S. 1981. "Decision Development in Small Groups. I: A Comparison of Two Models." *Communication Monographs* 48:1–17.

Ross, R. S. 1974. *Speech Communication: Fundamentals and Practice.* (3rd ed.). New York: McGraw-Hill.

Scheidel, T. M., and L. Crowell. 1964. "Idea Development in Small Groups." *Quarterly Journal of Speech* 50:40–45.

Schein, E. H. 1969. *Process Consultation: Its Role in Organizational Development.* Reading, Mass.: Addison-Wesley, pp. 46–52.

chapter 7

Making Effective Decisions

The second phase of problem solving, the focus of this chapter, begins after potential solutions have been identified. Dividing the problem-solving task into two phases is largely an arbitrary one, since every step in the problem-solving process calls for some type of decision, whether you are defining a problem, choosing among alternatives, or planning what action to take. Nonetheless, one of the more important tasks your group will face is to decide which of the examined alternatives should be chosen. The question is, How should a group choose? What decision-making methods can participants use? How do they ensure that they will make the "best" decision?

This chapter explores these issues and their effect on decision making in the group. Three perspectives are offered: (1) how to decide among proposed solutions, (2) how to implement solutions, and (3) how to evaluate the effectiveness of solutions. The chapter also discusses the problems groups have in reaching decisions, methods of decision making, and effective decision making.

THE GROUP AND THE DECISION PROCESS

Every decision creates some degree of tension. As individuals we often agonize over a choice we have to make. When we are working in a group, our problems may be exacerbated. We may continually face conflicts between what we believe is a good course to follow and

159

what other members of the group may advocate. There is doubtless an ongoing struggle between our desire to be a good group member—open, tolerant of the views of others—and our need to have our view be the prevailing one (Stein and Tanter 1980; Steiner 1972).

Although we might like to have our own way, we can acknowledge that tough decisions are rarely made by one individual alone. We tend to call upon others, seek advice, or, at the very least, ask others whether they agree or disagree with our choice. Part of the problem is that we lack the time to investigate the many alternatives that would aid us in making a decision. Along with a lack of time is the problem of our own biases, as well as our inability to know, with a sufficient degree of certainty, which alternative is the best one. Since it is rare for any one individual to have all the information bearing on a decision, consulting with others seems justifiable.

And there is another concern. It is difficult to estimate how what we decide to do in the present will be the right decision in the future. That is the reason for so much tension and anxiety that accompanies the making of a decision. The choices we have to make, as an individual or as a group, represent cost–benefit outcomes. Doubtless our anxiety increases when we realize that we may have to live with our decision for some indefinite time.

Reaching a decision in a group can be troublesome. For one thing, group members may lack procedures for their interactions. Randy Hirokawa (1980) found in his research that the one distinctive difference between effective and ineffective groups was that effective groups paid more attention to the procedures they used to solve problems. Effective groups seem to have members who provide direction (with such questions as, "Why don't we look at some other proposals?") and others who go along with these suggestions.

Another problem that groups have is how to deal with the information they have. Sometimes they are overburdened with too much information. Or they may not have a systematic approach for searching and evaluating information. As Herbert A. Simon (1960), a Nobel Prize winner in economics, observed, what gets in the way of good decision making is the decision makers themselves. While they all try to do their best, to be rational and thoughtful, they are limited in how much information they can process. It may also be that the information that groups need is not readily available. Hackman and Morris (1975) found in their review of decision-making behavior that people seldom spend time planning how they will get information, assimilate information, or apply that information in ways that would assist them in making choices.

Thus group decision making, like individual decision making, is not always an easy task. As in other group activities, group participation offers the advantages of shared responsibility and greater resources, and the disadvantage of possible friction among group members. Using a structured system to weed out ineffective or undesirable choices and to identify effective ones can be a help, however.

THE SECOND PHASE OF PROBLEM SOLVING

The primary task for a group in the second phase of problem solving is to choose a solution that will be the most effective for changing the condition that brought the problem to its attention in the first place. In this section we'll examine the three steps in the second phase of problem solving.

Deciding Among Proposed Solutions

Knowing what their chief goals are, analyzing both the quality and the acceptability of a proposal, and determining to what extent they can, or cannot, rely on precedent—these are some of the factors group participants should consider when faced with two or more alternate solutions to a problem. Weighing each factor can provide members with a gauge by which to measure the suitability of a proposal, so that the choice is not just the result of guesswork or compromise.

Spending time getting information can assist a group in making choices.

1. Understand Goals   When choosing among alternatives, group members need to ask: What can be done to make sure that the decision processes we use will help us reach desirable outcomes? A model, developed by Simon (1960) offers some valuable advice, in the form of the discrepancy model.

A discrepancy model   Simon believes that if a group is to come to decision, the members must understand their goals. Intuitively, we know that it is difficult to make choices among proposals without such understanding. Yet, as Simon explains, although goals are worth working for, they are seldom achieved as stated. To overcome this difficulty, he suggests that a group *fractionate* the problem.

To *fractionate* means to break a problem down into a number of subproblems. By exploring a subproblem of a larger problem, and by dealing with a very specific, concrete issue, a group can avoid the frustration and disappointment that comes from a large, complex problem perceived to be insoluable.

In contemporary terms Simon's approach is called a *discrepancy model,* for it allows a group to understand where it wants to go and how far it must move to get there. Simon's model, which he labeled the *general problem solver,* offers group members a chance to sort out their reasoning processes, allowing them to assess the discrepancy, or distance, between their goal and the present state. The model was designed to be used in any problematic situation for which a decision has to be made. Four steps are involved.

1. Erect goals.
2. Determine the differences between the present situation and the goals put forth.
3. Find by a search process (memory, past experience, new information) the tools for reducing the discrepancies between the goals to be achieved and the present situation.
4. Apply the tools (suggestions, ideas, proposals, recommendations) that have emerged from the search process.

As an example, suppose you have formed a committee of citizens concerned about your city's water. Your group has collected information from health officials, and you are aware that a recent investigation of all the states' water supplies indicates that the drinking water in your state, as well as in most other states, is contaminated with dangerous or potentially dangerous chemicals. Your goal would be to make the water in your area as free as possible of contamination. How would you fractionate such a problem?

You would examine some of your subgoals: (1) making citizens aware of the problem—this may take the form of consulting a variety of agencies to help you disseminate information about the seriousness of the situation; (b) bringing pressure for change—your best bet would be to deal with the problem locally, but still there is a need to get those in control to act; (c) analyzing the cost of changing filtering systems. While some states have already altered their water treatment facilities, the costs may be too dear for your state or city to bear. You would have to consider proposals for rearranging priorities in the city's budget, for example. The issues are enormous. Yet, working with one issue—say, creating an awareness among the public—may allow your group to begin the process of change.

The importance of learning to *fractionate* is that groups can pursue some issues that help them realize doable goals. Many times a group will have in its repertoire ways of dealing with parts of a problem. If the members continue to work on each subproblem, they would have a solution that could come close to realizing their overall goal. But if not, they can still derive satisfaction from having made a decision affecting some aspects of the problem. It keeps participants from being bogged down so that they cannot see any progress.

2. Examine Decision Quality and Acceptance N. R. F. Maier (1963), an astute researcher of problem-solving groups, suggests that there are two ways a group can evaluate the effectiveness of a proposed solution: one way is to analyze objectively the *quality* of the solution and the second way is to determine the likelihood of its *acceptance.*

How a group searches for potential solutions—the criteria the members use, as well as knowledge of what would keep a proposed solution from being realized—influences the quality of a solution. Although individuals may have any number of reasons for choosing one solution over another—"It fits the facts," "It's the only one that comes to mind," "It seems logical," or "I like what Jim says, and I agree"—a *quality* decision is more likely to emerge from the following pragmatic test: "This is the solution that produces the desired objective most completely, most efficiently, and with the least number of undesirable risks." (Maier 1963, 1).

Using *acceptance* as a criterion means knowing how people responsible for carrying out a decision feel about it. If individuals in the group withdraw from participation, become angry or aggressive toward one another, or signify that they cannot enthusiastically support the decisions of the group, then the effectiveness of the decision is markedly reduced.

Maier proposes the formula "ED = Q × A" to stress that an effective decision is equal to the quality of a decision proposal multiplied by the group's acceptance of the proposal. While quality refers to the best formulation that members can achieve, acceptance encourages members to help bring the decision to pass. A solution that has not allowed an expression of acceptance will not likely be effective.

Maier's equation also helps to differentiate among decisions. They are not all of equal importance, nor do they require the same degree of calculation. For example, some decisions will require high acceptance but can be of low quality, such as the work of a task group assigned to plan vacation schedules, coffee breaks, and other routine matters. Some decisions, such as the work of a task group preparing a highly specialized or technical report, would have to be of high quality but would need only low acceptance. Other decisions fall into a third category—they require both high acceptance and high quality.

The advantage of separating the dimensions of quality and acceptance is that you can reasonably question what the comment "This is a good decision" expresses. You can ask whether "good" means "acceptable," or whether "good" means "of high quality," or whether both elements are being considered. Maier's criteria suggest that for solutions to be effective, they have to take account of the available resources as well as the reactions of the people involved.

3. Estimate the Importance of a Decision   What can also help a group come to decision is to assess the amount of time and other resources a group will want to devote to its discussion. In an approach similar to that proposed by Maier, Simon (1960, 5–13) asks decision makers to acknowledge that not all decisions require the same amount of effort. He offered the categories *programmed* and *nonprogrammed* decisions to help a group ascertain how much of its resources should be expended on finding a solution.

Programmed decision, a term Simon borrowed from computer language, refers to a routine choice for which there are precedents or established procedures. It may include such apparently innocuous choices as whether your organization should bring in a coffee service, or the more substantial, complex decision of how a government should respond to an unauthorized plane flying over its airspace. If a group is faced with what can be designated a "routine" decision, then searching for precedents can help make it easier to come to decision.

An example: In everyone's house, the garbage has to be carried out on a somewhat regular basis. Although household members may complain about having to perform this task, no one has to deliberate for too long about how the job should be performed. Since in most households garbage disposal is a recurring task, the procedures are already in place. Whether the garbage has to be well wrapped in paper or plastic or perfunctorily placed in a can is usually not an issue.

Although *programmed* decisions are automatically less important than *nonprogrammed* ones, programmed decisions can also go awry, as was probably the case in the Soviet Union's shooting down of a Korean Air Lines passenger plane in 1983. The decision doubtless represented a response mechanism already in place: (1) When a foreign plane violates territory, and (2) does not respond to communication from officers in charge, and (3) is flying over sensitive areas (the plane was shot down over an area where missile experiments were going on), then (4) the plane is on a spying mission, and (5) for planes that spy, there is a "routine" response.

In contrast with the programmed decision, the nonprogrammed decision has fewer specific precedents and procedures to point to. It is a decision that has to be made for the first time. Nonprogrammed decisions have to be made when what should be done is not readily specifiable. Some examples would be: selecting graduate programs to support if enrollments continue to decline; predicting educational needs of a community in which birth rates are declining but in which high technology industry is being developed; determining which health programs to support for the aging population; and coordinating state and federal resources to combat acid rain. These decisions will require a great deal of time, energy, and resources, far more than a programmed decision will require on the average.

The optimizing decision If a group determines that a decision warrants such use of resources, then the members will have to decide how much time should be allotted for the project overall. According to Simon (1976), important decisions—decisions that demand a solution of high quality or excellence—can be thought of as *optimizing decisions.* When involved in searching for optimizing decisions, individuals would consider all possible alternatives, choosing from among these the course of action with the most likely best outcome. For these decisions the group will have to devote an inordinate amount of energy, time, skill, and expertise, and whether it is worth making the effort can be considered as another decision point. An optimizing solution should be distinguished from solutions that are overly ideal, however. Sometimes a group chooses a solution that far exceeds what can reasonably be done. But if the participants will take into consideration the pressing issues and reach a workable solution, excessive idealism need not deter the group from acting (Simon 1976, 153–157).

The satisficing decision According to Simon, *satisficing decisions* can be thought of as reasonable substitutes for optimizing decisions. Satisficing decisions fall into an intermediate category, between routine and optimal. In your consideration of possibilities, you would examine a somewhat narrower range of alternatives, perhaps choosing a solution that is not too different from the current situation but that still represents some desirable change. The strategy of "satisficing" can also be thought of as bringing about an incremental improvement. Such a solution is open to the type of criticism expressed by one analyst of decision-making processes as "the art of muddling through"; nevertheless, a "satisficing" solution, with its concern for workability and feasibility and its focus on finding specific solutions for specific problems, does aid a group in producing a reasonably good solution (Lindblom 1959).

The discussion thus far has elaborated a number of approaches for determining the adequacy of a proposed solution. Each of these methods will help ensure that there is a good enough match between the problem and the solution. Now your group is ready for the next process, that of preparing ways to get your solution carried out.

Implementing Solutions

After your group agrees on a best solution, the next task is to figure out how to make that solution work. It is far too easy to say, "Well, we have a solution; we've done our job," and then go on to other activities. The tougher assignment (although it certainly has seemed tough enough choosing a solution) is to provide the means for bringing about the desired changes. This is a procedure calling for a "following through" of the group's recommendations for change. It is a way of making certain that recommendations for change are made operational (Napier and Gershenfeld 1981).

Two procedures can help the group implement a solution. First, members choose a plan of action, and, second, they estimate what resources are needed to carry out the plan. Both tasks require a commitment among individual members to support the group's choice of solution and to rely on their unique talents, areas of expertise, and resources to bolster the group's solution. The overall effect of these commitments is that members become responsible for putting a solution into effect.

Accountability Accountability is an inherent component of the implementation process. The following questions can help you plan for accountability:

What is our task and how shall we do it?

Who will be responsible for carrying out the proposed plan?

When can our group reasonably expect results?

What unplanned events or accidents are likely to jeopardize our actions?

What people should we consult who can help us with our proposal?

What people should we consult who could threaten our proposal?

Nothing is more frustrating than to have a solution for a problem and then not be able to put the plan into action. Asking such questions as what limitations are placed on the group that would keep it from successfully implementing the solution is a way to apply a reality test. Implementation may not be easy to accomplish; it takes time, but it is more likely to occur when members understand what is expected of them (Patton and Giffin 1978, 170–171).

The Implementation Game   The following example illustrates the consequence of not including implementation plans as part of your solution proposal (Bardach 1977, 171–172).

A new superintendent of schools gave a directive to the faculty of an inner-city school, describing a number of innovative ideas for teachers to try out with their students. He asked the teachers to encourage more self-motivated behavior so that students could become more responsible for their own learning and education. The teachers were told to use their own skills and talents to devise plans; their efforts would be supplemented with a set of "stimulating, self-instructional, and pedagogically sound material." The superintendent urged immediate *implementation* of the program.

Although the teachers were eager to carry out the directive, they did not know exactly what to do. There were no specific directions as to how they were to be innovative, or how they were to interpret "self-motivated behavior," or how they were to make students more responsible for their own education. Nor were the supplementary materials distributed at the beginning of the project. The lack of clarity and direction, as well as of specific activities to promote the desirable goals, led, after a while, to disillusionment on the part of the teachers. The administration, while requesting that teachers carry out proposals requiring unique methods, did not provide sufficient advice or follow-up communication for implementation to take place.

Here is a contrasting example.

Massachusetts Fair Share is the name of a group of individuals interested in identifying and solving problems affecting citizens of that state. They have examined such problems as the cleaning up of polluted streams to the changing of voter registration procedures. The latter task involves the effort to change an existing policy, in which voters are permitted to register only in specifically designated places during business hours, to a more simplified procedure of voter registration by mail.

The group's implementation methods include such acts as hiring canvassers to encourage citizens to write letters into the legislature. The canvassers bring writing paper into the homes they visit and urge people to write the letter, then and there, asking legislators to bring a bill for mail registration out of study committee. Group members also are using paid lobbyists to work directly with legislators. In addition, they have sent articles about the need for change to local newspapers throughout the state, and they are distributing, door to door, their own newsletter advocating the proposed policy. Finally, they are conducting public education seminars on this issue around the state.

As the example shows, the members of Massachusetts Fair Share have drawn up highly specific and workable methods of trying to accomplish their goal of a change in the registration law. Because the tasks are clearly defined, members know what is expected of them. This makes implementation easier.

The search for ways to implement a solution means using a variety of support activities—meetings, discussions, inquiries, research, investigations, and consultations. Moving from a general conception of an ideal state of affairs to specific methods for accomplishing the ideal are different processes (Bardach). Implementation is difficult to do, and becomes even more difficult if, as part of a new proposal, members must also indicate in some detail how they think they can accomplish the proposed solution. Implementation, then, is a detailing of those acts that will help bring about a desirable outcome. It also involves accountability. When group members understand what is to be done, when they agree to be accountable for seeing a solution through to completion, and when they are willing to devote their resources to that effort, they are then ready to consider the next step, that of evaluating how effectively their solution meets the needs of the problem.

Evaluating Solutions

This is the final checkpoint for judging the effectiveness of a group's solution. Unquestionably, every time a solution is proposed, members are asking implicitly or explicitly: "Is it desirable? Can it be done? Are there any risks?" What remains is to decide whether a solution, after it is put into operation, will work as the group thinks it should. It is important for a group to be open during this analysis. If group participants receive new information, or have to reassess their examination of gains and losses, they will need to be sufficiently flexible to be able to offer additional alternatives or to move back to a reconsideration of the problem.

Let's assume your group has made a decision. After much deliberation, how can you know that the decision will bring about the desired effect? One way to make this judgment is to forecast—to project, to make predictions about what is likely to occur as a result of the proposed solution. Although predicting events is clearly risky, it can be done if group members are able to identify their reasons for forecasting outcomes (Gouran 1982; Gouran and Hirokawa 1983). To do so goes beyond mere hunch. It means that group members will employ evidence and sound logic in support of their predictions. The following questions can help them through this tricky prediction stage (Patton and Giffin 1978, pp. 148–155):

Are there other cases or events that are similar to what we are proposing?

Has a similar solution been tried anywhere else? What were the results?

Was the solution put into effect by a group such as ours? How was it done?

Do we know of any side effects in trying this solution? Are the risks greater than the potential gains?

These questions can help your group compare important similarities between events that have occurred in the past and the outcomes that are being predicted. By comparing past events with predicted ones, the group can estimate which is more likely to be the better.

Generally, a group's concern with the effectiveness of solutions means that members will be evaluating the feasibility of the solution, evaluating the extent to which it solves the problem, and, after putting a solution into effect, evaluating whether it has worked without creating unacceptable risks. Evaluating solutions depends on developing evaluation measures. These may take the form of surveys, questionnaires, in-depth interviews, paper and pencil tests, inquiries of those who have to live with the decision, or other measures that can be applied to the particular solution.

After a solution has been tried, the group, in effect, is asking whether the solution has produced the largest result, "the most bang for the buck." Sometimes the effectiveness cannot be known until it has been tried for a period of time. It would be useful for a group to meet at a later time to check on how well the solution meets the needs of the situation. The important learning is that groups need to think about developing evaluation measures if they are to know how well their solution has worked to remedy the problem (Nisbett and Ross 1980).

METHODS OF DECISION MAKING

Thus far you have looked at decision making as a process of choosing a "best" alternative, implementing that choice, and evaluating how well it works. You know that the acceptability and quality of a solution can influence a group's choice. You have also made distinctions among types of decisions—programmed and nonprogrammed, optimizing and satisficing—with each type helping to determine how much time and resources a group should use in making a decision. A group's choice is also affected by the methods it uses in coming to decision.

The method of decision making has consequences both for the group's satisfaction with the decision and for the group's commitment to carry out the decision. What method a group uses will be determined by (1) how much time is allotted for the task, (2) the complexity of the task, and (3) consideration of the social climate of the group. While each method will be useful in some circumstance, groups should be concerned about the different outcomes each method brings. Below are decision-making methods that groups frequently use (Schein 1969, pp. 46–58).

1. Decision by Lack of Response

Decision by lack of response occurs most commonly when a member suggests an idea, but nobody responds to it. There is neither praise nor criticism. Although it may seem as if a decision has not been made, the effect is the same as if a vote had been taken. Group members suggest ideas, and until the group finds a proposal it is willing to act on, all the suggested but bypassed ideas have, in effect, already been rejected. Although no official votes have been taken, the impact for the proposers of these ideas is the same—their ideas have "plopped," a style of decision making that clearly affects a group's outcome. Valuable suggestions may be lost simply because no one bothers to respond to them. Groups working on a task need to be aware of this tendency so that they can participate actively when ideas are suggested, rather than submitting passively to proposals only when they seem to be enjoying group support.

2. Decision by Authority Rule

Groups are most often led by a "chair" who has legitimate authority for the decisions made by the group. Even when an official leader has not been appointed, a group may converge upon the views of a single person who is treated as a leader. Sometimes the decision process is so dominated by a single individual that other individuals appear to give up their decision rights. Whichever pattern occurs, decision by authority refers to the procedure by which a single person makes the final decision. Using authority as a method of decision often means that participants in the decision process are engaged in an "abdication of choice" (Simon 1976, 127). The authority figure need not be dictatorial or arbitrary. Rather, the group accepts the authority's position as the basis of its choice. The group may even be consulted but, after a time, the "in-charge" person may say, "Thank you for your help; this discussion has been useful, and I will make my decision."

How appropriate this type of decision making is will depend on the relationship established between group members and their leader. If the norms of the group permit a single person to make a decision, there may be no problem. If this is not the group norm but the group members feel that the chair or leader has listened carefully to their ideas, then the group may not quibble with decision by authority. Routine decisions would most likely fall into this category. On the other hand, when a decision calls for commitment and group support for its implementation, then decision by authority is not a good choice.

Groups may hesitate to carry out an action, or at least not do so with enthusiasm, if members feel they have contributed little to the decision. An even worse condition would be for the authority figure to go through the motions of calling a group together and asking for the participants' advice but, in reality, to have made the decision without the input of others. The pretense that there is consultative decision making can be more harmful than an up-front declaration of, "I would like your advice, but I will be making the decision." In sum, a routine decision, one that does not require the development of many proposals, or a decision in which the time for consultation is not available, as in an emergency situation—these can effectively be made by authority rule. This is not true of the decision affecting many individuals over a period of time, however.

3. Decision by Minority Rule

It is hard to conceive of situations in which a minority view becomes the prevailing view, since so much of our political rhetoric assumes that majority rule should prevail. Yet a small number of articulate, dominant, or powerful individuals can have this effect. They succeed because they employ tactics that promote their views. For example, a few members can agree on an action and present it to the group with a comment like, "Does anyone object to this?" If no one speaks up immediately, the presumption is that everyone agrees. Only after the fact, as researchers have discovered, do members who were silent during such a discussion indicate that they really did not agree (Janis 1982). They tend to go along with the majority because they do not want to obstruct what they perceive as group agreement. (We will talk more about this tendency to succumb to group pressure later on in the chapter.) Another tactic, similar to this one and also leading to a decision by minority, is to make statements such as, "Well, I think we can all agree that Amy's idea is the best we can get, so let's go with it"; or "If we don't decide something right away, we may be meeting here far into the night." Such statements have the effect of inducing other members to accept proposals they might not necessarily have chosen without the pressure.

A decision by minority also affects a group's decision about procedures. A leader can announce, "We don't have a great deal of time, so why don't we all express our views, and then we'll take a vote." If the group goes along, participants may lose a chance to determine what procedures they should be using, as well as the opportunity for a full, open discussion. Unfortunately, it sometimes takes a while before group members realize they have been "railroaded" into making a decision. Some decisions do not require a great deal of time, and there are occasions when a group will consider and subsequently accept a report proposed by a minority of members. Nevertheless, members should be aware when their decision rights are being forfeited to a few dominant individuals.

4. Decision by Majority Rule

If you want to know how members view an issue, you can ask them. This can be done by informal polling or, more formally, by asking members to vote. While this practice is the primary mode of our political system, its effectiveness as a method of group decision making is open to question. Most of its undesirable effect come from the polarization that accompanies voting. The act of voting brings with it an outcome of winners and losers. While being on the winning side can produce euphoria, a member of the minority may feel thwarted and even resentful. This is the difficulty with majority rule—it leads to the creation of coalitions, or even cliques, when it would be preferable for group members to work together, interdependently, to complete a task. Clearly, voting will be useful during many episodes of a group's life, especially when members agree that they are willing to abide by a vote. But just as the group should be watchful of rule by minority decision, members should also be alert for the appropriate and fair use of majority rule.

Majority and minority decisions in groups are not the same phenomena as in political voting. A presumption of our political system is that political minorities have the right to compete on equal terms in an election. Thus they have the potential to become the majority. On the other hand, if polarized coalitions are permitted to develop in groups, then members who find themselves in the minority may justifiably feel that they will *never* have a chance to prevail. The question for a group becomes, Will the use of voting be detrimental to the maintenance of a healthy climate? Unless voting is necessary for deciding some procedural or routine issue, or if there is not enough time for extended deliberation, it may not be the best method to use.

5. Decision by Consensus

Consensus decision making is thought to produce more desirable outcomes for the group than polling and majority decision making. The assumption of decision by consensus is that everyone has agreed to a position after a fair and reasonable discussion, although not everyone will hold the same view. Consensus requires having a "sense of the group." It is based on a presumption that all participants have had an equal opportunity to raise issues and to influence the direction a group will take. E. H. Schein (1969), a theorist of organizational behavior, describes consensus as a process in which a participant would express something like the following:

> I understand what most of you would like to do. I personally would not do that, but I feel that you understand what my alternative would be. I have had sufficient opportunity to sway you to my point of view but clearly have not been able to do so. Therefore, I will gladly go along with what most of you wish to do (p. 56).

For consensus to take place, a group must be willing to spend a sufficient amount of time listening to all views. Members would have to agree that the decision warrants careful discussion—active participation and active listening—so that all members can feel that they have been understood.

Though potentially an effective method of satisfying the needs of group members for a full hearing, consensus has some problems as well. If members have been pressured to agree, or if they agree for the sake of unanimity, or if a group settles too soon for an agreed-upon position without an in-depth look at the merits of alternative positions, then consensus could very well produce decisions of poor quality. Other disadvantages are that it can be time-consuming and susceptible to abuse. The advantage of decision by consensus is that it provides participants with a setting in which they can be heard, present divergent views, argue, or bring forth new data.

What is evident from an examination of these methods of decision making is that each method has some advantages and some disadvantages. Each might be useful, depending on the context in which a decision is to be made. Which method should be used will be a function of the amount of time that is available, the complexity of the decision (programmed or nonprogrammed), the extent of group acceptance or commitment needed, and the consequences for group action. What is important is the fact that each method has consequences for group members' satisfaction with the decision as well as their commitment to carry out the decision, and how each decision method affects the quality and the acceptance of the decision. The failure to establish some type of systematic procedure for coming to decision as well as for estimating the likely consequences of a decision method could hinder a group's effort at reaching a good decision.

MAKING THE "GOOD" DECISION

If the members of your group find that the decisions they have made are neither satisfying to them nor confront effectively the problems that have been identified, then the question becomes, "What may have prevented the group from making the 'good' or 'effective' decision? How can it avoid similar mistakes next time?" This section will explore some answers to these questions.

Lack of Vigilance

According to Janis and Mann (1977), two social psychologists who have written insightfully about decision-making processes, a group is susceptible to making unfortunate errors, a condition they called *lack of vigilance.* Groups displaying a lack of vigilance are likely to engage in defensive avoidance. This is a reaction in which group members will not investigate viewpoints or data contradicting their own perspective. Nor will they allow anyone in their group to focus on potential defects in the group's proposed solution. Once participants have chosen a solution, these groups seem to develop an unwarranted optimism about their choice. They become the equivalent of "true believers"—individuals who are so convinced of the rightness of their cause that no amount of logical arguments will change their thinking. In these circumstances, members rely on shared rationalizations and stereotypic thinking to support their choice of solution. They may begin to use any number of slogans "We're the best," "Everyone else is wrong," and the like to bolster their choice, even though these slogans have little to do with the facts of the situation.

A group that suffers from a lack of vigilance displays some of the following interactions.

1. *Members are influenced by those they believe to be of high status* (Moore 1968). The influence of the high-status member may be an unconscious one. Members may simply desire to affiliate with

such a person or, depending on the amount of power that the high-status person has (or is thought to have), may fear that the person can do them harm. Whichever the case, the influence of status alters independence in decision making.

2. *Members may become too insulated from other groups and other resources.* When members of a group talk only to each other, they tend to reinforce each other's views. Groups that believe that they have all the appropriate and necessary information, expertise, and abilities, are apt to assume that they are making rational decisions. At the same time, they suspect that other groups are biased and irrational.

3. *Members seldom have a definite procedure for searching out information and evaluating solution proposals.* As Hirokawa (1980) observed, effective groups discuss procedural matters (how to go about solving the problem, how to evaluate the relevance of sources) to a greater extent than do the less effective decision-making groups. Decisions can also be faulty if based only on the views of the most persuasive advocate. This does not mean that individuals should not argue for their point of view. In fact, argument can be instrumental in allowing a group to make a choice among alternatives, provided that the group tolerates such a climate and that the evaluation of information and alternatives is thorough (Schultz 1982). What is important is that groups take the time to examine thoroughly their data and to establish some type of procedural system to aid the decision-making process (Gouran and Hirokawa 1983).

The Groupthink Phenomenon

Janis' concept of *groupthink,* a term he used to describe historical decisions that became fiascoes, evolved from his analysis of the conditions leading to a lack of vigilance. Janis (1982) points out how, even at the highest levels of government, decision makers are affected by the damaging symptoms of groupthink. Let's examine a few of these historical "fiascoes" to illustrate the difficulties a group may encounter when trying to reach a decision.

Pearl Harbor   The question Janis asked was, How was it possible for a large portion of the U.S. Pacific Fleet to be lined up in the Hawaiian harbor, exposed to air attack, when the admirals in command knew, or should have known, that Japan would enter the war on the side of the Axis powers (Germany and Italy) against the Allied powers (United States, USSR, Britain, France), and that they would attack the U.S. fleet somewhere in the Pacific? Janis uses the Japanese attack on Pearl Harbor in 1941 as an example of some of the symptoms of groupthink—a sense of "invulnerability," "shared rationalizations," "stereotypic thinking," and "unwarranted optimism."

Janis concludes that those in command probably engaged in the following scenario: The United States is the most powerful country in the world (invulnerable); thus Japan, a third-rate power (stereotypic thinking), would never do something so foolish as to attack the U.S. fleet; if Japan did, the U.S. would obliterate that country (shared rationalization, unwarranted optimism). Affected by the symptoms of groupthink, the admirals took no defensive precautions, and the rest is history. Japan attacked Pearl Harbor; all the ships in the harbor were destroyed. It was a stunning defeat for the United States.

Korea Janis cites U.S. decision making in Korea as another example of groupthink. Korea, after World War II, had been divided by the United Nations into two regions, North Korea and South Korea, at the 38th parallel. In 1950, when North Korea invaded South Korea, the United States entered the war between the two Koreas in support of South Korea. After several months of battle, the North Korean army was defeated, but the U.S. decision makers decided to pursue the defeated North Korean army across the 38th parallel up to the border of China. This decision was made despite numerous warnings that China would enter the war in support of North Korea, if U.S. and South Korean troops crossed the 38th parallel.

For Janis, the question is, Why was the threat by China discounted? The answer, as in the case of Pearl Harbor, was that U.S. decision makers assumed that their side was invincible and that the other side was inferior. The belief in their own invulnerability, along with shared beliefs about the inferiority of China, led to a disastrous decision. U.S. decision makers shared a belief that China was a "puppet" of the Soviet Union; and since it was known that the Soviet Union did not want to enter a ground war (it had suffered a loss of 22 million people in World War II), they believed that China would not act unilaterally. That the assumptions about China were erroneous was confirmed when our troops crossed into North Korea. Within a few weeks after the decision to pursue the defeated North Korean army, the Chinese attacked in massive force, trapping entire U.S. units and compelling the rest to withdraw hastily, in what has been labeled "the longest retreat in American history" (Janis 1982, 53).

Counteracting Groupthink

It is often very difficult for a group to admit that its decision processes were faulty or that its members have made an error in judgment (Gouran 1982; Nisbett and Ross 1980). Once a group has ac-

cepted a decision, even if the decision was a result of faulty processes or of unreliable evidence, the members tend to keep supporting the original decision. They may agree to "cover up" their error,
as in former President Nixon's Watergate fiasco, or use such strategies as attacking or ignoring an opposing view.

An unfortunate illustration of this tendency to push ahead,
disregarding negative findings, occurred with the decision to manu-
facture the drug thalidomide. The medication was to be used as an
antidote for the nausea women may experience in the early months
of pregnancy. Although one researcher employed by the Food and
Drug Administration (FDA) indicated that there were serious side
effects associated with using the drug, her opposition was not sufficient to overcome a majority view that there would be no serious
harmful effects. As we now know, the drug was marketed, and only
after the horror of babies born with severe deformities was it taken
off the market. As this example suggests, dissenting voices seem to
have a great deal of difficulty being heard. It is all too easy to demean
an opponent, to be too certain of the rightness of one's own view, and
to rely on stereotypes to discount opposing views.

There are a number of potential flaws in decision making that
keep a group from making the "good" decision. But groups can counteract these flaws. The potential for making effective decisions is
enhanced when groups employ the following steps.

1. *Groups need to reconsider alternatives initially evaluated as
unsatisfactory.* By being open to new ideas, groups counteract the
tendency to draw on limited amounts of information or their inclination to take "cognitive shortcuts" (Stein and Tanter 1980). In this
way members can learn whether they have overlooked potential
gains of previously rejected proposals. They will need to engage in
a thorough search for essential information. And, in so doing, the
emphasis should be on "search," employing a large number of activities to help ferret out possible routes for making a choice.

2. *Groups need to re-examine their choices.* They should look
again at the risks and drawbacks that may not have been given
sufficient attention when their decision choice was first evaluated.
In the initial stages of inquiry, some proposals get rejected when
they may be worth considering. Going over the process again can
often be a fruitful practice. The larger picture may come into view.
As Simon observed in his comparison of decisions made by chess
masters and novices, the two groups go through similar decision
processes, but the repertoires of the masters are larger (Janis and
Mann 1977, 388). They simply see more of the potential consequences of alternative moves, not only for the immediate play but
for what each move portends for subsequent moves.

3. *Groups need to consider how easy it is to accept the information and judgments of the people who support them and to neglect*

the views of critics who oppose them. Groups that acknowledge this tendency would make certain that they take steps to surmount this proclivity. A group could benefit by consulting with experts who could provide additional evaluation of the advantages and disadvantages of proposed courses of action. Hearing from sources not directly involved in the group's deliberations offers a group the potential for fresh insights. Critical evaluations within and outside the group can help offset pressures for group conformity.

4. *Groups need to put together contingency plans to use if they cannot get their original policy enacted.* They also should recognize that the objectives they wish to achieve could be thwarted by poor information, by political opposition, by organizational failure, or by some other unanticipated event. Even when a group believes it has analyzed the decision carefully, it is still wise to double-check.

A FINAL COMMENT

Decision making is an intricate process. While it is difficult to understand all the factors that allow a group to make any decision, let alone a "good" decision, some of what we know can help. For one thing, groups do better if they have agreed on some procedure for a systematic gathering of information. For another, to reach a decision of quality, one that meets the requirements of the task, a group must use several process components—a search for information, an examination of alternatives, and an estimation of how good the match is between the solution and the objectives of the group. Throughout its deliberations, a group has to be certain that the processes and methods for decision have allowed the quality and acceptable decision to emerge and, at the same time, to be mindful of the constraints that prevent a proposed solution from taking effect.

A group should consider setting reasonable standards and reasonable goals. Participants should realize that excessive idealism can lead to solutions that are unreasonable. On the other hand, it is also important to recognize that good decisions do not necessarily promote desirable outcomes. For example, because of time pressures, a group may have made a good decision to take a direct flight to a conference, even though it was not as economical as a flight with intervening stops. But if the flight was delayed because of mechanical problems, making the group later than would have been the case with the less direct flight, the original decision was not a "bad" one, even though the outcome was. To increase their likelihood of success, however, group members can, as William Morris observes, play with an "eye to the odds or probabilities of various cards being drawn and various hands occurring" (1972, 21). In making a decision, a group will have to estimate what the relationship should be among goals, experiences, and expectations to satisfy members' criteria for reasonableness.

Members should recognize that a group is usually in a stressful situation during the decision-making stage. Therefore, a group should be watchful of the interpersonal needs of its members (Phillips 1973). They should understand that people will not perform adequately if members do not feel secure, accepted, or competent about their participation. Members need to examine the degree of trust that has been established, the extent to which power and influence are shared in the group, and the possible existence of unresolved issues stemming from differences over personal goals and the goals of the group (Napier and Gershenfeld 1981).

To be in a group that fails to come to decision can be a very frustrating experience. But before participants conclude that their group has failed because of "personality clashes" or "irreconcilable differences," they should examine some of the other conditions that can bring failure. They should be leary of the search for the "right" solution or such killer phrases as, "It can't be done," or "We've tried that before." If members can learn to reduce the number of barriers that keep them from looking at a problem in new and different ways, if they can learn to "reframe" the problem—to say it in other ways, to try other definitions, to filter out the extremes, to compare the problem with other problems that have been encountered—then the group is going beyond the typical, ordinary way of looking at a problem. Participants will have learned that the decision-making task, complex as it is, can become a very creative and satisfying experience.

SUMMARY

This chapter has discussed the second phase of problem solving, when groups make choices among alternative proposals. Groups can be aided in this process by "fractionating" the problem—breaking it down into subproblems. This will help the members focus on the various issues related to the major problem. If participants are able to resolve more manageable problems, then they can more likely deal with the larger problem. Fractionating a problem also helps members to work on achieving more reachable goals.

In deciding among proposed solutions, participants should concentrate on understanding the differences between the quality of a decision and it acceptability, on weighing the importance of the decision task—whether it is a routine or a complex decision—and on determining how much time and resources to devote to the task. "Optimizing decisions" are those that merit greater expenditure of resources. "Satisficing decisions" are the result of a concern for feasibility.

Another step in the second phase of decision making involves the implementation of a solution and, especially, members' accountability for carrying out the proposed solution. Without specific instructions for implementation, even the best-intended proposals may fail.

The final checkpoint in the second phase is evaluation—measuring the effectiveness of a group's solution. Groups can use forecasting; by comparing their solution with others that have been tried, members can attempt to predict likely outcomes. Participants can also use such techniques as questionnaires, interviews, and surveys to evaluate their proposal.

While there are many paths for arriving at effective decisions, a group is more likely to make a wise choice if it considers a goodly number of reasonable alternatives and determines what procedures will be adopted for making the decision. Five methods are discussed. Decision by lack of response occurs when ideas are suggested but bypassed simply because no group member reacts to them, either positively or negatively. In decision by authority rule, the final determination is made by a leader or by a single individual rather than by the group. A small group within the larger group may agree on an action and present it to the group; if no one raises objections or other comments immediately, it is assumed that the entire group accepts the proposal, and thus the decision is by minority rule. Decision by majority rule takes place when at least 51 percent of the members agree on an idea. Although such democratic practices are widely acceptable in the political process, they may be less desirable in a small group setting. Victory by the majority may lead to the formation of polarized coalitions. Finally, in what may be the most useful method of decision making, members can achieve decision by consensus. In this practice, the views of every member are aired, so that everyone has an equal chance to try to persuade the others. Ideas that are not acceptable by the group are eventually discarded. One problem with this procedure is that members may accept a proposal simply to be accommodating; another drawback is that it is time-consuming.

In the last section, the chapter explores how groups can make good decisions more likely to occur. For one thing, members need to be alert to the phenomenon known as lack of vigilance. They should be sensitive, for instance, to the influence of high-status people or experts who make them feel less confident about their own judgments, deterring them from questioning the experts; they should also avoid insulation from other groups and resources. Moreover, participants will have to be watchful that they do not become susceptible to the symptoms of "groupthink." They will have to check any inclination to be overly optimistic, to engage in rationalizations, and to believe that they are invulnerable. They will need to learn to be leary of any proposal that keeps them from a thorough examination of the information and the objectives they wish to achieve. With a commitment to making the "good" decision, incorporating counteracting measures for decision flaws, and evaluating both the adequacy of the decision process and the consequences of their choice, groups can learn to make effective and satisfying decisions.

REFERENCES

Bardach, E. 1977. *The Implementation Game: What Happens After a Bill Becomes a Law.* Cambridge, Mass.: MIT Press.

Gouran, D. S. 1982. "A Theoretical Foundation for the Study of Inferential Error in Decision-Making Groups." Paper presented to Conference on Small Group Research, Pennsylvania State University.

Gouran, D. S., and R. Y. Hirokawa. 1983. "The Role of Communication in Decision-Making Groups: A Functional Perspective." Paper presented to the Speech Communication Association Convention, Washington, D.C.

Hackman, J. R., and C. G. Morris. 1975. "Group Tasks, Group Interaction Process, and Group Performance Effectiveness: A Review and Proposed Integration." In L. Berkowitz (ed.), *Advances in Experimental Social Psychology* (vol. 8). New York: Academic Press, pp. 1–55.

Hirokawa, R. 1980. "A Comparative Analysis of Communication Patterns Within Effective and Ineffective Decision-Making Groups." *Communication Monographs* 47:312–321.

Janis, I. L. 1982. *Groupthink: Psychological Studies of Policy Decisions and Fiascoes.* Boston: Houghton Mifflin.

Janis, I. L., and L. Mann. 1977. *Decision Making: A Psychological Analysis of Conflict, Choice, and Commitment.* New York: Free Press.

Lindblom, C. E. 1959. "The Science of Muddling Through." *Public Administration Review* 19:79–99.

Lott, A. J., and B. E. Lott. 1961. "Group Cohesiveness, Communication Level, and Conformity." *Journal of Abnormal and Social Psychology* 62:408–412.

Luft, J. 1970. *Group Processes: An Introduction to Group Dynamics.* Palo Alto, Calif.: National Press.

Maier, N. R. F. 1963. *Problem-Solving Discussions and Conferences.* New York: McGraw-Hill, pp. 1–19.

March, J., and H. Simon. 1958. *Organizations.* New York: John Wiley, pp. 140 ff.

Moore, J. C., Jr. 1968. "Status and Influence in Small Group Interactions." *Sociometry* 3:47–63.

Morris, W. T. 1972. *Management for Action.* Reston, Va.: Reston Publishing.

Napier, R. W., and M. K. Gershenfeld. 1981. *Groups: Theory and Experience.* Boston: Houghton Mifflin.

Nisbett, R. E., and L. Ross. 1980. *Human Inference: Strategies and Shortcomings of Social Judgment.* Englewood Cliffs, N.J.: Prentice-Hall.

Patton, B. R., and K. Giffin. 1978. *Decision-Making Group Interaction.* New York: Harper & Row, pp. 148–155.

Phillips, G. M. 1973. *Communication and the Small Group.* Indianapolis: Bobbs-Merrill.

Schein, E. H. 1969. *Process Consultation: Its Role in Organizational Development.* Reading, Mass.: Addison-Wesley, pp. 46–58.

Schultz, B. 1982. "Argumentativeness: Its Effect in Group Decision-Making and Its Role in Leadership Perception." *Communication Quarterly* 30:-368–375.

Shaw, M. E. 1981. *Group Dynamics: The Psychology of Small Group Behavior.* (3rd ed.). New York: McGraw-Hill.

Simon, H. A. 1960. *The New Science of Management Decision.* New York: NYU School of Commerce, Accounts, and Finance.

Simon, H. A. 1976. *Administrative Behavior* (3rd ed.). New York: Macmillan.

Stein, J. G., and R. Tanter. 1980. *Rational Decision-Making: Israel's Security Choices.* Columbus: Ohio State University Press.

Steiner, I. D. 1972. *Group Process and Productivity.* New York: Academic Press.

chapter 8

Conflict in the Group

How do you react to the term *conflict?* One scholar has predicted three types of responses. Kenneth Benne (1980) believes that if you were asked to free-associate to the term *conflict,* you might use words with morbid and negative connotations: *war, death, destruction, aggression, violence.* Some few individuals would name words that have positive connotations: *fun, excitement, drama, adventure.* And, for the third group of responses, the choices would be relatively neutral: *bargaining, mediation, competition.* While some people might produce terms belonging to two or all three groupings, the variation in responses indicates a fundamental ambivalence toward conflict.

What is noticeable about Benne's findings is how apt people are to view conflict in negative terms. On the other hand, theorists of conflict believe that a negative interpretation ignores a basic tenet of human life: conflict is a part of all human interaction and, indeed, an integral part of all enduring relationships (Coser 1956) As Raymond Mack (1975) observed in his study of social conflict, wherever human beings are, there is bound to be conflict, and yet the idea of conflict is generally deplored.

Studies of group communication reveal the consistent presence of conflict and, at the same time, a persistent effort to avoid conflict. Group members tend to hide their feelings of frustration, their disagreements with proposals, or their dissatisfaction with the progress of the group because they do not like to be involved in a conflict situation. Their antipathy toward conflict is so great that they will even sidestep issues, declaring that they are essentially in agreement, even though such action is detrimental to the group's decision-making ability (Wood 1976).

This chapter examines conflict, particularly as it affects the small group. You will find some general propositions about the nature, components, and levels of conflict. The focus will be on the effects of conflict within groups and between groups, including an exercise that will allow you to apply what you have learned about the nature of conflict. In the next chapter we will explore ways of managing conflict so that your group can work on tasks more effectively and with more satisfaction.

THE NATURE OF CONFLICT

You can learn about conflict by exploring the generalizations people hold about its nature. For example, one of the more accepted beliefs is that harmony is the norm in human affairs. Lewis Coser, in his study *The Functions of Social Conflict* (1956), offers a contrasting view. Coser sees conflict as the normal state of affairs for any relationship where people interact. The belief in harmony as normal behavior in all relationships is a powerful myth in our society. When you become aware of how potent these myths about conflict are and examine the contrasting realities, you should have a better understanding of how conflict functions in your everyday world (Doolittle 1982).

The Myths and Realities of Conflict*

Myth. We tend to believe that conflicts are unnatural. We assume that as humans with rational minds we should be able to live in conflict-free relationships.

Reality. From our research on organizations we learn that conflicts are both natural and inevitable. Not only are they natural but, if well used, they can stimulate creative ideas and promote good decision making. Charles Redding, in his survey of the role of communication within organizations (1972), found that a good, healthy organization allowed and even encouraged some degree of disorder and conflict.

Myth. Conflicts occur because of a lack of understanding between individuals in the group or among groups of individuals.

*This section on myths and realities is based on R. G. Doolittle, 1982, "Communication and Conflict." In R. L. Applebaum and R. P. Hart (eds.), *Modcom: Modules in Speech Communication.* Chicago: Science Research Associates.

Reality. There may be some truth to this view, although it is more likely that we will continue to be in conflict, even when we understand someone else's point of view, because we hold such distinctly opposing philosophies. For instance, supporters and opponents of the Equal Rights Amendment probably understand each other, in the sense of grasping the words that express the positions each group has taken. But, undoubtedly, these groups will continue to be in conflict, since their interpretations of how a constitutional amendment would affect the status and civil rights of women are so fundamentally different.

Myth. Conflicts can always be resolved.

Reality. This view reflects an underlying belief that somehow conflict is wrong. It also may be wishful thinking—a desire to be free of the emotional strain that often accompanies a conflict. As one can discern from conflicts such as those between pro- and anti-abortion groups, some clashes are enduring and will continue. For some conditions, it is probably a good thing that conflicts do continue, and even escalate. For instance, the continuing conflicts over race relations, as well as the continuing struggles, have been instrumental in bringing about changes for blacks in job opportunities, education, housing, and civil rights (Doolittle 1982).

Myth. Conflicts should be avoided because they represent breakdowns and deterioration of the social fabric of society.

Reality. Undoubtedly, conflicts are and have been destructive, as in the conflicts between ethnic or religious groups—the recurring clashes between the Protestants and the Catholics in Northern Ireland or the battles between the Palestinians and the Israelis, for example. But, at the same time, suppressing conflicts or not allowing dissenting groups to challenge existing laws does not mean that conflicts will go away. The dissident groups may go underground, but the conflicts do not end.

Myth. One of the more persistent myths is that conflicts represent breakdowns in communication. When Cool Hand Luke, as a prison escapee about to be shot in the motion picture of the same name, shouted at the sheriff, "What we have here is a breakdown in communication," he was, alas, confirming what many of us assume: "breakdown," or the absence of communication, is responsible for the problem.

Reality. The term *breakdown* does not describe what is actually happening. Although we tend to believe that disagreement occurs when people have stopped communicating with one another, "breakdown" is more likely to take place when the communication has not been handled well. It is a result more of not knowing how to manage a conflict situation than because communication has been avoided. When we are in conflict with another person, we may indeed avoid communicating with him or her. But adding "more" communication that is "bad" communication does not help with the management of the conflict (Fisher 1980).

We are confronted, then, with two divergent views about the nature of conflict: (1) conflict is inherently destructive; it can lead to the breakup of a relationship or destroy a group; and (2) conflict, although stressful, can stimulate ideas, spur creativity, and inspire innovativeness (Coser 1956; Torrance 1957). There is some merit in both positions. Whether conflict will be perceived as natural or unnatural, however, will depend on how the conflict is defined.

The Components of Conflict

All conflicts, whether between family members, friends, teachers and students, professors and administrators, labor and management, or nations, have certain features in common. The key elements are (1) interdependence, (2) perceived scarce rewards, and (3) incompatible goals. In addition, conflict theorists insist that a conflict is not a conflict until it is expressed (Hocker and Wilmot 1985). We must recognize and admit that a conflict exists before we can settle it. Although a conflict may be expressed in subtle ways, as when two people speak politely to each other but do not engage in any real conversation, the important point is that we cannot deal with a conflict unless we acknowledge verbally (although there may be nonverbal clues as well) that a conflict exists.

How do you know when you are in a conflict? It may surprise you that a shouting match is not the only way to tell. Conflicts can indeed be noisy, but more often than not, people in conflict may not tell each other what disturbs them. In any event, we can recognize the presence of conflict by its distinct components.

1. *Conflict occurs in a context of interdependence.* Interdependence cannot be defined objectively—it is defined by the perceptions and beliefs of the parties in conflict (Folger and Poole 1984). This definition assumes that there cannot be conflict if people interacting do not have an impact on one another. If the action of one does not affect the other, then conflict does not occur. The fact of interdependence helps to explain, in part, why there is such a fear of conflict. Some people may resist telling their roommate to clean up their side of the room because they fear the consequences of a potentially angry partner. A student clashing with a professor over a grade cannot afford to antagonize the professor if the desired change is to be effected. Nor can the professor afford to alienate the student if his or her reputation as a fair teacher is to be upheld. A leader of a task group cannot insult one of the members and expect others in the group not to be affected by such behavior.

The concept of interdependence also provides the basis for learning how to deal with conflict. Interdependence implies that since conflict affects all parties (whether a group, organization, or a community), they will need to find some mutually satisfactory and acceptable resolution of the dispute. An assumption of interdependence, then, is that when people are able to recognize their common values, there is hope for some constructive resolution of their problems.

2. *Conflict occurs when there are similarities in needs and values, but the rewards to satisfy these needs and values are scarce or are perceived as scarce* (Hocker and Wilmot 1985). The rewards may be *tangible,* as in money, prizes, bonuses; or *intangible,* as in love, respect, self-esteem. If there is one scholarship available in the history department but two eligible juniors vying for the award, then this is potentially a conflict situation. It is not the difference in needs that is at issue but rather the perceived scarcity of the resource.

Hocker and Wilmot underscore this point, stating that in a conflict, regardless of the substantive issue, the parties in conflict usually believe that there is a scarcity—a shortage of power and/or self-esteem reward. Finding a way to increase the scarce goods (scholarships) or finding other cooperative ways for both students to gain support and recognition may be a way to offset the potential hostility between the two contenders.

Conflict is an inevitable feature of any group's interaction.

3. *Conflict occurs when there are perceived incompatible goals, whether stated or unstated.* Goals represent a multiplicity of desires, some of which are tangible and others of which are merely hoped for and thus intangible (Hocker and Wilmot 1985). I may

oppose the establishment of a fruit and vegetable market across from my apartment complex because I like an unobstructed view from my window, but other apartment dwellers would be in favor of the market because it would be convenient for shopping. My desire for an unobstructed view and their desire for convenient shopping are goals that are clearly incompatible. Handling this type of conflict will take more than a statement of positions. It will require learning some methods for managing conflict, a topic we will discuss in the next chapter. Sometimes, however, goals are only perceived as incompatible, and when we are willing to discuss our positions, we may find that they are not so different after all.

Levels of Intensity of Conflict

Conflict appears in many forms. We are in conflict with other group members when we do not want to meet with them outside of class. We have conflict when we favor a "no smoking" regulation for dining rooms and smokers say, "What about our rights?" Other types of conflict emerge between nations over boundary lines and territory or within a nation between ideological factions—conservatives and liberals, Democrats and Republicans. Conflict is more obviously exposed when, for example, we read of armed struggles between supporters of the Sandinistas and supporters of the "contras" in Nicaragua.

Another point: Although most of us would rather not have conflict, we do not always respond to conflict negatively. Conflict appears to be an essential part of our political system. We live in a system that emphasizes competition in the marketplace. We support the right of freedom of speech and believe that competing ideas should be debated. Our judiciary system pits plaintiffs against defendants.

Some conflicts can be exhilarating. We cheer winners in competitive sports. Who can doubt that conflict exists among swimmers trying out for the Olympics or for runners hoping to be first in the Boston Marathon? In these examples, conflict is viewed positively. But when people are asked to use conflict in working out their goals or in fine-tuning their ideas, conflict appears to arouse either ambivalence or a negative reaction.

Perhaps part of the problem comes from the many terms of varying intensity we use to describe conflicts: *disagreement, combat, confrontation, competition.* We also confound the problem by using qualifying phrases such as, "We're just having a friendly disagreement." People who like to distinguish between "conflict" and "disagreement" tend to think of the former as the more emotionally intense term, and the latter as the calmer, more rational term.

Hocker and Wilmot (1985) believe that such a differentiation may not be a useful one.

Doubtless we would like to believe that "conflict" is somehow different from "disagreement." What is evident is that we can express sarcasm, sadness, or even anger when we are having a disagreement. In this sense, disagreements, verbal attack, sarcasm, put-downs, and competitive or destructive behaviors refer to the different ways that we respond to a conflict, but these terms do not negate the fact that a conflict is taking place. Although the various terms represent differences in degree, the important learning is that while conflicts can vary in their level of intensity, they are all conflicts and will have to be handled (Doolittle 1982).

A VIEW OF CONFLICT IN THE GROUP

A basic premise of the use of conflict in general also applies specifically to the group. Conflict is both a natural and an inevitable feature of any group's interaction. What is worth emphasizing, however, is that while conflict can be useful to a group, if it is not well used, it can be detrimental. Conflict will be valuable to the extent that it is perceived as substantive and constructive. For example, as one participant in a task group explained:

> Phil often disagreed with our decisions. Even though he played the role of "blocker" sometimes, he really helped us with his criticisms. He made us see things that we, at first, were unwilling to look at. I think because we liked each other, we tended to agree with each other, rather than causing a conflict. Yet with Phil offering a different view, we found that our group could also disagree without thinking that our efforts were to no avail. In fact, the more we interacted and felt comfortable with each other, the easier it became to comment on where we did not agree. We seemed to be following George Simmel's theory that conflict is inevitably a "form of sociation."

In this situation, the writer saw the conflict as useful. Expressing disagreements allowed issues to emerge that needed to be confronted. On the other hand, if the conflict had been too prolonged, too heated, and with no resolution in sight, then it could have been seen as harmful to the group.

Sources of Group Conflict

The dynamics of the group provides the stimulus for conflict. Even when members of a group have some sense of what they want to achieve, they can become bogged down when it comes to making a decision. They may argue over what procedures to use. They may disagree with how tasks have been assigned, when and how often the group should meet, and how a decision is to be made and who is to make it. The more difficult the decision task, the more likelihood that there will be controversy and conflict.

Group members will disagree over a host of other matters: the roles that each member will play in the group, the leadership in the group, and the degree of influence that individual members will have. There is also the problem of the *hidden agenda.* Often group members have issues that are of concern to them, but they do not bring these out directly. Their underlying concerns are not revealed because of a fear that others will regard such matters as unacceptable or perhaps even foolish. Although there is not an overt conflict, the group seems not to be able to function well. The items in the hidden agenda are having an undesirable effect and will have to be aired if the group is to accomplish its task.

Any heterogeneous group is bound to have people with unique personalities interacting in their own unique styles, which can lead to additional clashes. Conflicts over status, for instance, can appear as conflicts over ideas. And as groups continue working together, other forces will also produce conflict—new members entering the group, old members leaving, deadlines, and other demands.

Even before a group meets, there is the potential for conflict. Members may have very different ideas about what is supposed to happen when they do meet. Members will disagree about goals. They will also disagree about the means to achieve these goals. Conflicts over goals can be very serious, and perhaps more serious than conflicts over means (Coser 1956). Most conflicts will occur, however, because of the differences between what some individuals want and need and what other members of a group want and need.

An example will illustrate the point. Some residents of an apartment house on Long Island, responding to a series of muggings in their vicinity, sent notices to their neighbors as well as to other apartment residents in the neighborhood, suggesting that people concerned about safety meet to discuss the formation of a neighborhood organization to do something about the problem. Because so many of the residents were elderly and frightened by the reported muggings, many turned out for the first meeting. Presumably, the participants shared the same goal. They would all want to form an organization that would deal with the problem.

The assumption of shared goals was not borne out, however. There was immediate conflict over whether an organization was needed. Some residents felt that a large organization would be unable to deal with the problem. Others did not think they had any power to deal with the issue—it should be left to the police. Still others thought that a private detective agency should be hired. And so it went. That a group will have conflict over goals is predictable. Indeed, that there will be differences in what group members want to accomplish should be considered a fundamental tenet of group behavior.

When Interests Clash

When the differences among individuals result in a clash of interests, we have a condition called a *mixed motive situation* (Gouran 1982). This is a situation in which people have to make choices between their own needs and what appears to be the divergent needs of the group. Many situations bring about mixed motive interaction. It could arise between people who have to work together but have different styles in the way they tackle a project. It can stem from a perception of inequity. One individual may believe that he or she is putting more effort into a project than the the other person is. More often, a mixed motive situation reflects the ambivalences as well as the interdependencies of participants in the group. The question becomes, How do individual members serve the interests of the group without sacrificing their own interests?

A number of researchers have used game theory to illustrate the ambivalent reactions to conflict situations (Rapoport 1960; Deutsch 1969; Schelling 1960). They have used the game Prisoner's Dilemma to prove how difficult it is to make choices when there is such uncertainty about what course of action to take.

Prisoner's Dilemma   In this classic example, two thieves in cahoots have been caught and await trial. They are locked in isolated cells and kept incommunicado. The district attorney goes to each one and offers a deal. They are informed that they have only two choices: "Confess and implicate the other or keep silent." If only one confesses and implicates the other, then he goes free, while the other "takes the rap," a prison sentence of five years. If both confess, then they will both go to prison, but with shorter sentences of four years. If both remain silent, however, each will go free because the D.A. cannot make a case without a witness.

How should each thief act? In all conflict situations, each person's moves influence the structure of the conflict (Hocker and Wilmot 1985). If you are having a hard time jumping into the pool and your friend yells, "If you don't jump in, I'll splash you," she is setting out the *choices* for you—stay out or jump in—and the *payoffs*—get splashed or don't get splashed. As individuals contemplate what to do, they have a choice of using cooperative or competitive behavior. In the example of the Prisoner's Dilemma, thief A can think to himself, if thief B does not confess, then I can go free by confessing. But what if thief B does confess and I do not? Then I get five years in jail. So regardless of what B does, I had better confess and implicate B. Of course, thief B will reason in the same pattern. So both confess, and both get four years.

Obviously, the best solution would have been if neither had confessed, but this would have required that each thief act with the interests of both in mind. The game hinges on the uncertainty about what the other would do. Although it takes a while, most individuals playing this game eventually learn that the way to maximize their gains is to go for a collaborative solution. When individuals cooperate, they find more productive ways of dealing with conflict, whereas in the Prisoner's Dilemma, a lack of trust and competitiveness led to destructive behavior. Game theory shows us that human beings, corporations, nations—all could benefit if they were to trust one another and go for equitable, cooperative solutions.

Types of Group Conflict

Before a group can deal with a conflict, members have to sort out what type of conflict they are having. The most frequently used labels describing types of conflict are *productive* and *destructive* (or *realistic* and *unrealistic*). Two other terms, *integrative* and *distributive,* also describe opposing ways of approaching conflict.

Productive and Destructive   Productive conflict promotes the finding of the good solution or the accomplishment of a goal; destructive conflict leaves issues unresolved and relationships strained (Deutsch 1969). Lewis Coser (1956), using different terminology but emphasizing a similar concept, labeled the productive conflict as *realistic* and the destructive conflict as *unrealistic.* Productive or realistic conflict is desirable conflict, consisting of a discussion of controversial issues, of opposing issues, and of argument—all of which are means to an end.

In contrast, members may lose sight of issues and may use argument to attack another's credibility, to express dissatisfaction with the leader, or to have the last word. Then conflict is no longer a means to an end but an end in itself. While it may satisfy an individual need, it becomes argument disassociated from a group's goal, and thus destructive and unrealistic. The point to be stressed is that conflict is valuable to the extent that it is productive and realistic.

Integrative   Our choices for settling an issue can range from *cooperation* at one end of a continuum, to *competition* at the mid-point, to *warfare* at the end (Doolittle 1982). While it is not obvious that the terms *conflict* and *cooperation* should be linked, we have learned from the definition of productive and destructive conflicts that conflicts can and do take place within a cooperative context.

Integrative is the term used to describe this approach to conflict (*National Training Laboratory Reading Book* 1968). In this context, members of a group will argue over their differences, but because their conflict is over ideas, their focus is on the substantive issues. They do not engage in a personal attack on the honesty or integrity of others. Rather, they explore differences in productive ways.

Individuals who approach a conflict seeking an integrative solution do not typically think in terms of winners and losers (Blake and Mouton 1961). From the sound of it, you may think that a cooperative conflict is really not a conflict, for it goes against your tendency to think of conflicts as inherently destructive. An important assumption of a cooperative conflict, however, is that all parties gain from an agreed-upon solution. While members accept the fact that all participants are motivated by good intentions, they also recognize that to reach an integrative solution, participants will have to use argument and persuasion, and display emotional fire; but with it all, there is an implied agreement that they will work together to find a solution.

Distributive In a competitive type of conflict, participants expect that one side will win and the other side will lose. Although most people enjoy participating in games that test their skill, such as chess or word-building games, the game becomes more damaging when the stakes are high, or in winner-take-all contests. The term used to describe this win–lose situation is *distributive* (*National Training Laboratory Reading Book* 1968).

Distributive means playing a "zero-sum" game—somebody wins at somebody else's expense. When real-life issues are involved—salary, jobs, educational opportunities—then the game imagery of winners and losers can turn destructive. When the psychological costs or the social and economic costs of being on the losing side are too high, then a win–lose concept is fundamentally destructive. If, for example, people are led to believe that there will be a shortage of gasoline and begin hoarding large amounts for themselves, even though they know that others will suffer, then competition can become harmful. When some members of a group make all the decisions and essentially invalidate the contributions of other members of the group, this behavior is bound to make it hard for the group to accomplish its tasks. We probably all have been in this type of situation and have not liked it very much. The negative feelings we experienced undoubtedly account for our negative associations with the term *conflict*.

The extreme position is undoubtedly warfare. When people view themselves as enemies and feel free to use any number of tactics, from verbal abuse to weapons, to take revenge or to subdue their opposition, then they have reached the most destructive form of conflict (Doolittle 1982). In these circumstances, it is difficult to arrange an end to the conflict because the participants do not trust one another and have stopped communicating or do it so poorly that attempts to talk exacerbate the conflict (North, Koch, and Zinnes 1960).

Signs of a Good Conflict   How can you know when you are having a productive conflict? Within your group you can observe that people are flexible in their behavior. As the group searches for a decision, members may engage in a wide range of behaviors—from threat to negotiation, from compromise to withdrawing. But the important observation is that people are using conflict to arrive at mutually acceptable solutions. A productive conflict is based on an assumption that all factions within a group can attain important goals. Therefore, as an observer, you should be able to see people working hard to reach their goals (Folger and Poole 1984).

In a group where a destructive conflict is in process, people behave differently—they operate with a different assumption. Some believe they must win and, thus, others must lose. In this context, there will be much less flexibility among group members; their goals are more narrowly defined, and their aim seems to be directed at each other rather than at what the group desires to achieve. As you observe such a group, you may also see an escalation of the conflict or a number of passive people unable either to de-escalate the conflict or to deal with the issues at hand. In these instances, productive behavior would be impossible. Such destructive patterns of behavior lessen the opportunities as well as the motivation to work together (Deutsch 1968).

While these are two highly contrastive views of conflict in a group, you should also consider an important qualification. Within a productive conflict there will still be competitive elements. People will argue and defend their positions. There may even be a considerable amount of tension and hostility. Or within a destructive conflict, there may be efforts at conciliation. The difference between the two is that the participants in a productive conflict are more willing to change; they are more open to a reconsideration of their positions. In a destructive conflict, with individuals under a great deal more stress than they are able to withstand, views become polarized and members become defensive; it is a situation hardly conducive to resolution.

Benefits of Group Conflict

Learning how to use conflict well can be a bonus to a group. Among the benefits the group receives are the following:

1. A consideration of diverse ideas and perspectives.
2. Participation from many people.
3. More intense involvement with the task.
4. A better understanding of the problem.

Our research shows that groups can make better decisions when they care enough to argue about alternatives (Fisher 1980). In contrast, not accepting the fact that conflict should be a part of a group's inner workings means suppressing dissent, a behavior that interferes with a group's productive exchange of ideas.

Let's examine more specifically why individuals and groups should allow conflict to surface (Coser 1956).

Conflict serves as an antidote to apathy. When you know that it is all right and, indeed, desirable to share differences and that there is support for such expression, you help participants bond together and feel excited about what they are accomplishing. The sharing of emotions allows members to get to know one another in more human ways.

A consultant to small groups expresses the point this way: "Show me a quiet group, and I worry about whether the members will complete their task successfully. A good group is a noisy group. People shout at one another, and they are excited. There is a great deal of satisfaction watching a truly active, noisy, excited group."

Conflict provides a safety valve for the group. When people do not have to deny their feelings because the group accepts expressions of disagreement, then whatever feelings they need to express—disapproval, anger, fear—are allowed. On the other hand, negative feelings that are repressed at the time they occur will come out at another time, when it might not be as appropriate.

Sometimes a group is amazed when a relatively minor incident causes an explosion entirely out of proportion to what was going on in the group—an unexpected Vesuvius. To the observer of such a group, it is clear that some problem in the group's past was not handled when it should have been. Rather than let such emotions build up, an effective group will take the time to deal with a conflict before a burst of emotion takes over.

Conflict encourages a group to examine and manage problems. As noted in Chapter 6, it is only when a "felt difficulty" confronts us that we undertake to diagnose and remedy a problem. During the 1960s in our country, it took riots in the cities, the burning down of buildings, and sit-ins in restaurants, before the United States re-examined existing racial policies and civil rights violations. On the campuses, experimental programs and courses were instituted in response to the demand for more "relevant" education. It took groups marching against U.S. involvement in the war in Vietnam to bring about a change in U.S. policy. And as Lewis Coser points out (1956), it has been the continuing conflicts between labor and management that have brought about the changes in working conditions in our major industries.

Conflict encourages a group to make more accurate decisions. Decision accuracy improves because every individual, with his or her own unique experiences, can bring a singular frame of reference to the group. The clash of ideas opens proposals to more scrutiny and testing than if the clash had not occurred. As Janis observed in his work on "groupthink" (1982), when group members consciously avoid conflicts of ideas, they pay a price. They impair their consideration of important information and alternatives for solution.

Conflict assists a group in reaching decision by consensus (Horowitz 1962; Reicken 1952). Fisher, in his research on group development (1980), found that successful groups apparently will all go through a conflict phase. During this phase, every idea is tested, with some ideas accepted, others modified, and still others rejected. But the way a group goes through a conflict will have differing effects.

When people are in conflict over ideas, they are participating in a communication process in which divergent views are allowed to be expressed. In permitting a diversity of judgments, the group is more likely to reach a "true" consensus, in contrast with a consensus gained from group pressures for conformity. Although groups with emotional conflict may reach consensus, it could be at the expense of dealing with the real problem. In such circumstances, members tend to look for agreement on a less controversial issue, one with which they are more comfortable, while an analysis of the real problem is postponed (Fisher 1980).

Conflict can stimulate useful tension. Experiencing tension and performing better is a concept that permeates the creative arts. Musicians, dancers, actors—all testify that the shot of adrenalin stimulated by their tension before a performance actually improves their performance. For a group working on a task, tension accompanying conflict may encourage a group to make a greater effort to find a way to reduce that tension.

As long as the anxiety does not become destructive, increased tension in a group can often result in a useful examination of goals as members seek ways to understand and to address a conflict situation. Experiencing tension may stimulate the group to reconsider its goals, perhaps to choose one goal over another (Hocker and Wilmot 1985). In this way, the tension can lead to a redefinition of the conflict, because the group is motivated to engage in adaptive behavior that can reduce and even eliminate the conflict.

Why Conflict May Be Resisted

Given the fact that a group can be aided by using conflict well, what keeps a group from promoting conflict as a way to sort out the good from the bad proposal, the relevant from the nonessential idea, the substantive from the unimportant suggestion?

There is no doubt that the myths of conflict, as well as the negative effects people feel in a conflict situation, influence their willingness to use conflict in the group in productive ways. Clearly, emotions are involved when individuals are in a conflict situation. They may feel threatened, or even vulnerable and frightened about their ability to control a tense situation. They may feel embarrassed and unable to face the pressure. In addition, because of a basic fear of conflict, group members may not have the competence to deal with it, or may not have methods for handling dissension. Thus, when a conflict arises, group participants may try to suppress it or get it over with quickly. Such action, as we noted earlier, could lead to a feeling among members of resentment, dissatisfaction, and disappointment with the way the group was responding to their needs.

The avoidance of the underlying tensions can be harmful to the group as a whole too. A presumption that conflicts should be settled quickly carries with it the possibility that the conflict will be resolved in inappropriate ways, either by an unsatisfying compromise or by an inadequate solution.

"Managing" Group Conflicts

On the other hand, research data suggest that a more satisfying resolution of group conflicts can be achieved if members learn the methods for managing them. In fact, the term *managing* has become a replacement for the term *resolving* because managing implies that there are several ways that conflict situations can be settled (Pood 1980; Robbins 1978).

In his study comparing conflict management strategies with conflict resolution strategies, Walker (1976) found that those who adhere to a philosophy of *resolving* conflict view dissension as a disruption of the system, while those who use the term *managing* view conflict as a normal part of any system. The belief in the former leads to steps to eliminate the conflict, even with inappropriate means; an acceptance of the latter facilitates the search for reasonable procedures for dealing with the conflict.

This change in terminology is useful for learning methods that will mediate conflicts. It also leads to the understanding that some conflicts will continue, and in those situations, participants can agree to disagree, yet still be able to work together on other matters. Learning to manage conflicts can mean that the issues in dispute will be handled in ways that are more positive or, at the least, less destructive. What "management" of conflicts implies is that individuals and groups will have to learn to establish and to abide by a set of rules, deciding on areas of agreement, even though not all the conflicting views have been resolved. Chapter 9 will discuss more specifically how you and your group can learn to "manage" conflict. For now, the exercise "Role-Playing an Intergroup Conflict" will help you understand how conflicts once begun can become difficult to handle unless they are managed.

ROLE-PLAYING AN INTERGROUP CONFLICT

This exercise will give you experience participating in an intergroup conflict. By assuming the role of a member of a group that has goals in conflict with those of another group, you can explore how conflicts get started and how people may behave in a conflict situation. Role-playing is an insightful way to learn about your responses and a chance to learn new behaviors.

Procedure

1. The exercise works well with a large group (approximately 15–30). The larger group should be divided into three smaller groups of approximately equal size.
2. Three separate locations would be optimal, but the exercise can be done in one reasonably large room. Each group should be able to huddle as members work on the problem. The groups will need movable chairs, notepaper for recording scores and for sending messages, and large sheets of paper for displaying their proposals.
3. Each group considers the following conflict situation that actually confronted an urban community in the 1970s.

The Situation

During the early part of the 1970s, the issue of busing children to school became a tumultuous one for the residents of South Boston, a largely Irish Catholic, closely knit community. Although other ethnic groups resided in the area, no blacks did. In 1974, when federal judge Arthur W. Garrity ordered the Boston schools to desegregate, the reaction in South Boston ranged from protest marches to violence directed at the buses and at black students. South Boston schools, where the first steps toward desegregation had been ordered, were tremendously affected by the violence.

Residents from South Boston protested vehemently against the concept of busing any of their children out of the neighborhood. Their protests took the form of marches, verbal attacks on the children being bused in, and, unfortunately, some physical violence as well.

Role-Play Activity

Assume that you are a group of white parents of school children who have always gone to their neighborhood schools in South Boston. Now with a federal order handed down, your children are to be part of an experiment for desegregating the schools. The plan is to allow black children from other neighborhoods to attend your previously all-white schools and, at the same time, have your children bused across the city to black neighborhoods to help desegregate previously all-black schools. The role-playing proceeds according to the following steps.

1. Participants in each group, assuming the role of white parents, discuss why they are opposed to busing. Even if these are not your views, you are being asked to try to understand what other parents might be thinking and why there might be good reasons for parents to oppose busing. In this way, the dimensions of the conflict and the depths of feelings associated with it can be articulated.

2. Each group works for approximately 20 minutes constructing its case against busing. After the groups have discussed the case and formulated their arguments, they display their major arguments on sheets of paper. Their arguments are posted for everyone to observe.

3. Now the members of each group choose a spokesperson to be their representative in what will be a three-person debate. The purpose of the debate is to allow everyone to hear each group's case. The objective for the representative is to present the best case that could be used to persuade the City of Boston to continue to oppose busing for South Boston schools, and especially to urge the mayor and the City Council to fight the judge's order in higher courts.

4. The representatives come forward, forming a small inner circle, and their groups sit closely behind them. Then each representative presents the case worked out by the group. The order of presentation can be determined by a toss of a coin.

5. After the cases have been presented, all participants vote by secret ballot for the presentation they consider to be the best one. The method of voting is as follows: Everyone is given a sheet of paper and asked to rank-order the participants. That is, put "1" for the representative with the best case, "2" for the next best, and "3" for the third place. Then, on the same sheet of paper, assign a value to each presentation, from 1 to 10, with 10 signifying the highest rating. After the results of the ranking and the scores for each group are computed, they are posted on sheets of paper or on the blackboard.

6. Each group then consults with its representative. Members discuss ways to change the case to make an even stronger presentation. After approximately 10 minutes, the representatives again come to the center. (The order of presentations may be changed.) They now have the task of persuading the participants that one of them is the best person to present the case to the City Council. They can provide new arguments as well as criticize the presentation of the others.

   Although there is to be no direct communication between group members and representatives during the presentations, members can assist their representative by writing their suggestions on notepaper and passing their notes to their representative. If a group or representative desires, a brief conference can be called.

7. When the presentations are completed, another vote is carried out using the same procedures as before. The participants are to vote for the representative who has presented the best case. These results are also posted.

8. After this tally, members can discuss what they have gained from the role-playing exercise. They can explore how each group voted, and why. They can talk about the general purpose of the exercise and how it affected them. After the discussion the groups can compare their learnings with what theorists have extracted from their research on intergroup conflict, as described under "Comments on the Exercise."

Comments on the Exercise

Conflicts emerge when groups compete for scarce or perceived scarce rewards or when they clash over differing values. Conflicts have a way of continuing with their own momentum and groups become polarized. When groups feel unsuccessful because they believe that other groups stand in their way, or when they see themselves in competition with another group over how resources will be used, the result is an intergroup conflict.

Often these conflicts are exacerbated. Once the conflict begins, the inclination is for groups to stop communicating with each other, to become isolated, to build separate systems for themselves (North, Koch, and Zinnes 1960). Groups will move through a series of changes affecting behavior within the group as well as between groups. When faced with intergroup conflict, groups seldom look for answers within their own group. Rarely will they examine their own methods of working—their procedures, their strategies, their failures. Rather, they will look outside their group for the source of their frustration.

Intergroup conflict has been studied by several researchers (Sherif and Sherif 1953; Blake and Mouton 1961). They have found that groups involved in these conflicts display certain responses that make it difficult to resolve conflicts. Did any of these tendencies occur in your groups?

Did members express a greater sense of loyalty within their groups? Researchers have found that when groups are faced with a common enemy, members will become more tightly knit. They are expected to demonstrate their loyalty to the group. Even when members disagree with the group's position, they are under quite a bit of pressure to go along. At the same time, the climate between themselves and other groups deteriorates. Rather than seeing other groups as diverse, each with their own objectives and skills, they begin to distort or to stereotype what the other group represents (Coser 1956).

Did your group develop greater solidarity because of the conflict? As members become more unified, they begin to display more hostile behavior to the other groups. They will also reduce their communication with the other groups. The decrease in interaction further reduces opportunities for lessening hostile feelings (North, Koch, and Zinnes 1960). It becomes increasingly more difficult to alter distortions and reduce the hostility.

Did members in your group tend to see themselves as superior and the rival group as inferior? What seems to be the case is that negative information about one's own group is discounted, and positive features of the other group are ignored. For example, did your group listen carefully to what their representatives were saying, but pay little attention to what their opponents were saying? Also, under competitive conditions groups are more accepting of authoritarian leadership. They may succumb to less democratic behavior, if they believe that they are in a situation that is not in their control (Blake and Mouton 1961).

The Effects of Conflict Between Groups

In this experiment, the arguments presented by the three groups tend to be fairly similar. Yet asking people to choose a best representative, to strive to be competitive so that they stop working for a common goal, motivates them to become divided. As you may recognize from observing your own behavior and the behavior of others in your group, conflict can occur even when there does not seem to be good reasons for conflict. The role-play experiment simulates competition, which in turn leads to conflict.

Distortions, the inability to see beyond our own position, and the unwillingness to look at mutual goals and interests affect the ability to deal with conflicts. Then the conflict becomes one of argument from personal feelings or loyalty to the group. But when people can alter their focus on personalities, emphasizing instead what needs to be accomplished, then they can learn to use conflicts in productive ways.

Researchers have learned from their analysis of intergroup conflict that if groups are to reduce their hostile behavior toward each other, they will have to look for mutual goals, for what can be called *superordinate* goals (Sherif and Sherif 1958). Looking for mutually accomplishable objectives, or outcomes that all parties believe are worth achieving, is a technique that diverts attention from the differences that divide group members. Learning to collaborate is one of the important methods for minimizing the hostile effects of conflict. The next chapter will explore some methods that individuals and groups can apply to help them manage their conflicts.

A FINAL COMMENT

In managing conflict, a group has to be aware of potential problems. If participants have not engaged in a thorough analysis of the problem, the solution they reach may be a weak one. This is more likely to occur if they have not allowed a sufficient amount of dissent to take place. Additionally, if members ignore tension within the group, they may not be able to accomplish what they had set out to do.

To make conflict a useful part of a group's process, a group must learn not only to accept differences but to confront those differences so that they may be worked out. Participants must learn how to be cooperative and to trust, to be flexible and empathic toward the views of others, but a willingness to be cooperative does not negate using conflict to reach effective solutions. In short, managing conflict is a process of using communication and collaboration to achieve the group's goals.

SUMMARY

This chapter has addressed the issue of attitudes toward conflict in general and, specifically, the behavior of individuals in dealing with conflict in the group. We have stressed that just as conflict is an inevitable occurrence in our everyday lives, it is also an ongoing, natural phenomenon within and among groups. When groups have to decide which solution to adopt, members will have to deal with divergent and competing interests. What makes the management of conflict so difficult is the myth that conflict is unnatural and unwarranted. Negative perceptions and pervasive myths keep people from learning how to manage conflict.

Conflict offers many tangible benefits to a group if issues are discussed openly and thoroughly, but conflict can also be detrimental to a group's morale. The difference in outcomes will depend on whether members engage in productive or destructive conflict. A conflict is considered productive when a group is able to focus on common goals. When a group works collaboratively, participants are more likely to use conflict for productive solutions. When conflict is destructive, members engage in competitive strategies leading to distrust and escalating tension.

The exercise simulating intergroup conflict illustrates how perceived incompatible goals and scarce rewards are the bases of all conflict situations—where negative stereotypes, hostilities directed at an opposing group, and substantial internal group loyalty are likely to arise when one group believes that its goals are unattainable because of the other group. A learning for all groups is provided by the experiment in intergroup competition: to reduce distrust and hostility, establish a superordinate goal. It contributes a framework for achieving mutually satisfying goals.

REFERENCES

Benne, K. D. 1980. "The Management of Conflict." Presented to the Allied Health Professional Training Institute, San Antonio, Texas.

Blake, R. R., and J. S. Mouton. 1961. "Reaction to Intergroup Competition Under Win–Lose Conditions." *Management Science* 4:420–435.

Coser, L. A. 1956. *The Functions of Social Conflict.* New York: Free Press.

Deutsch, M. 1968. "The Effects of Cooperation and Competition upon Group Process." In D. Cartwright and A. Zander (eds.), *Group Dynamics.* New York: Harper & Row, pp. 461–482.

Deutsch, M. 1969. "Conflicts: Productive and Destructive." *Journal of Social Issues* 25:7–41.

Doolittle, R. J. 1982. "Communication and Conflict." In R. L. Applebaum and R. P. Hart (eds.), *Modcom: Modules in Speech Communication.* Chicago: Science Research Associates.

Fisher, B. A. 1980. *Small Group Decision-Making.* New York: McGraw-Hill.

Folger, J. P., and M. S. Poole. 1984. *Working Through Conflict: A Communication Perspective.* Glenview, Ill.: Scott, Foresman.

Gouran, D. S. 1982. *Making Decisions in Groups.* Glenview, Ill.: Scott, Foresman.

Hocker, J. L., and W. W. Wilmot. 1985. *Interpersonal Conflict* (2nd ed.). Dubuque, Ia.: Wm. C. Brown.

Horowitz, I. A. 1962. "Consensus, Conflict, and Cooperation: A Sociological Inquiry." *Social Forces* 41:177–188.

Janis, I. 1982. *Groupthink* (2nd ed.). Boston: Houghton Mifflin.

Mack, R. 1975. "The Components of Social Conflict." *Social Problems* 22:-388–392.

National Training Laboratory Reading Book. 1968. Washington, D.C.: Institute of Applied Behavioral Sciences.

North, R. C., H. E. Koch, and D. A. Zinnes. 1960. "The Integrative Functions of Conflict." *Journal of Conflict Resolution* 4:355–374.

Pood, E. A. 1980. "Functions of Communication: An Experimental Study in Group Conflict Situations." *Small Group Behavior* 11:76–87.

Rapoport, A. 1960. *Fight, Games, and Debates.* Ann Arbor: University of Michigan Press.

Redding, W. C. 1972. *Communication Within the Organization.* New York: Industrial Communication Council.

Reicken, H. W. 1952. "Some Problems of Consensus Development." *Rural Sociology* 17:245–252.

Robbins, S. P. 1978. "Conflict Management and Conflict Resolution Are Not Synonymous Terms." *California Management Review* 21:67–75.

Schelling, T. C. 1960. *The Strategy of Conflict.* Cambridge, Mass.: Harvard University Press.

Sherif, M. 1958. "Superordinate Goals in the Reduction of Intergroup Conflicts." *American Journal of Sociology* 63:356.

Sherif, M., and C. Sherif. 1953. *Groups in Harmony and Tension.* New York: Harper & Row.

Torrance, E. P. 1957. "Group Decision Making and Disagreement." *Social Forces* 35:314–318.

Walker, B. A. 1976. "An Exploratory Study of Conflict Management and Conflict Resolution Strategies in Problem-Solving Groups." Ph.D. dissertation, Michigan State University.

Wood, J. T. 1976. "Leading as a Process of Persuasion and Adaptation." In J. W. Pfeiffer and J. E. Jones (eds.) 1976 *Group Facilitators' Annual Handbook.* Lajolla, Cal.: University Associates, pp. 132–135.

chapter 9

Learning to Manage Conflict

In Chapter 8, we examined attitudes toward conflict, the nature, levels, and benefits of conflict, the forces that generate conflict, and the effects of conflict within a group and between groups. Now it is time to look at measures you and your group can use to improve your handling of conflict. This chapter outlines some basic approaches to managing conflict. It explores the management of conflict from three perspectives: (1) the styles in which people approach conflict, (2) what you as an individual can do to manage conflict, and (3) what the group can do to confront conflict and use it for productive ends.

INDIVIDUAL STYLES IN THE MANAGEMENT OF CONFLICT

A number of researchers have been interested in the styles or strategies that people use when they are in a conflict. They have been studying how effective these styles are in different situations (*National Training Laboratory Reading Book* 1968). Two classification systems emerge from this research: the use of conflict behaviors to satisfy the individual's own needs, and the use of conflict behaviors to satisfy the needs of others. Researchers have broken down these two classifications into five rather distinctive styles (Folger and Poole 1984). As you read over the following list, you can check to see which of the descriptions is closest to the way you would respond to conflict, and which might be your secondary approach, or your back-up style.

1. *A competitive style.* People who use this style have been called "tough battlers," people who are dominant, aggressive, controlling, and demanding (Filley 1975). They tend to be more concerned with their own positions, and lack sensitivity to the views of others. You can recognize this style in such responses as: "Do you call that an offer?" or "I really don't have time for a lengthy discussion. Can we just deal with getting a settlement now?" When competitive people pay attention only to their own needs, they fail to see that at some point they will have to depend on others to help get things done.

2. *An accommodative style.* People who use this style might be thought of as "friendly helpers" (Filley 1975). Although they are cooperative, they are unassertive. Expressions like, "Whatever you want," or "It doesn't matter to me" may be signs of accommodation. Accommodative individuals will give you their friendship, offer you understanding and kindness, but, at the same time, they will not assert their own needs. Because they do not feel comfortable when there is dissension and conflict, they may appease, smooth over, or give in too soon. It is a style that is sometimes characterized as a self-sacrificing and weak approach.

3. *An avoiding style.* In this case, the person is neither assertive nor cooperative. He or she withdraws from or seems to be indifferent to the people or the situation in conflict. "I don't want to be bothered. You settle the matter" or "Don't involve me" are responses that typify the fundamental approach. People who use this style appear to be apathetic, evasive, and isolated. Sometimes there are good reasons to avoid conflicts, but most often avoiders simply refuse to get involved.

4. *A compromising style.* Most of us probably accept this is the best style—a sort of middle point in both cooperation and assertiveness. It reflects a willingness to give up some of what is desired, if the other party is also willing to do so—a "Let's split the difference" phenomenon. Sometimes this approach works. The readiness to engage in a tradeoff will allow both parties in a conflict to gain.

But it is also possible that both sides may lose with a too quickly agreed upon compromise. A rather well-worn tale used by trainers in conflict management illustrates the folly of reaching for compromise too soon.

There are two people and one orange, and both people would like the orange. Well, that's easy, if one uses a typical approach and splits the orange, with each person getting half. But what if you were to learn that one of the parties takes the half, peels it, and throws away the juicy part, while the other party eats the orange sections and throws the peel away? Each had a different need: one wanted the peel to bake a cake, and the other wanted to eat the fruit.

The moral is obvious. Why not look for solutions that meet the needs of both parties? While some people may opt for compromise as the easiest path out of a conflict, such an orientation may not be the best way to resolve a dispute, especially if a bit more time spent working together for a solution could provide an even better outcome.

5. *A collaborative style.* With this style a person has put together a unique combination—he or she ranks high in both cooperation and assertiveness. This is a person who looks at the broader picture, seeking solutions with the other party or parties so that the needs of all parties to a conflict can be met. This style is most often characterized as a problem-solving approach. A collaborator asks, "How can we develop solutions that will meet both our needs?" It is a style in which individuals combine their search for information with an awareness of their own feelings and the feelings of others. They are willing both to express and to clarify their feelings and their reasons for their views.

Did any of these descriptions fit your approach to conflict? Although these are abstractions of generalized behavioral patterns, oversimplified and capable of being distorted, there are some things you can learn from these descriptions. For one thing, each style is appropriate for some situations, but not for others. If you are dealing with a noncooperative person, then being accommodative would not necessarily encourage a good resolution. For another, you would be advantaged if you know when and how to use several styles. If, for example, you perceive yourself to be more of a "friendly helper," you will need to learn how to stand up for yourself, to hold onto your reasoned-out views despite pressure from others. On the other hand, if you are a "tough battler," you would benefit from learning how to be more sensitive to the views of others.

Knowing that there are different styles increases your understanding of your own role in confronting conflict. Although no one style is appropriate for all conflicts, you can experiment with behaviors that are decidedly different from your predominant style. This should help you become more aware of the value of trying to achieve a balance of behaviors. By becoming attuned to your own behavior in a group, you will not only improve the way you approach conflict but you can help others in the group gain skills in managing conflict.

THE INDIVIDUAL AS MANAGER OF CONFLICT

One of your first tasks as a participator in a group is to accept conflict as necessary and even essential to the good functioning of the group, even though, at times, it may be difficult for the group. With such acceptance you can resist strategies of avoidance, especially the cries of "Let's get this over with!" or "Let's hurry up! Why don't we just vote?" When you realize that avoiding conflict is far worse than the problems brought on by a conflict, you will be able to emphasize that it is good for the group to examine conflicting ideas. Groups that avoid confronting a conflict show deteriorating signs— whether it is that some members have withdrawn from participation, or that the group is stalled, yet avoiding dealing with important issues.

Second, you can accept the fact that conflicts will move either in destructive or productive directions, but that you can influence the direction. There are several things you can do to move a group to productive ends.

a. You can impress upon the group that all members will gain if they search for a common solution.
b. You can stress the importance of the group's overall goals and values.
c. You can let the group know that the conflict is worth working on so that the dissension does not keep a group from getting their job done.
d. You can encourage or, if necessary, sustain a conflict as a way for members to increase their interest both in the group and in their problem. You can tell your group what R. C. North and his colleagues (1960) found in their investigation of conflict: that "if members are committed to sustain a conflict over issues, they are more likely to remain committed once consensus is achieved."

Third, you can also reinforce the point that constructive confrontation is good for the group by suggesting, when the group is having a rough time, that members try out a new procedure. For example, you can recommend that the group designate someone to be a "process observer," a person who will take notes about what is happening in the group and report back to the group. Any individual willing to examine group process can help a group understand how well the participants are doing in solving their problem.

Fourth, you can take a turn as a "process observer." If the group will accept this procedure, you can talk about how the group is doing its work. When you comment about the group's process, you are letting members know that certain behaviors are having certain effects. This activity can be useful when the group seems to be rushing along, quarreling over whether a proposed solution will work, and settling for a less thoughtful solution because the higher-quality solution has been doomed by a "They'll never let us do it" type statement.

When that happens, you can influence the group's decision

process by saying something like, "I'm having some trouble with your observation that 'They'll never let us do it.' You may be correct, but I would still like to spend a little more time analyzing each proposal." By taking exception to a point of view, or by asking for more time for discussion, you affect the group's procedures. Members may then take more time, look at different alternatives, and reconsider the solution they seem to have hurriedly accepted.

Your willingness to comment about process need not be thought of as "interfering." Rather, it can be seen as a genuine attempt to move the group in the direction of finding the best solution. As a member you are in a position to state that conflicts over issues are acceptable, whereas conflicts involving personalities are not. When members come to understand that disagreements represent each member's sincere involvement with the problem, and that eventually this process will lead to a far better solution than not hearing every member out, the group will have an incentive to cooperate.

As a process observer you can watch the group as members interact, and then provide feedback about how they are handling conflicting views—whether they are being open-minded, whether they are considering a number of alternative views, and whether they are working together for a common goal. In one group where Annette was appointed a process observer, for instance, she provided the following feedback:

"I notice that every time Judy gives an idea, other people look away. I think she needs to hear from you what you think about her ideas. Otherwise, she may get the feeling that she isn't being heard."

At another point, Annette interrupted the group with, "Wait a minute. Everyone is shouting here. Is something going on in the group that warrants attention at this time? Is there something going on that is making you interact in this way?"

This approach could be extended by allowing several members to become process observers. This would allow members to become sensitive to procedures that are getting in the way of the group's completing its task. Using process observation as part of a group's procedures can be an effective preventive measure. It can help keep a group from being incapacitated by a conflict that has become unmanageable. (More detail about observing and providing feedback will be found in Chapter 10.)

Finally, you can serve as an exemplary model for your group. You can use communication interaction patterns that favorably affect the outcome of a deliberating group. As a group member interested in promoting constructive conflict, you can engage in a careful analysis of the specific behaviors that seem to lead to conflict and the interaction patterns that prolong a conflict. As an individual you can establish desirable patterns of communication.

Some recent research suggests that there are really only two categories of responses we can use in a conflict situation: *regulated* and *unregulated* responses (Pood 1980). Regulated responses allow us to confront a conflict without hurting other participants or belittling their contributions. For instance, when asked why you support a given proposal, you can show a willingness to explain. You can elaborate about what a concept, idea, or issue means to you. You can do it without being sarcastic or making demeaning statements about what others may believe. You can show a willingness to argue, using argument in its best sense—presenting evidence and reasoning—and you can refrain from being defensive when your views are being scrutinized (Gouran 1982).

The other form of responses, those labeled *unregulated,* are remarks intended to put down, undermine, or disregard the other person's viewpoints. The use of unregulated responses is clearly damaging to the productive management of conflict. As Patton and Giffin point out (1974), trust is an essential element in constructive human relationships. And the degree of trust that we have for another person will influence the way we communicate about a conflict. Communicating defensively or arrogantly will clearly damage the trust needed to work on issues in conflict.

To be able to use conflict constructively means accepting and understanding the perspective of the other party.

When you interact with others, you want to know that you are not being misled. You also want to know about the intentions of others. Indeed, most people require some certainty about the risks involved when they attempt to influence or allow themselves to be influenced by others. Therefore, to be able to use conflict constructively means accepting and understanding the perspective of the other person. This means listening well and using language that promotes trust. Only then can the destructive conflict be minimized, and only then can constructive conflict come into play.

THE GROUP AS MANAGER OF CONFLICT

There are several approaches that the group can use to ensure that the conflict it is experiencing can be managed productively. One of the first tasks would be to determine whether the conflict is a productive one. When the conflict can be characterized as a discussion of controversial issues, consisting of argument and persuasion— components used as a means to an end—then it is a good conflict. As a group, participants can agree that unproductive conflicts—arguments used to attack someone's honesty or credibility—are to be avoided. Sometimes these attacks are prompted because an individual feels left out or does not share in the power resources of the group. Other times, people express their dissatisfaction with an idea because they do not like the presenter of the idea. In these instances, the conflict is no longer a means to an end, but an end in itself. It is conflict disassociated from the group's goal, a rift that may satisfy one person's individual needs, but clearly not those of the group.

When people differ and begin to argue, we often assume that they are opposed to one another because they have clashing personalities. Small group researchers offer a different view. When people are in conflict, it is more important to look at their behavior and the effect of that behavior on furthering the group's agenda (Fisher 1980). When people are working with others in a group, they are almost always dealing with competing viewpoints. There will of necessity be differences of opinion and all groups will have emotional episodes—outbursts of anger, expressions of sadness or frustration—that at the time of their occurrence may seem detrimental to the group. But if the group has as its motivation, "Let us find ways to give and take so that eventually we can reconcile our differences," then the participants are more likely to find a mutually agreeable solution (Gouran 1982). When the clash is over personal issues, or when the motivation is to win at somebody else's expense, then such conflict leads to disruptions.

Making the Conflict More Productive

Once the group members have decided that they are willing to be involved in a productive conflict, there are several steps they can take to help reduce the impasse that a conflict produces.

1. *Identify the issues.* The first step is to specify, in a "brainstorming" session, all the issues involved in the conflict (Hocker and Wilmot 1978). This is a time for every conceivable issue to be brought out, examined, and understood. It is more productive to

engage in this process openly with all participants expressing their views.

2. *Translate the issues into goals.* This step involves understanding the larger aims of the group. The development of goals becomes more realistic when they emerge from a discussion of issues that have become troublesome to the individuals involved in a conflict.

It would also be helpful if group members would take some time to rank-order their goals. The ranking can take the form of a "wish list" in which each "wish" is ranked 1, 2, 3, and so on, according to desirability; or a more practical approach can be taken by rank-ordering goals according to feasibility. Getting agreement and experiencing a shared sense of what the group is striving for can strengthen the group's ability to withstand divisive or incompatible positions.

3. *Determine direction and strategies.* One model of conflict management that has been found useful delineates three directions—argument, persuasion, and agitation—each with numerous strategies to apply (Schultz and Anderson 1984).

Argument: If some members of the group were to choose argument as their direction, then their aim would be to present the best case for their side—using such strategies as description, interpretation, presentation of fact, and reasoning—with minimal attention paid to emotional appeals. On the whole, argument is a conservative (in the political sense of the word—a more traditional approach, involving less risk) direction that, if successful, achieves results with optimal harmony on all sides.

Persuasion: When argument as direction fails, participants can turn to a more progressive direction (a more liberal approach, entailing greater risk) of persuasion. The aim of persuasion is to change attitudes and beliefs. It requires an in-depth analysis of group members, using strategies based on appeals to the emotions and to action, as well as the use of refutation and counterarguments. Because it engages the emotions of those who hold views differing from the speaker's, persuasion is less comfortably put aside or ignored. On the other hand, because emotional appeals personally involve the group, participants have to be careful when resorting to persuasion. A reliance on persuasion can create a defensive climate and alienate participants. If persuasion fails, the speaker can turn again to argument, although it may be more difficult to re-establish an open, neutral, and supportive climate after persuasion has been employed.

Agitation: Members can choose, finally, the more "radical" direction of agitation. When neither argument nor persuasion has allowed the participants to manage a conflict, agitation may be used. With its emphasis on fear and anxiety, agitation as direction encompasses the greatest amount of risk. Agitation is intended to coerce others to change their views. A speaker who is using agitation as direction is employing such strategies as threats, disruption, protests, verbal and nonverbal obscenity, and so on. When successful, agitation can achieve results most rapidly, but it also guarantees that other parties involved in the conflict will be alienated. And if agitation fails, there are usually no other directions that a group member can select that would have any chance of achieving success.

The advantages and disadvantages of each direction are summarized in Table 9.1.

When the group has used argument and persuasion but still cannot agree on a common goal, or has found that neither the proposed solutions nor agitation as a direction is acceptable, then there may be only one other possible route for the group, that of dissolution. It may be better for a group to dissolve, even for a temporary period, than to continue meeting in an environment that is unfavorable for an agreement. However, if group members can agree to stop what they are doing and work specifically on their conflict until they reach a consensus, or can agree to set a definite time for confronting the conflict, then this approach may be a more appropriate one than that of temporarily withdrawing.

Creating a Favorable Group Climate

One of the more important steps that a group can take is to create a communication climate in which the good conflict can occur. Probably the best-known recommendation for encouraging the productive management of conflict is a model reported by Gibb (1961) describing the differences between good and bad communication climates. He concluded that small groups were more productive under conditions of supportive rather than defensive climates.

Supportive climates occur when people are willing to listen and respond in nonjudgmental terms; when they participate actively and show an understanding of each other's views; when they are willing to experiment with new ideas; and when they recognize their interdependence as well as their independence. Defensive climates occur when there are attempts at controlling the behavior of others; when people fail to understand the feelings of others; and when they use communication that is self-serving and competitive, directing criticism at people and not at ideas, or delivered with such dominance and certainty that a negative climate results.

Mabry (1980), in a somewhat different approach, using questionnaire responses from participants from more than 50 groups, found that four dimensions were associated with a group's favorable communication climate: participation, identification, power, and personalness.

Table 9.1   THE USES OF ARGUMENT, PERSUASION, AND AGITATION

	Argument	Persuasion	Agitation
Political definition	"Conservative"	"Liberal"	"Radical"
Aim	To present best case	To change other side's position	To coerce other side to change
Concerns	Facts, definitions, values	Attitudes, beliefs	Anxieties, fears, humiliations
Strategies	Description, interpretation, evaluation	Refutation, motive appeals, appeals to act	Threats, public exposure, disruption
Advantages	Based primarily upon logical reasoning; requires little audience analysis; less risk of alienating, less defensive producing; greater possibility for harmony	Based equally upon logical reasoning and emotional appeals; requires less time to gather and develop evidence; less easy to ignore	Requires no time to gather and develop evidence, cannot be easily ignored
Disadvantages	More time required for gathering and developing evidence; possible to comfortably ignore	More time required for extensive audience analysis; more risk of alienating, more defensive producing; possibility of disharmony	Based solely upon emotional appeals; more time required for extensive audience analysis; requires dedicated followers; most risk of alienating, most defensive producing; guarantees disharmony
Other directions if "it" fails	Persuasion, agitation	Possibly argument, agitation	None

Participation refers to the skill with which members share task and interaction responsibilities. The question for the group is, Are members working as a group? Does everyone feel that he or she is contributing to the task? Positive answers indicate a satisfactory level of participation.

Identification is concerned with the meaningfulness and enjoyability of the work of the group. Here, the group needs to examine how members interact. Do they seem glad to spend time together? Do they believe it is a worthwhile task?

Power has to do with the distribution of influence—that is, do members feel that they are, to some equal degree, influential?

Personalness relates to the effectiveness with which the interpersonal needs of members for inclusion and affection are being met.

These dimensions allow members to think about what is going on in the group. They help participants avoid what Folger and Poole have called "trained incapacities." Group members who are applying new techniques for managing conflicts will tend to avoid the ineffective ways that they have used previously. They will try some innovative approaches, rather than rely on methods that have proved ineffective in the past (Folger and Poole 1984). Moreover, these dimensions provide guidelines for encouraging participants to become more actively involved in promoting the conditions that allow the group both to survive and to prosper.

A FINAL COMMENT

Learning to manage conflict means being open to change—being willing to try new ways to approach a conflict situation. As an individual, you can set a standard by practicing different styles and urging your group to try different processes. You can encourage the members of your group to set aside time to analyze how well they are working, to examine whether they are handling tension and disagreement in the group productively. From the perspective that individuals and groups can learn the skills of managing conflict, you can use the following checklist to evaluate how ready your group is to allow the good conflict to take place:

1. Does everyone have a chance to talk?
2. Are everyone's comments understood? Is everyone given feedback?
3. Are group members open-minded about ideas and opinions? Do they allow arguments to surface?
4. Does each person get recognition even if his or her idea was not accepted?
5. Does the group avoid "win–lose" strategies?

6. Do members help the group examine its process of exploring problems and making decisions?
7. Do members urge others to confront their differences rather than simply agreeing to disagree?
8. Do members assist the group in working toward the group's goal?

SUMMARY

The focus of this chapter has been on steps that individuals and groups can take to manage their conflicts more effectively. Before approaching a conflict situation, a person can appraise the different styles available for entering into a conflict. Each of these styles—competitive, accommodative, avoiding, compromising, and collaborative—is useful in some circumstances but inappropriate in others. Knowing which style you typically use and learning to increase your repertoire of styles would be helpful for your management of conflict.

As an individual you can positively influence how your group works through their conflicts. You can help a group manage conflict by reinforcing the essential gains for a group willing to confront issues. You can encourage the members of your group to set aside time to work on their conflicts, and to use response styles and communicative patterns that will enable the group to manage conflict productively.

A group can learn methods to promote the good conflict by determining whether they are having a productive or a destructive conflict. Participants will have to recognize that expressions of anger, sadness and other unpleasant emotions are acceptable ways of dealing with issues, but attacks on the person are not. The group can establish a norm reflecting a supportive rather than a defensive climate. Another approach is to identify key issues, translate these issues into goals, and carefully work out the directions of argument, persuasion, and agitation, along with appropriate strategies for each of these directions. Group members attain more satisfaction with their task and with each other through the productive management of conflict.

REFERENCES

Filley, A. C. 1975. *Interpersonal Conflict Resolution* Glenview, Ill.: Scott, Foresman.
Fisher, B. A. 1980. *Small Group Decision Making.* New York, McGraw-Hill.
Folger, J. P., and M. S. Poole. 1984. *Working Through Conflict: A Communication Perspective.* Glenview, Ill.: Scott, Foresman.

Gibb, J. R. 1961. "Defensive Communication." *Journal of Communication* 2:141–148.

Gouran, D. S. 1982. *Making Decisions in Groups.* Glenview, Ill.: Scott, Foresman.

Hocker, J. L., and W. W. Wilmot. 1978. *Interpersonal Conflict.* Dubuque, 1a.: Wm. C. Brown.

Mabry, Edward A., and Richard E. Barnes. 1980. *The Dynamics of Small Group Communication.* Englewood Cliffs, N.J.: Prentice-Hall.

National Training Laboratory Reading Book. 1968. Washington, D.C.: Institute of Applied Behavioral Sciences.

North, R. C., H. E. Koch, and D. A. Zinnes. 1960. "The Integrative Functions of Conflict." *Journal of Conflict Resolution.* 4:355–374.

Patton, B. R., and K. Giffin. 1974. *Interpersonal Communication.* New York: Harper & Row.

Pood, E. A. 1980. "Functions of Communication: An Experimental Study in Group Conflict Situations." *Small Group Behavior* 11:76–87.

Schultz, B. and J. Anderson. 1984. "Training in the Management of Conflict: A Communication Theory Perspective." *Small Group Behavior* 15:333–348.

chapter *10*

Diagnosis and Change

Have you ever thought, when you were working on a task with a group, "If only I could change the way this group is doing things"? Maybe this desire came because you detected a lack of spirit or you believed that some group members were not contributing as much as others. You may also have thought that the solutions offered were not the best ones. The question becomes, How accurate were your diagnoses? And if accurate, how do you go about intervening in the group? Are there things you could do to change the group's way of working?

Your need to be able to do something is a desire shared by many others, both theorists and practitioners (Bradford, Benne, and Gibb 1964; Bennis, Benne, and Chin 1969; Baird and Weinberg 1981). The concept of intervention is based on an assumption that changing "natural" ways of behaving to more consciously chosen acts will significantly improve both group process and outcome (Back 1974). Indeed, intervention in groups has had a long history. The scientific study of groups began in the late 1930s and early 1940s with studies of leadership and its effect on group performance. In the mid-1940s, the phenomenon of training, based on experiential learning, began in the National Training Laboratories in Bethel, Maine. It was a method of learning through analyzing one's own behavior and trying to improve it (Napier and Gershenfeld 1983).

Many types of organizations—community and volunteer groups, social agencies, businesses, and government—have been concerned, and continue to be concerned, with motivating and satisfying their members, as well as with enhancing the quality of the organization's products or services. As a result, training or coaching is offered by many organizations, either by an in-house staff or by specialists invited in to provide education and training in particular skills. Sometimes even intact groups are sent outside the organization for specific skills training (Blake and Mouton 1962).

The underlying premise of this chapter is that learning to observe and to give feedback, with the aid of both qualitative and quantitative data, can help group members work together more effectively. Although we know that some behaviors and processes help a group become more effective, we also know that members do not always use appropriate behavior nor do the processes that groups use necessarily serve their interests. Why should this be so? Part of the problem is that groups are often hampered by the traditional ways in which members have learned to operate. They may follow norms for group behavior that suppress creativity, or encourage conformity and discourage dissent. Along with the tendency to adhere to implicit rules, some groups may believe that they lack the resources for completing a task—they seem more willing to opt for a weak solution or to spend all their time studying a problem and never reach a satisfactory decision. When either the implicit rules or the inability to take action stifles group action, it is not at all surprising that members might wish for change (Dyer 1984).

This chapter offers approaches for evaluating and changing small group behavior. The discussion of ideas and the evaluation instruments are designed to help you use your knowledge of small group interaction to gain more satisfying and productive group experiences. In some ways, this chapter is a grand summary of what you have learned in previous chapters. Your understanding of such processes as membership, group development, leadership, and decision making already provides you with some of the skills for effective participation. But with a specific focus on methods that you can adapt in order to change ineffective processes to more effective ones, you will be able to integrate your knowledge with helpful actions.

The chapter addresses changing a group's performance from two perspectives: (1) *the evaluation process*—how specifically chosen individuals—a facilitator, a consultant, or members within the group—can observe group behavior and provide feedback to the group; and (2) *the intervention process*—how group members with a knowledge of group processes can alter a group's performance by changing the group's internal dynamics.

The chapter begins with a brief history and description of the intervention process. You will then learn how to collect data through observation and feedback. You will also be provided with several instruments for evaluating important group components: group interaction and communication, roles, task and social behaviors, cohesion, leadership, and decision making. The final section discusses some of the obstacles that groups encounter along with suggestions for remedying them.

ORIGINS OF INTERVENTION

Following World War II, a host of studies focused on group dynamics. The new concern was reflected in the study of groups as social systems—family groups, group psychotherapy and counseling, minority groups, and groups in formal organizations. In each of these areas, researchers looked for methods that would help train leaders and members to learn more about self and others as they worked together on tasks (Friedlander 1967). Group researchers produced data indicating that carefully designed interventions into a working group can alter group dimensions, such as risk taking, problem-solving effectiveness, and productivity (Blake and Mouton 1964; Bennis, Benne, and Chin 1969; Bednar and Battersby 1976). Both the researchers and the facilitators involved in training defined their task as a "re-education" process. Re-education was interpreted as distinctly different from indoctrination; re-education implied a deliberate, planned change in which all people affected were aware of what and how to change (Benne and Birnbaum 1960).

Many of the early experiments with intervention were accomplished in laboratory training groups (Back 1974). The emphasis was on changing the internal dynamics of the group largely by using new groupings of people in unfamiliar structures. Sometimes the training involved *team training*—people who worked together would be trained together (Friedlander 1967). The premise on which the training was based was that removing traditional restraints would allow freer participation and produce new ways of behaving in a group (Bennis, Benne, and Chin 1969). In addition, the presence of a trainer, an outside person, was considered essential to the re-education process.

The Role of the Trainer

The trainer would encourage group members to share their observations of their own and others' behavior. Participants were asked to establish new structures to offset their tendency to operate in highly ritualistic ways (Back 1974). They were expected to find or create their own goals, their own rules of operation, and their own leadership. As Bennis, Benne, and Chin (1969) report in their analysis of laboratory training groups, when training groups were working without a definite structure, they would try to create an order because they did not like to work without a structure. Under these circumstances the trainer as well as the participants could observe the contrasting needs and styles of the participants. Some would discover that they had unrealistic attitudes toward other members; others acknowledged their stereotyping of particular kinds or classes of people. Some would recognize that they had problems with authority figures, while others realized that they were avoiders of conflict. As a result, trainees were able to identify their typical patterns of group behavior as well as the behaviors that needed to be changed (Back 1974).

This emphasis on changing the internal dynamics of a group was a major thrust of laboratory training. For example, Hall and Williams (1970) found that when groups were given specific training in problem solving, they became more adept at handling new problem-solving tasks. A potent research finding was that groups intent on changing could do so with the use of instruments designed to give them feedback. And as Blake and Mouton discovered (1962, 1964), even the use of self-administered tests could bring about an increased understanding of personal and group reactions. Participants learned through the feedback of quantitative data—such as checklists and ratings—what behaviors to change.

Whether your group uses a trainer to provide feedback or relies totally on member feedback derived from quantitative measures, the training goals are similar. The purpose is to help you become a more effective participant. The group may examine any number of issues—from individual and group decision making to interpersonal relations and communication; from roles undertaken and role conflict to strategies of action; from intragroup and intergroup conflict to evaluation of group performance and outcome.

Intervention requires an ability to observe a group in action and to determine what needs to be done to improve the group situation. Feedback becomes the key to learning about member and group behavior. But seeing what needs to be done without the skills for creating change would not be meaningful without knowing how to intervene. On the other hand, knowing which techniques would help a group change would be useless if unaccompanied by valid diagnoses. Thus, to bring change to your group—to intervene— means to learn some special skills (Dyer 1984).

1. Observing—discovering what is happening in the group.
2. Evaluating—measuring group processes and outcomes.
3. Diagnosing—determining what changes would help the group become more effective.
4. Training—practicing new skills.

THE INTERVENTION PROCESS: LEARNING TO OBSERVE

You have already gained some insights from reading nine chapters that groups will perform more effectively if the following conditions are present (Napier 1985):

- Members are given equal opportunities for influencing group direction.
- Leadership is participative and functional.
- Members are flexible about the roles they undertake.
- Members share their feelings openly and respond with sensitivity to the interpersonal needs of others.
- Members encourage participation and the contributions of ideas.
- Members apply systematic problem-solving procedures.
- Members view conflicts as substantive and essential to the decision process.

You can explore with other members of your group whether they perceive that they are following these guidelines and to what extent they actually are. For example, you can create a scale that would measure "responding with sensitivity" relying on the information provided in Chapter 3. Or you can create a scale using items from several chapters, with questions such as:

1. Do members feel listened to?
2. Is there a perception of equal participation?
3. Are roles necessary?
4. Are the decision choices quality decisions?
5. Are procedures developed for evaluating ideas?
6. Are plans made for implementing solutions?
7. Do the internal dynamics of the group allow relationships to develop?
8. Are leadership behaviors demonstrated?
9. Are the resources of the group well used?

These are the types of questions you can use to help your group understand what is going on. Additional insights will come from *direct observation,* with feedback given by one or more group members or a trainer. Members can examine their group processes while they are still working on a task. This can take the form of stopping their group action so that they can examine particular components: goal achievement, membership responsibilities, and decision-making procedures. Or the group may prefer to receive feedback after members have completed their task. The discussion that follows will show you how to report your observations.

Observing and Providing Feedback

The difficulty with observation is to decide what you want to observe and which of your observations you want to communicate to others. When you first enter a group, you already are engaged in what Bennis and Shepard call "the subtle art of observing group process" (1956). You try to size up the group—who the leaders are, how the members line up, and what rules the group seems to be following. Every statement that is made, however cautiously at first, is an attempt to appraise signs of approval and disapproval. Without doubt, everyone in the group has his or her antennae out, trying to decipher the group. And, as groups continue to work, it is also true that members continue to make observations.

Although members are equipped to make observations—and, indeed, possess a good set of observation instruments—they probably do not make the total effort that is possible, unless they are specifically invited to share the data they have collected. It is also the case that no one person can see everything that is going on. Thus evaluation will be aided by scales, questionnaires, and other instruments to record what is going on in a group (Nicholas 1979).

With permission to engage in an observation-and-feedback process, participants can become more sensitive to specific components of group interaction. For example, if you are asked to be an observer, you might begin by observing only the interaction process, recording who is speaking to whom and who is not speaking or being spoken to. Or you can focus on only nonverbal factors, such as seating patterns and facial expressions. As you concentrate on group interaction, you will become sensitive to additional data: the language and style of each participant, the roles different individuals take in the group, and the way certain behaviors affect the group. As you continue to collect your observation data, you will become aware that you are reacting to what you see, and your reactions become the data for feedback. The exercise "Three Forms of Feedback" will provide practice in observing and communicating your findings.

THREE FORMS OF FEEDBACK*

The exercise described here is designed to help you practice two important components of the intervention process—how to observe and how to provide feedback. This exercise may be used as an in-class or out-of-class activity, either for observing

Source: This exercise has been used by this author as a co-trainer with K. D. Benne in the Applied Social Science Laboratory, Boston University.

your own group or for evaluating other groups. The exercise works well in a "fishbowl" pattern. You will need two groups— one, a discussant group, and two, an observer group. The groups can be of any size. Although both observers and the observed will feel somewhat self-conscious—at least in the beginning— each of you will learn much about self and others by following the procedures. The exercise should stimulate an insightful discussion when you are finished.

Procedure

1. The discussant group can choose any topic the members would like to discuss. When consensus on a topic is reached, the group begins the discussion even though members of the observer group will be in another location getting their instructions. The discussant group is not bound to stay with the first topic chosen. If the topic appears not to be satisfying, the group can move onto another.

2. After receiving their instructions, members of the observer group form an outer circle around the discussant group in progress. It is important that both the discussants and the observers act as if a barrier existed between the two groups. They do not acknowledge each other's presence. After approximately a 20-minute discussion, the two groups will share their observations and reactions.

3. When the discussant group has completed its discussion, the observer group explains the feedback procedure it will be using. Each observer then tells who or what he or she has observed, using the three forms of feedback described below. The observers also talk about why they chose to concentrate on an individual or why they chose to examine the entire group. Each person receiving feedback, as well as the group, is invited to reflect and share his or her reactions with the group. Both groups discuss the implications of the several ways of providing feedback.

Instructions to Observers

Observers, in their separate location, are instructed as follows:

1. When you walk into the room, you should position yourself so that you can observe a specific individual or, if you would rather, you can observe the group as a whole. Whether you

choose an individual or the group, you will be concentrating on the communicative acts, both verbal and nonverbal, that members display. You may be examining such components as the ideas proposed and exchanged, the way people respond to ideas, the patterns of interaction—who talks with whom and with what frequency, the spirit of the group, attempts at leadership, and the like. If you are centering your observations on one individual, please do not reveal your choice, either verbally or nonverbally, to the person you are observing. You can take notes, however. When the discussant group is finished, you will be asked to feed back the data you have collected.

2. The procedure you will be using is based on three forms of feedback. The first form is *descriptive,* and it is probably the easiest to use because there is not as much risk in giving description as there is in giving evaluations. When you are being descriptive, you are telling, without being judgmental—without commenting on whether the behavior was right or wrong—what you have been seeing. For example, your feedback may take the form of, "I saw you sitting back in your chair, holding a pencil in your hand. You were continually nodding your head, but you did not speak. You were not looking at any other member of the group. Your foot was tapping lightly on the floor."

3. The two other forms of feedback are both *evaluative.* The first form of evaluation is to give your perception of how the observed behavior affects the group. This is a judgment call, but it also is informed by your knowledge of effective participation in groups. Therefore, in estimating the effect a person is having, you are weighing what you think is good participant behavior. The second form of evaluation, and perhaps even more difficult to share, is to tell what effect the person has had on you, the observer.

　　The two forms of evaluative feedback will sound something like this. (1) *Effect on group:* "When I see you not looking at other members, I think you are not having as much of an impact on the group as you could. Others in the group do not get the benefit of your thinking." (2) *Effect on you:* "It seems that you do not wish to be active, and I would feel more rewarded if you took a more active position in the group."

Comments on the Exercise

As the two groups discuss the implications of this exercise, they will certainly touch on many important issues. For example, we noted that descriptive feedback is easier to use than evaluative feedback. Was that true for your group? The statement was based on research data (see Chapter 3) that evaluative comments tend to stimulate defensive communication. On the other hand, you have probably found that it is probably quite difficult to stick to descriptive statements without including evaluative terms like "more" or "less" and "better" and "worse."

Your discussion might lead you to inquire about any difficulties that observers had in providing feedback. You could focus on how those who were observed and received feedback reacted to this process. You could check on whether participants experienced the feedback as negative and, if so, what effect this had. While some people may react positively, and even with delight, to the fact that someone has paid attention to them, others may have very different responses.

You might also find out why some people were observed but not others. And if you were among the participants *not* observed, what were your reactions? Sometimes who one observes is dependent on physical placement—some participants are easier to watch; in other cases, there may be particular reasons why one person was singled out, and this issue would be worth discussing. A discussion of the results of this experiment can lead to a better understanding of the effect of communication in the group, individual satisfaction, and group morale.

Being observed and getting feedback can be a profitable experience, especially if members are able to provide a balanced account (Argyris 1962). Giving feedback can be thought of as a way to intervene in the group. It can lead to change because it can make you aware of information that you would not ordinarily have. But at the same time, you should avoid giving an analysis that is too negatively focused. Feedback is valuable, but it requires considerable skill and tact.

The value of this exercise is in demonstrating that you have choices in the way you use feedback. Generally you will not risk as much if you are able to tell descriptively what you have been seeing. As you move into the area of evaluation, you will be taking a greater risk, but at the same time, you create an opportunity for greater learning. When you use evaluative feedback, other people can reflect on your comments, and perhaps be willing to try some new behavior in this or other groups. Learning how certain behaviors affect you is also learning about which communicative acts are necessary for the group to prosper.

By observing interaction, group members can become more sensitive to the specific components of the interaction.

INSTRUMENTS FOR OBSERVATION

Measuring Group Interaction

As was discussed in Chapter 1, some of our major theorists have developed schemes for observing and measuring group interaction. For example, Moreno's sociogram (1953) and Bales's interaction category scheme (1950) can provide additional data about what is happening in the groups you are observing. Moreno's sociogram is useful for analyzing the interpersonal climate of a group. An interaction diagram, based on a chart of the communicative patterns of group members, can tell you who are the active and inactive

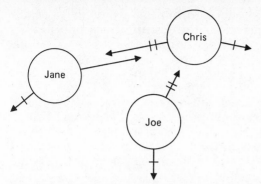

Figure 10.1 Group interaction sociogram. The circles represent group members; the arrows and crossmarks indicate direction and frequency of communication.

participants. Since groups that have more members participating actively are usually cohesive groups, you can use the data to estimate the attraction that members have for the group.

With Bales's Interaction Process Analysis (IPA), you can categorize members' comments and then evaluate whether they were helpful or disruptive to the group. You can also evaluate the contributions that each participant makes to the group, the potential leaders, and the phases of group development. We will examine each of these instruments.

Group Interaction Sociogram   The sociogram is a schematic rendering of the communication patterns in a group. Below are the steps in the process.

1. Draw a circle for each member of the group, and have your circles represent as closely as possible the seating arrangement of group members.
2. When one person speaks to another person, draw an arrow to show the communicative exchange between them.
3. Draw arrows every time someone speaks to anyone. A short crossmark can be used to indicate repeated communication between participants.
4. When a member's comment is directed to the group rather than to a specific individual, draw a line pointing away from the center of the group. Each additional comment can also be shown with crossmarks. Figure 10.1 illustrates a typical group interaction instrument.

   As you examine the sociogram, you can probably draw some reasonable conclusions about leadership status, attraction, and friendship patterns. These data allow you to answer questions about what is going on in the group, such as: "Are there pairs who communicate more with each other than with the rest of the group? Does one person receive more communication than others? Are there potential leaders in the group? Are there people who do not speak very often, or do not receive many messages? Are these people isolated from the group interaction?"

The sociogram gives you a graphic recording of the communicative patterns shaping a group. These conditions may be true only for the meeting you are observing, but by diagramming the communicative patterns over several meetings, you would be able to determine whether your initial results were accurate.

Interaction Process Analysis   One of the more powerful and widely used instruments for measuring group interaction was developed by Robert F. Bales. (See Chapter 1 for a more in-depth discussion of Bales.) The Interaction Process Analysis (IPA) consists of twelve classes of statements. Six of the statements make up the task dimension of a group. In the task dimension, members are either giving information, suggestions, and opinions, or they are asking for information, suggestions, and opinions. The other six statements represent the social-emotional dimension of a group. This dimension refers to the positive and negative responses that members give to ideas, suggestions, and opinions. The interaction process analysis is not easy to use (Bales trained the people who were assigned the task of coding the group's communicative patterns). If you have sufficient practice in coding group communication, however, the IPA can give you valuable information about what is happening in the group. Table 10.1 illustrates Bales's category scheme. There are also suggestions for recording your observations.

To be able to use this system, you will need to construct a matrix with the 12 categories on the left-hand margin. You then construct columns across the top of the page and number them to represent each participant. In each column, you record the type of interaction you observe. For example, who speaks to whom, and the type of statement it is, is recorded by a series of coupled numbers. You can use "0" to stand for a remark made to the group as a whole, and use a different number to stand for a remark made to each individual in the group. Thus, a 3–0 next to category 10 means that member "3" disagreed with or failed to respond to the group; 3–1 next to category 8 indicates that member "3" was asking for an opinion or an evaluation.

When you have completed your recording of the group's interaction, you will have collected data for evaluating how members participated in their group. You can determine who are the "high" and "low" talkers. You can assess whether there is a balance of

Table 10.1   BALES'S INTERACTION CATEGORIES

		Problem type[a]
Positive reactions	1. Shows solidarity; raises others' status, gives help and rewards.	f
	2. Shows tension release, jokes, laughs, tell stories, shows satisfaction.	e
	3. Shows agreement, shows passive acceptance, understands, concurs, complies.	d
Attempted answers	4. Gives suggestions, direction; takes the lead, tries to assume leadership.	c
	5. Gives opinions, evaluation, analysis, expressions of feeling or wish.	b
	6. Gives information, orientation, repeats, clarifies, confirms.	a
Questions	7. Asks for information, clarification, repetition, confirmation.	a
	8. Asks for opinion, evaluation, analysis, expression of feeling.	b
	9. Asks for suggestions, direction, possible ways of action, while maiautonomy.	c
Negative reactions	10. Disagrees, shows passive rejection, withholds help, does not respond.	d
	11. Shows tension, anxiety, withdraws from discussion	e
	12. Shows antagonism, deflates others' status, defends or asserts self.	f

[a]*Problem types: a = problems of orientation; b = problems of evaluation; c = problems of control; d = problems of decision; e = problems of tension reduction; f = problems of reintegration.*

social-emotional and task behaviors. This information can help you estimate the effectiveness of the observed group. For example, if a major project was to be accomplished but your analysis showed that the group spent a greater percentage of its time on the social dimension, then you can infer that the group probably needs a better balance of task and social dimensions.

Recall that Bales discovered from his use of the IPA that groups move through various phases in their development (orientation, evaluation, and control). You can learn from the IPA whether groups have spent a sufficient amount of time on orientation or whether they moved prematurely to the decision-making (control) phase. You can analyze the comments that were made in each phase. If there were too many negative reactions and insufficient information, you can assume that there were dissatisfied members in the group. Although the IPA system has limitations (Chapter 1), it is clear that using Bales's categories offers important insights about how well a group is performing.

Identifying Roles in the Group

In Chapter 2, we discussed how participating members in ongoing groups tend to assume certain roles, either because of the expectations of other members or because of their own perceptions about their competence and their past experiences in groups. As people begin to work in a group, they develop specialized roles for themselves. Some of the roles are beneficial to a group's deliberations; others are disruptive. The roles that are desirable are those that allow groups to make maximum use of the resources of their members. Examining role formation is important not only for recording what roles are being performed—group task and maintenance roles, and self-centered roles—but for noting which roles are *not* being undertaken. Identifying roles that contribute to effective decision making is an important task in evaluating group performance.

As Benne and Sheats (1948) explain in their classic work on classifying roles in the group, members who perform task roles contribute directly to the substantive work of the group by offering opinions, orientation, and coordinating and evaluating information. Members who undertake maintenance roles make statements that encourage group interaction and, by showing a willingness to go along with group suggestions, promote a good climate. In contrast, members who strive to meet personal goals tend to neglect group needs in their aggressive pursuit of their own interests. They may dominate a discussion, block action, or, by not taking the group's work seriously, have a disruptive effect on the group.

You can find out what roles members in your group engage in by having your group participate in the "Role Nominations: Functional Roles in Groups" exercise. It will let members know what roles other members perceive they are playing. The exercise should be used only by a group that has worked together and is willing to engage in self-assessment. When carried out in a spirit of learning, the exercise can give you important data about which roles are beneficial to the group.

ROLE NOMINATIONS: FUNCTIONAL ROLES IN GROUPS*

Procedure

1. Participants are given the role nominations form (page 233).
2. Everyone writes each member's name (first name or the letter A, B, C, and so on to stand for the individual) in the same order on all the forms.

*Source: K. D. Benne and P. Sheats. 1948. "Functional Roles of Group Members," *The Journal of Social Issues* 4, adapted from J. W. Pfeiffer and J. E. Jones, (eds.). 1974. *A Handbook of Structured Experiences for Human Relations Training,* vol. 2. La Jolla, Calif.: University Associates.

3. Each member places a check mark in the column corresponding to the roles the member (self included) has played most often in the group (based on an overall impression during a group task).
4. When everyone has completed the form, a facilitator or member calls out the marks he or she has put down. The roles for the entire group are summarized.
5. The group then discusses the perceptions members had about the roles being played. The discussion can focus on the appropriateness of individual roles, whether they are desirable and effective. Information can be gathered on the extent to which members are employing dysfunctional roles and the way the group has coped with these roles. Participants should also ask for feedback on how the distribution of roles was determined.

ROLE NOMINATIONS FORM

Instructions: For each member, place check marks in the column corresponding to the roles each has played most of ten in the group. Include yourself.

Roles	Members						
	A	B	C	D	E	F	G
Task Roles							
Initiator							
Information seeker							
Information giver							
Coordinator							
Orienter							
Evaluator							
Maintenance Roles							
Encourager							
Harmonizer							
Gatekeeper							
Standard setter							
Follower							
Anti-Group Roles							
Blocker							
Recognition seeker							
Dominator							
Avoider							

Comments on the Exercise

There are several ways to do this exercise. If your group is using a facilitator, then that person can collect all the forms and read them aloud anonymously. Even before the data are fed back, individuals may want to predict the nominations they most likely will receive. Because the exercise is time-consuming (though the time spent on this analysis is worth it), the group may want to restrict the number of nominations to one role per person or restrict the number of roles to be considered.

The exercise permits members to become more aware of the roles each person takes in the group. Sharing perceptions offers an opportunity for learning whether the way you see yourself is the way that others see you. Sharing data allows members to discuss which roles are problematic, and, rather than directing the discussion to "who" is a problem, members can talk about how to redirect their energies in more profitable ways. Members who express dissatisfaction with the role expectations that have been placed on them could offer suggestions for change.

If the group members want to, they can establish a practice session in which they work on employing desirable task and maintenance roles. Then the group can repeat the nominations exercise. Learning to evaluate roles provides an essential awareness of the variety of role functions employed in a group. Such an examination can also demonstrate that roles can be profitably shared among group members.

Measuring Group Cohesion

In Chapter 2, we explored the relationship between cohesiveness in the group and the group's performance. A cohesive group is a productive group, unless members become so overly friendly that they lose sight of the needs of the task. And the more cohesive the group, the more likely members are to derive satisfaction from the group experience. Because the development of cohesion is so important to a group, researchers have developed several instruments for measuring this variable. There are two widely used measures for cohesion. One is a questionnaire developed by Gross (1957) and Yalom et al., (1967) and another is by Seashore (1954). Either of these instruments will tell you about the internal bonding of a group.

The questions center on (1) the extent to which participants feel a part of the group; (2) whether they would be reluctant to leave the group, and (3) whether their group is more satisfying than other groups. The questionnaires are self-report measures and, like all self-report measures, are subject to biased reporting. Nevertheless, if members take care to report what they actually believe, rather than give what they think are expected answers, the self-report data help a group document what is happening and how members are experiencing the group.

The questionnaires can be administered by a trainer or by the members themselves. In the latter case, it would be useful to summarize the data so that individual members do not have to be identified. Table 10.2, from Gross and Yalom's work, consists of nine questions and can be used by various kinds of groups.

The index by Seashore, also a self-report measure, conceptualizes similar questions for measuring cohesion, but uses a paid-work group as its focus (Table 10.3). This questionnaire can be completed individually, or a group may decide that the members would like to answer the questionnaire together. In that case it could be a useful intervention for changing a group's climate.

From your analysis of the answers members gave in Table 10.2 or in Table 10.3, you should have a better idea how they perceive the climate of the group. For example, if on question 2 in Table 10.3 most members say they would very much want to change groups, this question should stimulate a discussion of what can be changed in the present group to make it a better experience. With the data collected from these instruments, either by examining individual scores or computing a group average on each question, you would gain additional information about how well the interpersonal needs of members were being addressed.

Table 10.2 QUESTIONS FOR MEASURING COHESIVENESS

1. How many of your group members fit what you feel to be the ideal of a good group member?
2. To what degree do you feel that you are included by the group in the group's activities?
3. How attractive do you find the activities in which you participate as a member of your group?
4. If most of the members of your group decided to dissolve the group by leaving, would you try to dissuade them?
5. If you were asked to participate in another project like this one, would you like to be with the same people who are in your present group?
6. How well do you like the group you are in?
7. How often do you think your group should meet?
8. Do you feel that working with the particular group will enable you to attain your personal goals for which you sought the group?
9. Compared to other groups like yours, how well would you imagine your group works together?

Source: J. P. Stokes. 1983. "Components of Group Cohesion: Intermember Attraction, Instrumental Value, and Risktaking." *Small Group Behavior* 14:167.

Table 10.3   SEASHORE INDEX OF GROUP COHESIVENESS

Check one response for each question.
1. Do you feel that you are really a part of your work group?
   ____Really a part of your work group
   ____Included in most ways
   ____Included in some ways, but not in others
   ____Don't feel I really belong
   ____Don't work with any one group of people
   ____Not ascertained

2. If you had a chance to do the same kind of work for the same pay in
   another work group, how would you feel about moving?
   ____Would want very much to move
   ____Would rather move than stay where I am
   ____Would make no difference to me
   ____Would want very much to stay where I am
   ____Not ascertained

3. How does your group compare with other similar groups on each of
   the following points?

	Better than most	About the same as most	Not as good as most	Not ascertained
a. The way the members get along together	___	___	___	___
b. The way the members stick together	___	___	___	___
c. The way the members help each other on the job.	___	___	___	___

Source: S. Seashore. 1954. *Group Cohesiveness in the Industrial Work Group.* Ann Arbor:
University of Michigan Institute for Social Research.

Measuring Leadership

Among the many variables that help shape a group, none is more
important than the way leadership functions are handled (Stogdill
1974; Argyris and Schon 1978). Leading a group means having members willing to take an active role in the group. Leadership also
means learning to communicate effectively, skills that include
showing a high regard for the ideas and feelings of other members,
setting goals, giving directions, facilitating the group's exchange of
messages, summarizing the group's progress, and taking steps to
counter disruptive influences.

The research data document that group task and social needs
can be met by one or more individuals and, even when there is a
formal leader, the group will prosper when several members take
on the responsibilities of leadership. It is more important that leadership functions be available to the group than that the group have
a designated leader (Benne and Sheats 1948).

There are two ways to think about measuring leadership. One

approach is to discover who are the potential leaders of an initially leaderless group. This would be useful information for anyone charged with choosing a leader for a group or organization. A powerful way of discovering the potential leaders in a group is to ask group members who they perceive are the leaders in the group.

If you are looking for someone to appoint as leader as your group takes on a project, you can more accurately obtain this information with the aid of a questionnaire based on members' perceptions. External observers can also provide data gathered from their evaluative instruments. You can create almost any type of rating or ranking scale from a combination of components associated with leadership: influence, status, power, sensitivity, and communicative expertise. Or you can rely on the questionnaire in Table 10.4.

The questionnaire has been used successfully to predict emergent leadership in initially leaderless discussion groups. By giving each person a form to rate each member of the group, self included (in a six-member group, each member would get six forms), you can learn from the perceptions of the group which member or members are leaders. The questionnaire is best used after a group has completed at least one discussion.

To score the questionnaire, sum the ratings each individual receives from every group member on each dimension. Divide the total by the number of group members.

The probable leaders in the group can be determined by noting which members are rated highest on the positive variables *Self-assured, Formulates goals, Gives directions,* and *Summarizes.* The positive variables are usually sufficient for predicting potential leaders, but, as Schultz reported (1974), higher ratings on the negative variables *Quarrelsome* and *Not sensible,* although not as potent as the positive variables, are associated with leadership perception.

In Schultz's study, members chosen as leaders were rated as more quarrelsome than non leaders, although the quality of quarrel-

Table 10.4   DISCUSSION EVALUATION QUESTIONNAIRE

Directions: Rate each member of your group, including yourself, on each of the following dimensions. Place a check mark at the point along the continuum that most closely represents your evaluation of each person's contribution to the discussion.

Self-assured	: _7_ : _6_ : _5_ : _4_ : _3_ : _2_ : _1_ :	Hesitant
Formulates goals	: ___: ___: ___: ___: ___: ___: ___:	Does not formulate goals
Quarrelsome	: ___: ___: ___: ___: ___: ___: ___:	Harmonious
Gives directions	: ___: ___: ___: ___: ___: ___: ___:	Does not give directions
Summarizes	: ___: ___: ___: ___: ___: ___: ___:	Does not summarize
Sensible	: ___: ___: ___: ___: ___: ___: ___:	Not sensible

Source: B. Schultz. 1974. "Characteristics of Emergent Leaders of Continuing Problem-Solving Groups." *Journal of Psychology* 88: 167–173.

someness was not so extreme as to block the discussion of issues by other members. Rather, a quarrelsome or argumentative person was perceived as helping a group examine alternative decision proposals. And in a complementary way, members rated highest in "sensibleness," while often rated as "best-liked" members in a separate questionnaire, were less likely to be chosen as leaders. Being seen as a somewhat less sensible person was more valued because such a person is more willing to take risks, a quality that aids a group's consideration of issues.

The second approach to measuring leadership is by judging its effectiveness. This assessment can be made by asking whether the leaders are performing functions that are appropriate to the needs of the group. The Barnlund–Haiman leadership rating scale measures more directly the adequacy of leadership activities in ongoing discussion groups (Table 10.5). The assumption of this rating scale is that leadership consists of three dimensions: *influence in procedure, influence in creative and critical thinking,* and *influence in interpersonal relations.* Because the scale is both evaluative and diagnostic, it is particularly valuable for pinpointing specific leadership functions that are either missing or need to be strengthened.

To score the scale, take each category and sum the ratings for each member. You will have a numerical score that will tell you the variables that are positively and negatively perceived. Then you can take steps to work on those attributes that would make a difference to your group.

Table 10.5 BARNLUND–HAIMAN LEADERSHIP RATING SCALE

Instructions: This rating scale may be used to evaluate leadership in groups with or without official leaders. In the latter case (the leaderless group), use part A of each item only. When evaluating the actions of an official leader, use parts A and B of each item on the scale.

INFLUENCE IN PROCEDURE
Initiating Discussion

A. 3   2   1   0   1   2   3

Group needed more help in getting started	Group got right amount of help	Group needed less help in getting started

B. The quality of the introductory remarks was:

Excellent	Good	Adequate	Fair	Poor

Organizing Group Thinking

A. 3   2   1   0   1   2   3

Group needed more direction in thinking	Group got right amount of help	Group needed less direction in thinking

B. If and when attempts were made to organize group thinking, they were:

Excellent	Good	Adequate	Fair	Poor

Table 10.5 (*Continued*)

Clarifying Communication

A. | 3 | 2 | 1 | 0 | 1 | 2 | 3 |
|---|---|---|---|---|---|---|

Group needed more help in clarifying communication	Group got right amount of help	Group needed less help in clarifying communication

B. If and when attempts were make to clarify communication, they were:

Excellent	Good	Adequate	Fair	Poor

Summarizing and Verbalizing Agreements

A. | 3 | 2 | 1 | 0 | 1 | 2 | 3 |
|---|---|---|---|---|---|---|

Group needed more help in summarizing and verbalizing agreements	Group got right amount of help	Group needed less help in summarizing and verbalizing agreements

B. If and when attempts were made to summarize and verbalize, they were:

Excellent	Good	Adequate	Fair	Poor

Resolving Conflict

A. | 3 | 2 | 1 | 0 | 1 | 2 | 3 |
|---|---|---|---|---|---|---|

Group needed more help in resolving conflict	Group got right amount of help	Group needed less help in resolving conflict

B. If and when attempts were made to resolve conflict, they were:

Excellent	Good	Adequate	Fair	Poor

INFLUENCE IN CREATIVE AND CRITICAL THINKING
Stimulating Critical Thinking

A. | 3 | 2 | 1 | 0 | 1 | 2 | 3 |
|---|---|---|---|---|---|---|

Group needed more stimulation in creative thinking	Group got right amount of help	Group needed less stimulation in creative thinking

B. If and when attempts were made to stimulate ideas, they were:

Excellent	Good	Adequate	Fair	Poor

Encouraging Criticism

A. | 3 | 2 | 1 | 0 | 1 | 2 | 3 |
|---|---|---|---|---|---|---|

Group needed more encouragement to be critical	Group got right amount of help	Group needed less encouragement to be critical

B. If and when attempts were made to encourage criticism, they were:

Excellent	Good	Adequate	Fair	Poor

Table 10.5 (*Continued*)

Balancing Abstract and Concrete Thought

A. 3	2	1	0	1	2	3

Group needed to be more concrete	Group achieved proper balance	Group needed to be more abstract

B. If and when attempts were made to balance abstract and concrete, they were:

Excellent	Good	Adequate	Fair	Poor

INFLUENCE IN INTERPERSONAL RELATIONS
Climate-Making

A. 3	2	1	0	1	2	3

Group needed more help in securing a permissive atmosphere	Group got right amount of help	Group needed less help in securing a permissive atmosphere

B. If and when attempts were made to establish a permissive atmosphere, they were:

Excellent	Good	Adequate	Fair	Poor

Regulating Participation

A. 3	2	1	0	1	2	3

Group needed more regulation of participation	Group got right amount of help	Group needed less regulation of participation

B. If and when attempts were made to regulate participation, they were:

Excellent	Good	Adequate	Fair	Poor

Overall Leadership

A. 3	2	1	0	1	2	3

Group needed more control	Group got right amount of control	Group needed less control

B. If and when attempts were made to control the group, they were:

Excellent	Good	Adequate	Fair	Poor

Source: D. C. Barnlund and F. S. Haiman. 1960. *The Dynamics of Discussion.* Boston: Houghton Mifflin, pp. 401–404.

Evaluating Decision Making

As with leadership, decision making is closely related to the effectiveness with which a group accomplishes its goals. It is also the area most connected to enduring satisfaction—a sense that members did their best to arrive at a decision proposal that is appropriate for the job required (Goodall 1985).

In using the post-decision reaction questionaire (Table 10.6), your group will be able to assess how well the members have handled some important elements that affect good decision making: the quality of the decision, the commitment of members, the influence each member felt, and the satisfaction derived by the members. You can add to or modify the questions on this form. The insights you gain should help your group's performance in subsequent meetings.

Table 10.6 POST-DECISION REACTION QUESTIONAIRE

1. To what extent do you feel listened to and understood?

1	2	3	4	5	6	7	8	9

(Not at all)   (A great deal)

2. How satisfied are you with your participation in the group?

1	2	3	4	5	6	7	8	9

(Very dissatisfied)   (Very satisfied)

3. How satisfied are you with the social climate of the group?

1	2	3	4	5	6	7	8	9

(Very dissatisfied)   (Very satisfied)

4. To what extent do you feel you influenced the group's decisions?

1	2	3	4	5	6	7	8	9

(Not at all)   (A great deal)

5. To what extent do you feel committed to the decisions the group made?

1	2	3	4	5	6	7	8	9

(Not at all)   (A great deal)

6. How satisfied are you with the group's performance as a whole?

1	2	3	4	5	6	7	8	9

(Very dissatisfied)   (Very satisfied)

7. What recommendations would you make for improving the group's discussion?_____

_____

8. What adjectives best describe the way you feel about the group's overall decision-making processes?_____

_____

Source: Adapted from J. K. Brilhart, *Effective Group Discussion.* 1982. Dubuque, Ia.: Wm. C. Brown.

LEARNING TO INTERVENE IN THE GROUP

Let's assume that your group has information about some of the problems the participants have experienced—the cohesiveness of members, leadership functions, individual commitment to the group's decision—and that these results have been fed back to the group. What then is supposed to happen? The research on intervention indicates that knowing a problem exists can often help a group identify remedies to treat the problem (Stogdill 1974; Bednar and Battersby 1976; Argyris and Schon 1978). On the other hand, the mere identification of a problem may not be sufficient for a group to know how to work on the problem.

Interventions are presumed to be able to lead a group into a conscious awareness of their own processes. Intervening will work if members use analysis and feedback to help them activate the change process. To bring about a planned change requires that members suggest what has to be changed and how a change can be implemented (Benne and Birnbaum 1960). You now know that much of what goes on in a group is taken for granted. Nevertheless, if members wish to change what is going on, they will have to question such procedures as decision making, conflict resolution, and the development of roles and role relationships.

Dyer (1972) indicates that a diagnostic intervention is somewhere between giving an opinion and developing a theory or insight about what is keeping the group from performing at a satisfying level. Thus an intervention is exploratory. Members have to be willing to question, suggest, and propose hypotheses that perhaps can help them examine conditions within their group. By suggesting or hypothesizing what might account for some of the difficulties, the group can more ably examine possible remedies.

The exercise "Individual Experiment" can help the members of your group heighten their awareness of which behaviors affect them positively and which have a negative impact. While it is an exercise that identifies symptoms and not causes, it still can raise the group's awareness of what has to be changed.

Barriers to Change

Many of the barriers to change are embedded in our own culture. Within the group we may experience any of the following elements that affect our willingness to change: role expectations, the influence of status, the assumption of formal leadership, and biases and stereotypical behavior. As group members examines their behavior, they can question or suggest hypotheses concerning the content of

---

INDIVIDUAL EXPERIMENT

1. Ask group members to write down on a small piece of paper *four* types of behavior that they feel might block the group in its effective development. No member should sign these papers, and no other names should be mentioned.
2. Ask each member to record *four* types of behavior that each has experienced in other work groups that have had a positive effect on the group's problem-solving ability.
3. Tally the responses under headings of "Helpful" and "Nonhelpful" behaviors, and present them to the group. A six-member group will have 24 helpful and 24 nonhelpful behaviors, although many of the responses will be overlapping.
4. Now your group can spend 10 or 15 minutes establishing some clear ground rules to ensure the maintenance of the positive behaviors and the removal of those behaviors that tend to block group progress.

Source: Adapted from R. W. Napier and M. K. Gershenfeld. 1985. *Groups: Theory and Experience.* Boston: Houghton Mifflin, p. 480.

---

the discussion, their internal communicative processes, and their procedures (Dyer 1972).

If group participants are examining the *content* of their discussion, they might ask whether they have considered sufficiently the available research data. They can explore whether they have shared their experiences and opinions in ways that affect either positively or negatively the quality of their discussion. A focus on *communicative processes* would entail exploring what is happening in the group in the "here and now." It is a concern with the way they are exchanging messages and responding to ideas.

As an illustration, a group member could state, "I was wondering if the group was aware that only two people talked about this issue." Another person might inquire about particular types of reactions: "I wonder, Richard, how you felt when your idea was rejected." If there is apathy in the group, someone could ask what has contributed to this situation. Or group members could inquire whether the goals were too broad or perhaps not clearly stated. When the focus is on *procedures,* the group's rules are examined with questions such as, "Does the group begin meetings on time? Do they take a break during a rough period of the discussion? How do they get back on track when they have been socializing?"

To be able to intervene so that barriers to change are overcome means using a *meta-discussion* process. It is essential during this process that members talk about what keeps them from attaining their goals. It should not be a "let it all hang out" session where personality difficulties are emphasized. Rather than focus on personalities, group members are encouraged to talk openly about structural and procedural barriers they perceive are thwarting the group's process.

A process analysis is typically used in connection with group meetings. For a process analysis to succeed, members have to provide a climate that encourages an open discussion. Anyone should be able to express, without fear, satisfaction or dissatisfaction, either with his or her own goals or the goals of the group. To bring about change, people need to be permitted to talk about and explore the reasons for their current performance. They also need to be able to set their own goals for improving their performance (Bennis, Benne, and Chin 1969).

It is the group's responsibility to discuss the possible changes to be adopted for improving the members' working relationships, the way they make decisions, their problem-solving ability, and their individual satisfaction. But in carrying out an assessment session, a group will have to be cautious about its methods of inviting and responding to criticism. It is not very helpful for someone to impose on another, "If only you would change!"

A part of the intervention process is also being protective (Bradford, Benne, and Gibb 1964). In a training situation, the trainer would intervene to protect certain individual members from inappropriate or unnecessarily severe comments. Without a trainer, group members need to take on this responsibility. Despite the difficulties arising from a sharing of criticism, group members can overcome many of the barriers to change by discussing barriers openly, by examining their own behavior, and by employing regular assessment sessions.

One final and significant effort that a group can make to implement change is to allow people to practice new ways of behaving. In the preceding chapters, there are exercises that you can employ to help you practice: from brainstorming, to examining roles, to reducing conflict. They were designed to encourage you to examine specific features of the discussion process—communication patterns, feedback responses, leadership styles—and to analyze your problem-solving and decision-making procedures.

The exercise "Alter Ego: A Task in Group Development" will allow a group to diagnose and propose remedies for any of the specific problems that surface as the group engages in a discussion. The exercise is for practice. A group can choose an issue to discuss that

ALTER EGO: A TASK IN GROUP DEVELOPMENT

Procedure. The exercise depends on two groups (groups of seven are ideal). One group is the discussant group; the other takes on the task of coaching the members of the discussant group. (This group assumes the role of the other, but in a more idealized way—an alter ego). The concept behind this activity is that groups can evaluate their behavior by making an intervention themselves.

The task is best accomplished in a large room with space in the center for members of the small, interacting group (the discussant group), who sit in an inner circle, and the coaching group, individually seated behind members of the discussant group (see Figure 10.2). The people who are not active participants are observers and respondents for both groups. A skilled group member is asked to serve as a facilitator.

Action. The discussion group members begins exploring a topic of their choice. After approximately 10 minutes, the facilitator interrupts the discussion and asks the coaches (alter egos) to talk to their partners. This is the time for giving advice, for suggesting a new behavior, if it is warranted, or makes general comments about improving the group's discussion.

The group continues discussion, with time out for consultation with the coaches for two more 10-minute periods. After the second 10-minute consultation, the players are asked to reverse roles—with the coaches now the discussant group, and the discussants serving as coaches. The discussants can begin the discussion anew or continue the discussion where it left off. The maximum time for the entire discussion should be about 50 minutes.

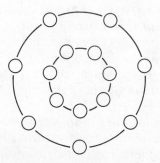

Outer circle = coaches
Inner circle = small group interacting

Figure 10.2 Alter ego exercise. The inner circle is the discussant group. Seated in an outer circle are the coaches.

Results. After the discussion is completed, the role players discuss openly their reactions to the advice and intervention. Then the observing audience is asked for comments. The discussion is centered on the implications for the group of learning to take advice, of learning to put oneself in another person's shoes, of the norm of trying out a new behavior. By asking members to consider other positions, other views, and other styles of interacting, the group comes to recognize a wider range of acceptable behaviors.

pertains to what the participants are currently working on. Or members can choose any issue they would like to discuss just so they can practice.

A FINAL COMMENT

Learning to intervene in a group is the equivalent of being an effective member. Effective membership means knowing how to participate in a group. It involves learning how to structure a task and to create a climate of cohesiveness. It means learning to express doubts and to take action to convert inappropriate interactions to more effective ones. The underlying assumption of evaluation is that learning to observe and to provide feedback helps a group identify problems that interfere with achieving goals.

There are many ways of going about helping groups. One way is to encourage members to think about how other people may be perceiving their interactions. Another way is to have members examine how they contribute to a group. It is also important that groups take the time to integrate their findings from this exercise into a theoretical framework.

Without an understanding of the theoretical basis of group development, members of a group would be unable to conceptualize measures for bringing about change. Thus, by examining the theories that explain what has happened to them, participants gain insight into the essential needs of the group. Obviously, it takes a great deal of skill to be able to apply theory to the problems that you are diagnosing, but asking some pertinent questions about content, process, and procedures is an important step to help you see what suggestions would help the group.

When members have an awareness of the group, the needs of members, and what is happening within the group at any given moment, they can facilitate the group's development by establishing attainable goals, by constructing workable norms, by improving cohesion, by fostering open communication, by strengthening the quality of problem solving, and, in so doing, contribute to the overall effectiveness of the group.

SUMMARY

This chapter has emphasized the processes that bring change to a group. Based on a historic concept that carefully designed interventions into a working group can alter both the processes groups use and the effectiveness of their product, the chapter presents a number of ways that groups can observe, measure, and evaluate their own performance. Two approaches are considered. One is to examine the observation process itself. For this purpose an exercise is provided for practicing what and how to observe, as well as the forms of feedback that can be used.

A second approach is to provide instruments for collecting data, so that an intervention for changing group behavior would be based on accurate data. The instruments assist the evaluation process by allowing members to examine both qualitative and quantitative data. These include interaction and role behavior analysis forms, leadership emergence and leadership effectiveness forms, and questionnaires for evaluating cohesion and decision making. A final exercise provides practice in diagnosis and intervention.

REFERENCES

Argyris, C. 1962. *Interpersonal Competence and Organizational Effectiveness.* Homewood, Ill.: Richard D. Irwin.

Argyris, C. and D. A. Schon 1978. *Organizational Learning.* Reading, Mass.: Addison-Wesley.

Back, K. 1974. "Intervention Techniques: Small Groups." *Annual Review of Psychology* 25:367–387.

Baird, J. E., Jr., and S. B. Weinberg. 1981. *Group Communication: The Essence of Synergy.* (2nd ed.). Dubuque, Ia.: Wm. C. Brown.

Bales, R. F. 1950. *Interaction Process Analysis: A Method for the Study of Small Groups.* Reading, Mass.: Addison-Wesley.

Barnlund, D. C., and F. S. Haiman. 1960. *The Dynamics of Discussion.* Boston: Houghton Mifflin.

Bednar, R. L., and C. Battersby. 1976. "The Effects of Specific Cognitive Structure on Early Group Development." *Journal of Applied Behavioral Science* 12:513–522.

Benne, K. D., and M. Birnbaum. 1960. "Change Does Not Have to Be Haphazard." *The School Review* 68:283–293.

Benne, K. D., and P. Sheats. 1948. "Functional Roles of Group Members." *Journal of Social Issues* 4:41–49.

Bennis, W. G., and H. A. Shepard. 1956. "A Theory of Group Development." *Human Relations* 9:415–437.

Bennis, W. G., K. D. Benne, and R. Chin. 1969. *The Planning of Change.* (2nd ed.). New York: Holt, Rinehart and Winston.

Blake, R. R., and J. S. Mouton. 1962. "The Instrumented Training Laboratory." In *Issues in Training.* Washington, D.C.: National Training Laboratories, pp. 61–67.

Blake, R. R., and J. S. Mouton. 1964. *The Managerial Grid.* Houston: Gulf.

Bradford, L. P., K. D. Benne, and J. Gibb (eds.). 1964. *T-Group Theory and Laboratory Method.* New York: Wiley.

Dyer, W. G. 1972. *The Sensitive Manipulator.* Provo, Utah: Brigham Young University Press.

Dyer, W. G. 1984. *Strategies for Managing Change.* Reading, Mass.: Addison-Wesley.

Friedlander, F. 1967. "The Impact of Organizational Training Laboratories upon Effectiveness and Interaction of Ongoing Groups." *Personnel Psychology* 20:289–308.

Goodall, H. L., Jr. 1985. *Small Group Communication.* Dubuque, Ia.: Wm. C. Brown.

Gross, E. F. 1957. "An Empirical Study of the Concepts of Cohesiveness and Compatibility." Honors Thesis, Harvard University.

Hall, J. and M. S. Williams. 1970. "Group Dynamics Training and Improved Decision-Making." *The Journal of Applied Behavioral Science* 6:39–68.

Moreno, J. L. 1953. *Who Shall Survive?* (Rev. ed.). Beacon, N.Y.: Beacon House.

Napier, R. W., and M. K. Gershenfeld. 1983. *Making Groups Work: A Guide for Group Leaders.* Boston: Houghton Mifflin.

Napier, R. W., and M. K. Gershenfeld. 1985. *Groups: Theory and Experience* Boston: Houghton Mifflin.

Nicholas, J. M. 1979. "Evaluation Research in Organizational Change Interventions: Considerations and Some Suggestions." *Journal of Applied Behavioral Science* 15:23–40.

Pfeiffer, J. W., and J. E. Jones (eds.). 1974. *A Handbook of Structured Experiences for Human Relations Training,* vol. 2, rev. La Jolla, Calif.: University Associates.

Schultz, B. 1974. "Characteristics of Emergent Leaders of Continuing Problem-Solving Groups." *Journal of Psychology* 88:167–173.

Seashore, S. E. 1954. *Group Cohesiveness in the Industrial Work Group.* Ann Arbor, Mich.: Institute for Social Research.

Stogdill, R. M. 1974. *Handbook of Leadership.* New York: Free Press.

Stokes, J. P. 1983. "Components of Group Cohesion: Intermember Attraction, Instrumental Value, and Risk Taking." *Small Group Behavior* 14:163–173.

Yalom, I. D., P. S. Houts, S. M. Zimmerberg, and K. H. Rand. 1967. "Prediction of Improvement in Group Therapy." *Archives of General Psychiatry* 17:159–168.

Appendix

For participants to improve their group processes takes both understanding and practice. Obviously, there is an interdependence between understanding and knowing what and how to practice.
Throughout this book you have been provided with concepts and
theories, as well as exercises, to enhance the skills of group participation. The assumption underlying group exercises is that you will
want to improve your own and the group's performance.

The material included in the Appendix will allow you and your
group to experiment more extensively with becoming effective
group members. You will find role-play suggestions, dialogues of
groups and case studies, and additional techniques for practicing
group skills. The more important learning for your group will come
when members gain a greater understanding of how people communicate in groups and how communicative patterns help the
group develop good interpersonal relations and task competencies.

CREATING PRACTICE SITUATIONS

Group members willing to confront their own performance can also
comprehend how they can change. One approach is to create a role-
play situation or case study that reflects the experiences members
have had as a working group. They can either portray themselves
or use their experiences to create fictional characters. What happens as members try to construct characters and provide them with

dialogue is that the group gains insights into the reasons for particular behaviors.

A willingness to focus on some troubling issue can help group members discover behaviors that have interfered with their goals. Examining one event or critical episode is usually more helpful than trying to address a host of issues (Fisher 1980). As an example of what a group can do to confront its own behavior, consider the following re-creation of a dialogue of a group meeting. This group is evaluating an issue that has caused considerable conflict. The case study format the members used provided data for their own group to analyze; it also provides data for other groups to identify problems and suggest possible remedies. Providing diagnostic questions can help a group get started, but is not essential in case writing. Your group may want to analyze this case or construct one of its own.

Case Study: The Spring Weekend Decision

Case Background

This is a task group examining a campus issue: which band to hire for a Spring Weekend event. The members are the following:

Mary—a political science major, a sophomore who lives in a dorm. She is hard-working, well organized, and gets good grades.

Jose—a freshman of Hispanic origin. He is the first of his family to attend college. He would like to get into the School of Business, but is worried about his grades.

Jill—a native of this university town, a junior, a marketing major, and a member of Delta Delta Delta sorority. She has confidence in her leadership abilities.

Ralph—a senior physics major. He is dedicated to his work, but has little time for other activities.

Steve—a junior, a physical education major who is also on the football team.

Case Log

MARY: Is Steve late again? Let's start anyway. We are running out of time.

JILL: Does anyone have any suggestions about who to get for Spring Weekend?

JOSE: How about a Reggae band, man!

JILL: I don't think enough people would go to see a Reggae band. Any other suggestions? How about you, Ralph?

RALPH: I haven't really thought about it. I had a physics exam yesterday, and now that I think of it, I have a lab in half an hour, so could we make this quick?

JILL: I personally think we should try to get Pat Benatar. She has a large following here and I'm sure that we could make money on her.

MARY: That sounds great to me. I love Pat Benatar. I just bought her new album. I play it all the time.

RALPH: I hate Top 40. How about having "The Jam"? But do whatever you want, just so long as we can get something decided today.

(Steve has just arrived for this meeting.)

STEVE: Sorry I'm late. Practice went overtime today because we had a holiday yesterday.

MARY: Steve, you missed it. We've been discussing Spring Weekend. Don't you think Pat Benatar would be a great idea?

STEVE: That junk! You couldn't pay me to see her.

JOSE: Yeah, I hate that stuff. Anything but her.

JILL: Well, then, who would you pick?

STEVE: I would choose Van Halen.

JILL: Don't you think that's a little expensive?

STEVE: Yeah, but more people would go see Van Halen than Pat Benatar.

MARY: Jill's right, Steve. We can't afford it. Why don't we take a student poll to see who students really want?

JILL: Yeah, great idea! I was just about to say that.

JOSE: The idea is o.k., I guess, but do we have enough time?

RALPH: Whatever you guys want. You have my support. I have to leave, so hurry up.

STEVE: Yeah, I could ask all the guys on my football team what they think.

MARY: Steve, I was thinking of an organized way of doing this, like having us pass out surveys at the Union.

JILL: We could ask people to decide on bands that we can get like Pat Benatar, Peter Tosh, South Side Johnny, and whoever else we can think of.

JOSE: Yeah, but who's gonna do all of that work?

STEVE: All of us will, Jose.

MARY: (under her breath) You mean Jill and I will!

STEVE: What was that, Mary?

MARY: Oh, nothing! I just have a feeling that when we get right down to it, the work won't be evenly divided.

RALPH: Well, listen, guys, I got to go. Let me know what you decide.

STEVE: Boy! That Ralph is always leaving early and he never says anything about anything.

JILL: Well, Steve, that's a little like the pot calling the kettle black! You are always late and you don't say much about the task.

MARY: Hey! Lay off Steve. He was just making a comment.

JOSE: Look, why don't we just finish this thing and stop wasting time.

JILL: Why don't we end this meeting and meet again tomorrow when everybody is in a better mood?

MARY: Good idea! Why don't we all leave and ask people what band they like?

JILL: Mary, why don't we get together tonight and write up that survey?

MARY: Sure. That would help me a lot.

Case Questions

1. What roles do each of the participants undertake?
2. What roles are missing?
3. Does anyone show leadership ability?
4. How should a group deal with a member who is late?
5. How can a group deal with members who do not work actively for the group?
6. Were stereotypes operating in this group?
7. Was it helpful for Mary to stop the conflict between Jill and Steve?
8. How could this group work more effectively?

The Spring Weekend case represents a mostly literal adaptation of some of the problems the group was experiencing. Writing the dialogue helped the participants understand their interaction patterns. A different example is represented below. In this case the group members cooperated in writing an analysis of their behavior. By agreeing to write their critical comments, they were able to see why they had not succeeded in achieving the high goal they had set for themselves. As you will read, the group had not originally planned to be so introspective, but because the participants were able to confront their problems, they became a very productive group in their next project.

Case Analysis: A Troubled Group

Group Analysis

When we began to write our case study, we thought of writing about fictional characters who had problems something like ours. We met one evening with the idea of completing the case study, but when we asked ourselves what problems we should illustrate, the tension among members was so great that we couldn't deal with creating a case. All the bad feelings we had, our disappointment in how our previous task had gone, affected us. We had too many unshared grievances. We decided that we would have to air them if we were going to be able to get anywhere.

We agreed to write down our gripes, whatever feelings we wanted to express and had not, and we would talk about them at another meeting. Finally when we met, we were able to openly and honestly deal with the problems we had encountered. It is unfortunate that we had to wait so long before we became an effective group, but in the long run our experience may benefit all of us.

Problems Identified by the Group

The problems we experienced began during our first two meetings. We had met in class briefly to exchange names and phone numbers. Then we thought it would be a good idea to "break the ice" by meeting at a local restaurant. Our meeting there seemed to set the tone for our group. We found that we had a lot in common and that we enjoyed socializing.

At our next meeting, it was becoming clear that socializing was going to haunt us. We found it hard to get down to work. We also encountered another problem. Even though everyone attempted to supply important information, some people's ideas were more valued than others. This meant that some people felt excluded. This also meant that some people carried more of the workload, which then led to further conflict, though none of this was expressed.

There was a lot of tension built up in our group. One example was that no one understood exactly what each individual had to gain from contributing to the group's effort. So when Dave worked with us, he didn't give us much help. His thinking was that since he was in a lot of groups, he didn't have much to learn from this task group. But he never told us that this was why he acted the way he did.

Such misunderstandings led our group into an disorganized pattern of communication, marked by interruptions, a lack of listening to others, and a disregard for the opinions and values of others. Steve (a low-talker) would come up with a good idea and Emily (high talker) would shoot down the idea before any of us could evaluate its worth.

Another problem was that no member felt responsible for the success of the group. There were too many instances in which some members did not show up for meetings or showed up late or, worst of all, came unprepared to help with the task. Only three of our seven-member group were prepared with the necessary research. Trying to get a meeting scheduled was the most difficult problem of all. For instance, Chuck is on the baseball team and Dave is on the tennis team. This means a big time commitment. And the rest of us work, so there really were not many good times for meeting.

To conclude, we feel that the following were our group's major problems:

1. Inclusion needs were not met.
2. Effective communication was not practiced—there was a lack of self-disclo-

sure, a lack of listening and understanding, constant interruptions, and "high-talker" dominance of the discussions.
3. There was little responsibility for completion of the project. People didn't show up for meetings; some did not do the required research.
4. There was a lack of honesty in dealing with each other, and a lack of positive reinforcement.

Other possibilities for practice would be case studies based on actual social, political, historical, or moral issues. Current public controversies, conflicts between nations, mock jury trials—such issues could provide a group with realistic decision-making tasks. As an example, consider the following case. While the names and details are altered somewhat, the case reflects events that touched the lives of real people.

Case Study: Who Should Decide?

Case Background

Dan and Barbara Robinson are a young married couple. Dan is 34; Barbara, 32. They both have Ph.Ds and are employed as research scientists at a major university hospital. They are also the parents of two children, a boy of 5 and a girl of 3. Mrs. Robinson has just given birth to another son. But neither parent is able to greet this birth with joy. They have been informed that their son has multiple handicaps.

He has been diagnosed as having spina bifida, a neural tube defect that prevents a complete closing of the casing of the spine. Children with spina bifida are likely to be incontinent, will be unable to walk unaided, will spend most of their lives in a wheelchair, and may also be severely retarded. The Robinsons' son will require many operations to correct this defect, and he will need constant care, especially during the early years of his life. The more immediate problem is that this child has a severe heart defect, and unless this defect is corrected, he may not live more than a few weeks. However, the corrective heart operation cannot be performed without the permission of the parents.

After much agonizing and consultation with their doctors and their minister, the Robinsons have refused to give permission for the operation. They believe that it would be better for all concerned—their children, themselves, the university hospital for which they do research, and society—if this disabled baby were allowed to die. When the hospital authorities are informed of the Robinsons' decision, they decide to oppose the decision. They immediately appeal to Judge Adele Vinson of the District Court to issue an order requiring the operation.

The Action

Assume you are members of a panel who have been appointed by Judge Vinson to aid her in ruling on the issue before her. The panel members represent various disciplines: psychology, social work, medicine, law, and philosophy. Your task is to decide whether the parents or the hospital should make the decision. If you agree with the parents, then the baby will be allowed to die, and you can discuss appropriate ways for carrying out this procedure. If you agree with the hospital, then there are other decisions to be made: Who should have responsibility for the care of the child? Who should bear the cost of lifetime care?

Discussion

This case is best accomplished in two sittings: a first meeting to identify issues, and, after researching the issues, a second meeting to reach a decision. Acting out the roles of the panel members or even discussing the case without taking on specific roles can give you greater understanding of how individuals participating in a group affect one another. In addition to the facts of the case, you may want to discuss the broader implications of whichever decision you make.

Comments on the Case

What makes this case a realistic experience for group members is that it illustrates the fact that decisions involve more than a mere outline of the pros and cons. Making decisions depends also on the assumptions and values of the people involved. Your group will be aided in its analysis by considering such issues as why certain factors were weighted more heavily than others, why individuals supported a particular view, and what the most important factors in the group's decision were.

Using a case such as this one, or other cases drawn from current issues and conflicts—say, for example, the Palestinian–Israeli conflict, the decision to launch the space shuttle *Challenger* in freezing weather—can give groups a substantial basis for understanding group interaction and decision processes. Participants will be able to realize how many factors influence a decision. Not only will members examine various viewpoints; they will also become more sensitive to the feelings and beliefs of others. Analyzing a case should create a greater awareness of the intrapersonal and interpersonal issues confronting a group.

PRACTICING OBSERVATION

With your understanding of the theories of group communication, you are now better able to analyze group behavior. If you are in a position to observe ongoing groups, you will learn a great deal about influences on groups. While observation is a complex procedure—there is much to concentrate on—deciding on what you will focus on will allow you to compile sufficient data to make some judgments about a group's effectiveness.

As an example, consider the following excerpt of one person's observation of a committee meeting of the Board of Directors of a university Student Union. This was one of the regular weekly meetings, open to the public, for the 18-member board. The Union board is a student-run organization that uses a modified parliamentary procedure to conduct its meetings.

Case Observation: The Student Union Board of Directors

An Individual Observer's Goals

As I observed the meeting of the Union board, I concentrated on seven major factors. First I was interested in what type of climate the group functioned under. Were they comfortable with each other or did they seem ill at ease? Second, I wanted to examine the task and social dimensions. Was there an equal amount of time spent on these dimensions or was the group focusing on only task with little regard for social relations? Were there conflicts and how would these be handled? The third factor I was looking for were the different communication styles, such as the extent to which participants offered opinions, stated facts, gave suggestions, and expressed feelings. I wanted to see how these styles affected members. The fourth factor was the role of nonverbal communication. How were members seated? Were their facial expressions reflecting interest or lack of involvement? What about their postures? Did the way they were sitting correlate in any way with their interest and participation?

For my fifth category I would be concentrating on their listening skills. When someone spoke, did other members acknowledge they had heard the member or were they more interested in what they had to say? Leadership factors were the sixth factor I would observe. Did leaders so dominate that other members had little to offer? The seventh factor was the social-emotional relations established among members. I was interested in appraising how members related to one another on a personal basis.

Results and Interpretations by the Observer

When I first entered the meeting room, I found the board meeting room to be a comfortable one. People were sitting around chatting, and most seemed familiar with one another. But as the meeting got under way, the friendliness was not as apparent. The climate seemed to get more hostile. This was especially true when the issues discussed were controversial. However, even though there were conflicts, the conflicts seemed to be beneficial. They seemed to help the members clarify what was at stake. For instance, when the group was discussing a policy proposal for the Student Pub, many conflicting views were expressed. After some discussion, some people realized that they were arguing over the wording, rather than over some real differences in policy. But it was the conflict itself that helped board members realize that they were nitpicking and that they could improve the wording without inflicting hostility on one another.

The Union board is an extremely task-oriented group. Judging from the length of the meeting (over one and one-half hours), I think it was necessary for them to handle themselves in this manner. Had the members spent as much time on social relations, the meeting would probably have gone on much longer to accomplish as much as they did. On the other hand, the members might not have seemed so bored toward the end of the meeting had they felt that their relational needs were clearly being met.

I noticed both good and not so good communication skills. Typically, when someone offered a suggestion or gave an opinion, people were more apt to listen if it was stated in a sincere fashion. Members seemed appreciative and included when they were asked for their opinions and suggestions. On the other hand, when one group member asked for an opinion from another member, instead of commenting on the opinion given, the questioner moved on to another topic. This had a negative effect. The first member did not speak after that, perhaps because he felt his opinions were not valued.

The leadership roles were of interest because the appointed leader was not the dominant figure in this meeting. Various members who had expertise on particular topics seemed to be in charge, and they used a round-robin system of asking each person seated at the table if he or she wanted to comment. I saw this as effective in helping the group accomplish its task. Although social-emotional factors did not play a strong role in this group, I did observe that some members went out of their way to make it known that they appreciated the work done by other members.

I learned many things observing this group. For one thing, while a modified form of parliamentary procedure can help a large group to complete a great deal of work, it can also stifle a lot of creative work. Most important, however, I learned that most people do not know how to listen. There were very few reinforcing comments made after someone presented his or her ideas. I think more people would have volunteered ideas if ways had been found to encourage more people to contribute. Too often, ideas were dropped when paraphrasing might have helped increase the number of ideas presented. I also think that if members would take some time to relate to each other, members would show more animation as they conduct their meetings. It would seem worthwhile finding a more interesting way to conduct meetings so that more people would be interested in playing an active role. After all, the Union board reflects a great many functioning student committees who are responsible for recreational, travel, social, film, media, and cultural events. It would be a noteworthy goal to involve a broad section of the student body.

COMMENTS

The more observations you are able to make, the more you will be able to learn about group effectiveness. A group observation can also be a useful way to gather data. If several of you divide the tasks of observation, then each person can concentrate on particular variables. The result should be a more in-depth examination of process variables that affect group behavior.

GROUP TECHNIQUES FOR PROBLEM-SOLVING SKILL BUILDING

The focus in this book has been on the problem-solving group. One of the more difficult issues for groups is to define a problem so that possible solutions can be recognized. Two factors influence the finding of potential solutions: (1) a heterogeneous group of people to ensure that a variety of ideas will be heard, and (2) the freedom to respond to ideas without fear or constraint.

Two techniques can markedly assist in this process. One is labeled *Nominal Group Technique,* and the other is *Ideawriting.* Both of these approaches to problem solving were designed to offset factors that sometimes negatively affect groups—verbal aggressiveness, the influence of status, the dominance of one or of a few members, participation by too few members, and the examination of too few ideas. They are especially helpful to groups who do not have a history of working together but have converging interest in finding a suitable policy, a desirable action, or a new program (Moore 1987).

Nominal Group Technique

Nominal Group Technique (NGT) was developed by Andre Delbecq (1975) as a method for increasing individual participation in a discussion group. One of its assumptions is that in a conventional discussion, some members may so dominate that others remain silent. Another assumption is that groups have a tendency to limit their consideration of ideas, perhaps because of uncertainty or disagreement about the nature of the problem and possible solutions. Therefore, a procedure is needed that will circumvent problems of group participation.

The technique consists of four steps.

1. *Silent generation of ideas in writing.* Participants, working silently and independently, jot down their ideas in response to a stimulus question.
2. *Round-robin recording of ideas.* A facilitator asks each participant for one idea from his or her list. These suggestions are recorded (on a flip chart or blackboard) and the process continues until participants have contributed all their ideas or have agreed that a sufficient number of ideas have been produced.

3. *Serial discussion of ideas.* There is no general discussion as ideas are being suggested and recorded. Participants may seek clarification so that they are clear about the meaning of each idea. It is not a time for arguing or debating the value of an idea, however.
4. *Voting.* Participants identify what each believes are the most important ideas. They rank-order their choices and the votes are recorded. By examining the pattern of voting, the group can determine which ideas have gained a consensus.

Using NGT For NGT to work, the groups should not be larger than 12 to 13 members, although many groups can participate at the same time. What is more important is that the questions addressed be appropriate for this technique, and that a leader who understands the process can act as a facilitator of the process. Examples of the kinds of questions that groups can consider are, "What are some of the obstacles that keep freshmen from learning about university facilities?" "How can the university encourage greater student participation in extracurricular events?" "What are the goals to be achieved in developing the city's downtown district?"

During the first step, for which only four to eight minutes need be allowed, it is important that participants work silently in creating their lists. What is being sought are thoughtful, independent, and creative formulations of ideas. Although the meaning of a question can be explained, excessive talk or explanation should be discouraged.

In the round-robin session, each participant can decide whether he or she has an idea that has not been recorded. Anyone may "pass" but also may add ideas later in the process. When ideas are recorded, only slight editorial changes should be considered. As much as possible, ideas should be recorded in the words of the participants because they are the producers of the ideas, although it is also possible to "piggy-back" on an idea or add new items for each round.

As ideas are recorded, they should be numbered. Then when participants are asked to rank-order their choices, they can use numbers rather than having to write out each idea. The use of numbers will make it easier both to tally the vote and to display where a consensus has taken place. Another approach for simplifying the task of rank-ordering, since there will be so many ideas—perhaps too many for manipulating a rank-ordering—is to ask participants to choose their top five ideas rather than to try to rank a dozen or more. (Using index cards so that each participant can record a single idea on a card can facilitate the tallying of the vote.)

In the serial discussion of ideas, any member may ask about the meaning of an item. It would be helpful for the contributor of the idea (and others may also do so) to give his or her interpretation. The facilitator can also help by adding, "It seems to me that this means . . ." While similar items can be combined, what should be avoided are attempts to arrange items in broader categories. The object of NGT discussion is to have members understand the meaning of an item. It is not appropriate to argue or to try to reach consensus at this time.

When the process is completed, group members will have before them a selected list based on consensual agreement according to their rank-ording of ideas. Since NGT is an initial process for identifying issues, group participants will have much more to do if proposals for change are to be explored. They will have to take these issues and develop ways to deal with them. For example, they can appoint task committees to develop proposals that would focus on the specific issues identified.

The real value of NGT is that it has the potential for producing a better generating and sorting out of ideas than even brainstorming can. By clarifying how a problem can be defined, NGT helps group members see possible solutions. It helps them avoid getting bogged down because a problem has been ill defined. By allowing a diverse, and often large, group of people to consider a problem in a way that encourages their serious contributions, NGT can stimulate more creative suggestions and a greater commitment for a group to continue working on a problem (Moore 1987).

Ideawriting

Just as NGT is a starting point for identifying issues and a stimulus for further thought, "ideawriting" is a technique that helps make more specific the ideas resulting from group interactions (Moore 1987). The assumption of this technique is that a group can achieve its goals by writing rather than by discussion. The technique also assumes that when members work on the same task at the same time, and also have an equal chance to express their ideas, the group can be more productive.

The process involves four steps (Moore 1987, 39).

1. *Organization.* A large group is divided into smaller working groups.
2. *Initial response.* Each participant reacts to a question and then places his or her written response (on a worksheet or a pad) in the center of the group.
3. *Written interaction.* Each participant then reacts, in writing, to all of the written responses.
4. *Analysis and reporting.* Each participant reads the comments made in response to his or her initial idea. Then the group as a whole discusses the major ideas arising from the

written reactions. The group members summarize their discussion and record the main points on large sheets of paper (or blackboard).

Ideawriting is most useful for stimulating both the development and the critique of ideas. It is especially useful for a large group when getting the views of many people would be difficult. The format demands, however, that smaller units work together; when a group is large, therefore, it can then be subdivided, with one leader capable of handling multiple groups.

Ideawriting is also an economical process for developing ideas. Each reaction and response can have a cumulative effect. With the opportunity to examine a variety of reactions, each participant has the benefit of multiple comments.

Using Ideawriting   An ideal size for the first step, organization, is a group of three or four members. Many small groups can be conducted at the same time, however. One person in each group can be asked to serve as group leader. The major responsibility will be to keep the group on track.

The most significant part of the initial response process is to react to a "triggering" question. The typical questions are openended, dealing with what policies or programs to establish or what goals to try to attain. Each participant writes his or her name at the top of the page, and then takes approximately 5 to 10 minutes to respond to the question. The second step is to select one of the "pads" (not one's own), read it, and give a written reaction to it. This process continues until everyone has responded to every other person's ideas.

Although the process could be considered completed at this point—since ideas have been suggested, modified, and elaborated—a group can also decide to discuss and summarize its findings. In this case, one member of each group can report to the other groups orally about his or her group's idea. Then the large group can examine all the ideas, discuss them, analyze, and synthesize them.

When the most promising ideas are identified, groups come away from such a session knowing that they have explored a number of useful ideas and that they have the benefit of critiques to help them further develop their ideas. From this exposure of ideas, groups can choose some of the options that would help them achieve their goals.

SUMMARY

None of the processes discussed in the Appendix is an end in itself. The techniques are designed to foster group learning, to help participants examine their own processes. They encourage a group to be more spirited and more committed to completing a task. By using these techniques to practice the skills of group participation, group members will be better able to gain insights into how to make their groups more effective.

REFERENCES

Delbecq, A. L., A. H. Van de Ven, and D. H. Gustafson. 1975. *Group Techniques for Program Planning: A Guide to Nominal Group and Delphi Processes.* Glenview, Ill.: Scott, Foresman.

Fisher, B. A. *Small Group Decision Making* (2nd ed.). 1980. N.Y.: McGraw-Hill.

C. M. Moore. 1987. *Group Techniques for Idea Building.* Newbury Park, Calif.: Sage Publications.

Index